"WE HAVE JUST BEGUN TO NOT FIGHT"

*An Oral History of Conscientious Objectors
in Civilian Public Service during World War II*

TWAYNE'S
ORAL HISTORY SERIES

Donald A. Ritchie, Series Editor

HEATHER T. FRAZER AND
JOHN O'SULLIVAN

"WE HAVE JUST BEGUN
TO NOT FIGHT"

*An Oral History of Conscientious
Objectors in Civilian Public Service
during World War II*

TWAYNE PUBLISHERS
An Imprint of Simon & Schuster Macmillan
New York

PRENTICE HALL INTERNATIONAL
London   Mexico City   New Delhi   Singapore   Sydney   Toronto

Twayne's Oral History Series No. 18

"We Have Just Begun to Not Fight": An Oral History of Conscientious Objectors in Civilian Public Service during World War II
Heather T. Frazer and John O'Sullivan

Twayne Publishers
An Imprint of Simon & Schuster Macmillan
866 Third Avenue
New York, New York 10022

Library of Congress Cataloging-in-Publication Data

Frazer, Heather T.
    We have just begun to not fight : an oral history of conscientious
  objectors in civilian public service during WWII / Heather T. Frazer
  and John O'Sullivan.
        p.   cm.—(Twayne's oral history series ; no. 18)
    Includes bibliographical references and index.
    ISBN 0-8057-9134-5 (alk. paper)
    1. World War, 1939–1945—Conscientious objectors—United States.
  2. Service, Compulsory nonmilitary—United States.   I. O'Sullivan, John,
  1939– .   II. Title.   III. Series.
DN810.C82F73   1996
940.53'162'0973—dc20   95-20068
                                                              CIP

The paper used in this publication meets the minimum requirements of American
National Standard for Information Sciences—Permanence of Paper for Printed
Library Materials, ANSI Z39.48–1984.∞™

10 9 8 7 6 5 4 3 2 1 (hc)

Printed in the United States of America

Contents

Foreword

Moral reasons drove thousands of young men to take the unpopular stand of refusing to fight during the Second World War. The military divided conscientious objectors into three categories, with the least cooperative sent to prison and the most cooperative put in uniform for noncombatant duties. Those in the middle, who offered limited cooperation, were sent to Civilian Public Service camps where they fought forest fires, worked in hospitals, and allowed themselves to be used in scientific experiments. With humility and humanity, these oral histories explain in the conscientious objectors' own words what brought them to their decision, how draft boards treated those who would not serve in the "good war," how life was in the camps, and what the experience meant to their lives. The nonviolent response to a brutal world has had increasing meaning since the Second World War, most notably in the civil rights movement and the opposition to the Vietnam War. Although these interviews deal with events that occurred a half century ago, they retain great relevance for the post–Cold War era as the United States redefines its world role.

Oral history may well be the twentieth century's substitute for the written memoir. In exchange for the immediacy of diaries or correspondence, the retrospective interview offers a dialogue between the participant and the informed interviewer. Having prepared sufficient preliminary research, interviewers can direct the discussion into areas long since "forgotten," or no longer considered of consequence. "I haven't thought about that in years" is a common response, uttered just before an interviewee commences with a surprisingly detailed description of some past incident. The quality of the interview, its candidness and depth, generally will depend as much on the interviewer as the interviewee, and the confidence and rapport between the two adds a special dimension to the spoken memoir.

Interviewers represent a variety of disciplines and work either as part of a collective effort or individually. Regardless of their different interests or the variety of their subjects, all interviewers share a common imperative: to collect memories while they are still available. Most oral historians feel an additional responsibility to make their interviews accessible for use beyond their own research needs. Still, important collections of vital, vibrant interviews lie scattered in archives throughout every state, undiscovered or simply not used.

Twayne's Oral History Series seeks to identify those resources and to publish selections of the best materials. The series lets people speak for themselves, from their own unique perspectives on people, places, and events. But to be more than a babble of voices, each volume organizes its interviews around particular situations and events and ties them together with interpretative essays that place individuals into the larger historical context. The styles and format of individual volumes vary with the material from which they are drawn, demonstrating again the diversity of oral history and its methodology.

Whenever oral historians gather in conference, they enjoy retelling experiences about inspiring individuals they met, unexpected information they elicited, and unforgettable reminiscences that would otherwise have never been recorded. The result invariably reminds listeners of others who deserve to be interviewed, provides them with models of interviewing techniques, and inspires them to make their own contribution to the field. I trust that the oral historians in this series, as interviewers, editors, and interpreters, will have a similar effect on their readers.

DONALD A. RITCHIE
Associate Historian, U.S. Senate
Series Editor

Acknowledgments

This book emerged from the convergence of two research interests. John O'Sullivan had written on the draft during World War II, then began examining the experiences of conscientious objectors during that war. Heather Frazer, with a background in women's history, brought a focus on the often neglected role of their wives and families. This collaboration resulted in a paper delivered by Heather Frazer at the University of Maryland (subsequently published in *Peace and Change*). By then we had decided to work together on an oral history of Civilian Public Service during World War II.

Our research benefited immeasurably from the discovery that Heather Frazer's uncle, Robert C. Turner, had been one of the 12,000 men who served in CPS during World War II and that he had been married to his wife, Sue, at the time. Not only did Bob and Sue Turner enthusiastically encourage us, they gave us one of our first interviews and were kind enough to share their copy of the 1947 *Directory of Civilian Public Service*. Using addresses that were more than 30 years out-of-date, we engaged in detective work to locate the present whereabouts of over 2,000 CPS assignees. These men, once contacted, shared the names and addresses of their CPS friends, and CPS reunions generated additional names.

From the late 1970s to the present, we have conducted over 100 interviews with CPS men and their wives; friends, colleagues, and students have done another 25. We made a number of trips up the East Coast as far as Maine to interview CPSers, and we traveled as far afield as Oregon, California, and England. We found some CPS men in our own backyard. During a talk on our research at Florida Atlantic University, we became aware of a man in the audience nodding responsively to our remarks; he later introduced himself as Bill Channel, a CPS assignee.

The men and their families not only generously shared their reflections, personal letters, and CPS memorabilia but graciously provided us with hospitality. In fact, the wealth of available material made it extremely difficult to select the interviews to include in this oral history. Each interview adds a compelling dimension to the larger story and provides a unique perspective on the CPS years. We extend our thanks to each participant: you have personally enriched our lives, and without your enthusiastic support, this study would have been impossible.

We are extremely grateful to our families, friends, colleagues, and students who helped us with the interviews, especially Barbara Bello, Karen Clark, Ed Money, Michael Morison, Tom Payzant, and Jeffrey Turner, who worked on some of the interviews in this study. They too experienced our sense of discovery as each CPS narrative unfolded. We also benefited from Nick Turner's assistance in locating the photographs for inclusion.

William Stafford was a singular inspiration to us. He shared his observations in two separate interviews and then allowed us to use as the book title the phrase he had coined at the CPS camp in Magnolia, Arkansas, to denote the commitment of the men in CPS: "We have just begun to not fight."

We extend our thanks to the American Historical Association for a Beveridge grant, the Schmidt College of Arts and Humanities for a summer research fellowship and a professional support grant, and to Florida Atlantic University's Division of Sponsored Research, the Palm Beach Council on the Humanities, the Eleanor Roosevelt Institute, and the American Philosophical Society for grants that helped with research and transcription expenses.

Thelma Spangler, the former History Department secretary at Florida Atlantic University, deserves special commendation for initially typing the bulk of the interview transcripts. A native of Amish country in Lancaster, Pennsylvania, she contributed enthusiasm for the project as well as superb typing.

Warren Hoover and William Yolton, past and present directors of the National Interreligious Service Board for Conscientious Objectors, encouraged us and provided names and addresses of CPS men. Bernice Nichols, J. Richard Kyle, and Wendy E. Chmielewski, curators of the Swarthmore College Peace Collection, furnished invaluable assistance in locating the CPS records in their splendid collection.

We are grateful to Gary W. Reichard, former chair of the History Department at Florida Atlantic University, for supplying sustained support for the project.

Sandy Norman and Lisa Turner proved to be perfect guides for recent arrivals in the land of computer literacy. They showed us the quickest routes and the alleys to avoid; best of all, they were always available. Special thanks also to Sandy for helping to proof the manuscript.

Above all, we thank our families for their unflagging sustenance and encouragement. Jim Turner, Heather's father and an officer in the Marine Corps during World War II, displayed forthright admiration for the CPS men and their experiences from the very beginning. Kimberly, Devon, and Carter, when they were children, may have wondered occasionally why Mom was away on all those trips or why she seemed glued to a tape recorder, but they always encouraged the project. More recently, the eagerness of my son-in-law Ross and daughters-in-law Leslie and Beth to see the finished manuscript helped spur its completion. Finally, and most of all, I thank my husband Perky, whose love, faith, and discerning questions made this book possible.

Research that focuses on family continuously reminds one of the centrality of family in all that we do. By their direct assistance, but more importantly by their presence and love, we are sustained. My wife Marjorie, as always, is my gentlest and most perceptive guide. My children, John, Michael, Shelagh, and Daniel, and my daughters-in-law, Josefina and Allison, are sources of continuing renewal. Finally, my first grandchild, John Joseph deVarona O'Sullivan, now a year old, is my guarantee that I will be regularly getting out of my study to play catch.

Introduction

World War II stands, for almost all Americans, as the just war, the necessary war, the "good" war. Yet a small but significant number said no to this war. They offered principled opposition by serving as noncombatants in the military, performing alternative civilian service as conscientious objectors, or taking an absolutist position and going to prison. Edna St. Vincent Millay captured their spirit: "I shall die, but that is all I shall do for Death; I am not on his payroll."[1]

Approximately 25,000 men opted to serve in the military in a noncombatant capacity, designated as 1AO. The Selective Service System referred to them as "conscientious cooperators."[2] Another 6,000 refused service of any kind and ended up in prison. Almost three-quarters of these prison objectors were Jehovah's Witnesses (JWs).[3] The third category of objector, those the Selective Service System characterized as offering "limited cooperation"[4] and designated 4E, are the subjects of this book: those who entered Civilian Public Service (CPS).

The CPS program eventually had close to 12,000 participants serving at 151 camps scattered across the country. They worked as aides in mental hospitals, volunteered as smoke jumpers in forest fires, and served as guinea pigs in medical and scientific experiments. They were a remarkably diverse group: blue-collar workers and college professors, Amish farmers and Pulitzer Prize winners. The communities they created in the camps, as well as their encounters with the local, often hostile, communities surrounding the camps, are a largely unexamined aspect of wartime America.

The creation of the Civilian Public Service program can best be understood by examining the experience of conscientious objectors (COs) in the First World War. The 1917 draft act (An Act to Authorize the President to Increase Temporarily the Military Establishment of the United States) provided that members "of any well-recognized religious sect . . . whose existing creed or principles forbid its members to participate in war in any form" would be exempted from service in any combat arm, but not relieved from serving "in any capacity that the President shall declare to be non-combatant."[5] Claimants for noncombatant status during World War I numbered 64,693; of the 56,830 who were finally recognized, 29,679 were found qualified for military service, and 20,873 were eventually inducted for noncombatant military service.[6] A more problematic group, from the military's perspective, were those who conscientiously opposed even noncombatant military service. They often suffered harsh treatment at military training bases, and of 504 men who were brought before courts-martial, 450 received a sentence. The penalties ranged from death (seventeen men) to terms of imprisonment averaging sixteen and a half years.[7]

Secretary of War Newton D. Baker, on 1 June 1918, created the Board of Inquiry to investigate the situation of conscientious objectors who refused to accept military authority. The board consisted of Maj. Walter G. Kellogg of the Judge Advocate's Office and two civilians, Judge Julian W. Mack of the U.S. Circuit Court of Appeals and Harlan F. Stone, dean of Columbia University Law School. Kellogg later wrote that, at the time of his appointment, "although I had never set eyes on a conscientious objector, I firmly believed that they were, as a class, shirkers and cowards." Kellogg's interviews with over 800 objectors between June 1918 and January 1919 "upset most of my ideas. . . . They are, as a rule, sincere—cowards and shirkers, in the commonly accepted sense, they are not." Having conceded their sincerity, Kellogg still viewed them as "no less a national problem."[8]

Part of this "problem" disappeared when those challenging military authority were allowed to work, under civilian direction. The Board of Inquiry recommended that 1,500 objectors be assigned agricultural furloughs and an additional 88 men granted permission to work in the European reconstruction unit of the American Friends Service Committee (AFSC).

War's end brought a reduction of the courts-martial sentences imposed on objectors. None of the death sentences were carried out, and the last military prisoner was released two years after the armistice.

What lessons had been learned from the experience of conscientious objectors in this war? The government, faced with objectors it deemed sincere who refused to work under military authority, eventually allowed alternative service here and abroad. Third Assistant Secretary of War F. P. Keppel wrote that what he had tried to accomplish on behalf of the War Department "was to make sure that any citizen, entirely apart from our agreement or disagreement with his views as to warfare, should receive treatment appropriate to America in the twentieth century rather than a Prussian reaction to an annoying situation."[9]

For many in the peace community, the government's response to conscientious objectors in the early part of the war had been "a Prussian reaction." CO status had been defined too narrowly and applied too rigidly. Courts-martial and death sentences served as blunt instruments to intimidate conscience. By war's end, however, a widening range of accepted expressions of conscientious objection provided for all but the absolutists.

Harlan Stone, reflecting on the evolving treatment the CO received during World War I, wrote in 1919 that "if unhappily we should again find ourselves in an armed conflict, the record of our experience with the conscientious objector, and especially the common-sense interpretation of it, will be found to be of value not only to the military authorities but to the public at large."[10] World War I forged closer bonds among the so-called Historic Peace Churches—the Mennonites, Brethren, and Friends. The testing of their shared peace witness brought them together, and this deepened relationship continued into the postwar period. It would intensify by the mid-1930s as unsettling events in Europe and Asia ominously increased the threat of world war.

In 1935 Mennonites met at Goshen College in Indiana to discuss the question of conscientious objection in wartime. One of the participants, the historian Guy Hershberger, noted that, "if in a future war there is any provision for exemption from military service it will probably be due to the fact that the nonresistant people themselves devised the plan."[11] Later that year 80 representatives of the Historic Peace Churches gathered in Newton, Kansas, and began exploring conscientious alternatives to military service. What they hoped to design was a program, administered by civilians, that would provide creative service, similar to the AFSC work camps. Such a program would offer their young men a more desirable option than prison or noncombatant military service.

The outbreak of war in Europe in September 1939 brought a sense of urgency to the peace churches' concern about conscientious objection. A delegation from the Historic Peace Churches met with President Franklin D. Roosevelt on 10 January 1940 to convey their strong commitment to alternative service. They informed the president of their sponsorship of various relief projects and recommended that "those whose conscientious convictions forbid participation in war in any form" could "render constructive service to their country and the world" by joining in these efforts. They noted that such arrangements had eventually emerged in the last war, but only after "months of confusion and distress" because of "the lack of any previous established policy." By meeting with the president, they hoped to be involved in "finding the best solution to the problem of the conscientious objector."[12]

What the peace churches saw as the best solution, humanitarian work under civilian direction, won little support in the broader community. A Gallup poll in January 1940, the same month as the meeting with President Roosevelt, asked what should be done with COs in wartime. Only 13.2 percent of the respondents approved of exemption from military service.[13]

On 20 June 1940, as banner headlines recorded the fall of France, Democratic Senator Edward Burke of Nebraska introduced a compulsory military service bill in the Senate. Republican Congressman James Wadsworth of New York presented the same bill in the House the following day. This proposed draft act incorporated the 1917 draft act's provision for COs, allowing noncombatant military service only for members of the Historic Peace Churches. Those seeking a broader recognition for conscientious objection would have to make their case in committee hearings and by lobbying members of Congress.

While some pacifists focused on defeating compulsory military service, most, acknowledging that a draft law would be enacted, sought to improve its provision for conscientious objection. The effort to include protection for absolutist objectors—those whose consciences prohibited any acquiescence to military conscription—proved futile. Absolutists were accepted under British conscription law, but Congress showed no such willingness. Success, however, came in broadening eligibility for CO status beyond membership in the Historic Peace Churches. Now eligible were those who "by reason of religious training and belief" were "conscientiously opposed to participation in war in any form." Also, the new draft act made provision for those opposed to noncombatant military service by allowing them to be assigned "to work of national importance under civilian direction."[14]

The Selective Training and Service Act of 1940, signed into law by Franklin D. Roosevelt on 16 September, had a markedly improved conscientious objection provision compared with the version introduced three months earlier. Nevertheless, one of the leading Quaker lobbyists, E. Raymond Wilson, would later ruefully acknowledge how much the peace groups had not addressed: "There was little discussion, as it unhappily turned out, on issues of pay, dependency, disability and death, service outside the United States, or the implications of 'work of national importance.' "[15]

The draft act provided for COs to do work of national importance under civilian direction but gave no guidance on how such a program should be organized and administered. The arrangements that eventually emerged represented a convergence of interest between the Selective Service System and the Historic Peace Churches. The Selective Service System, under its acting director Colonel (soon to be Brigadier General) Lewis B. Hershey, saw a real advantage in not being burdened with administering the alternative service program. Hershey hoped that the Historic Peace Churches, acting under the aegis of the Selective Service System, would create a joint committee to assume administrative responsibility for the program. The peace churches lacked as clear a sense of their interests. In addition, each church needed to resolve its questions about the alternative service program within its own denomination, and then with the other churches, before dealing with the government.

A two-day meeting in early October at the Mennonite Home Mission in Chicago, involving 65 peace church representatives, provided a forum for differing perspectives on an alternative service program. It also led to the creation of the National Council for Religious Conscientious Objectors, an eight-member body with M. R. Zigler of the Church of the Brethren as chairperson, Orie Miller of the Mennonites as vice-chairperson, and Paul Comly French, a Quaker, as executive secretary. The following month the council's name was changed to the National Service Board for Religious Objectors (NSBRO).

Clarence Dykstra left the presidency of the University of Wisconsin to become director of the Selective Service System on 16 October 1940, the day of the first draft registration. Dykstra began working with the NSBRO to develop the particulars of the alternative service program that would become Civilian Public Service, and they quickly agreed on a variety of arrangements. Dykstra met with President Roosevelt on 29 November and found little support for the conscientious objector program in the Oval Office. Dykstra told Paul French that when he informed the president of the evolving plans for work camps for COs, Roosevelt "expressed instant and aggressive opposition." The president told Dykstra that COs "were not even going into CCC [Civilian Conservation Corps] camps because it would make it too easy for them, and he proposed to see that they had an Army officer to drill them." Dykstra, taken aback by the president's vehemence, "immediately shifted the subject and decided to wait for a more opportune time."[16]

Roosevelt's hostility led Dykstra to scale back the CO proposal. The Selective Service director encouraged the Historic Peace Churches to assume financial responsibility for the maintenance of the men in the program. Some hesitated over accepting a financial burden of unspecified size, but Orie Miller of the Mennonites pledged that they "would gladly pay their share of the bill. They would do it even though every Mennonite farmer had to mortgage his farm."[17]

Dykstra presented this new arrangement to the president in a memorandum on 19 December. Government agencies would make available camp sites and equipment, but the Historic Peace Churches would supply "generally all things necessary for the care and maintenance of the men." Dykstra appealed to FDR's political instincts by noting that this "voluntary assumption of financial and supervisory responsibility . . . will meet with general public approval, if properly administered."[18]

Dykstra conveyed the president's approval to Paul French of the NSBRO on 20 December, thanking him as well for the "heavy responsibilities" that his group and the churches it represented had assumed.[19] These burdens proved not only heavy but increasingly contentious in time: the financial arrangement, designed as a six-month experiment, would be renewed for the duration of the war. By continuing this commitment, the Historic Peace Churches accepted a set of obligations very different from those they had assumed in 1940. The situation changed from a peacetime draft with service limited to one year to a wartime obligation of service for the duration. The peace churches, in addition to providing support for four or five years, were responsible for thousands of COs from other denominations.

This agreement in December 1940 would decisively affect the experience of conscientious objectors in World War II. The Historic Peace Churches saw it as the best available arrangement at the time, and a decided improvement over the World War I treatment of COs. Critics would later argue that the peace churches conceded too much to the government and had not been sufficiently committed to the need for pay, dependency allotments, and workmen's compensation for the men in CPS. Detractors also complained that the authority of the Selective Service System over CPS violated the draft act. President Roosevelt had named Gen. Lewis B. Hershey as draft director on 31 July 1941. Although the draft law provided for COs to do work of national importance under civilian direction, General Hershey now headed the agency and Col. Lewis Kosch directed the Camp Operations Division. This criticism merged into a broader critique that the Historic Peace Churches and the NSBRO had been co-opted by the government into playing a role in administering conscription.

The planning phase for CPS ended with the president's signing on 6 February 1941 of Executive Order No. 8675, which authorized the director of Selective Service to make assignments of conscientious objectors to work of national importance. Section 3 allowed the director "to accept voluntary services of private organizations and individuals," an acknowledgment of the collaboration with the Historic Peace Churches and the NSBRO.[20] The first contingent of CPS men was ordered to report to a camp at Patapsco, Maryland, on 15 May 1941.

The early camps utilized isolated CCC facilities; the government's intention was to remove and protect the assignees from society. CPS men engaged in soil conservation work, forestry service, and tree nursery projects under the supervision of the U.S. Forest Service, the Soil Conservation Service, and the National Parks Service. After work, many CPS units conducted Bible classes, planned future relief and reconstruction projects, and generated a wide variety of discussion groups. The men also played sports, wrote camp newsletters and literary magazines, and put on theatrical productions. Church agencies attempted to create a religious environment, and pacifist leaders visited the various camps and gave lectures.

CPS men were drawn from over 200 different sects and denominations, but the majority came from the Historic Peace Churches, with the Mennonites composing 39 percent of the total, the Brethren 11 percent, and the Friends 7 percent.[21] The rest represented mainstream denominations, dozens of sects as well as those nominally affiliated with organized churches, and atheists.

Why did these men choose to enter CPS? The answers are as varied as the men themselves. For the Mennonites and Brethren in particular, selecting the military would have been "frowned on," and it was expected by families and the churches that the men would choose to be COs. Some COs from other denominations charged that men from fundamentalist churches drifted into CPS from inertia rather than commitment; but going into the military would have been viewed as an act of active rebellion by groups such as the Amish. Strong religious teachings at home or at church also persuaded many men not affiliated with the Historic Peace Churches to become pacifists.

The World War I experience persuaded other men; novels such as Erich Maria Remarque's *All Quiet on the Western Front* (1929), atrocity stories, and revelations about the use of wartime propaganda validated the pacifist witness. The philosophies of Tolstoy, Thoreau, and Gandhi helped convince others to become COs. Some men were part of the peace movement of the 1930s and members of organizations, such as the Fellowship of Reconciliation (FOR) and the War Resisters League (WRL), that had been formed in response to the general disillusionment with war as a tool to resolve international disputes. For these men, alternative service provided an opportunity to fulfill citizen responsibilities while also gaining moral authority through a pacifist witness. In contrast to fundamentalists, they reached their decisions to enter CPS only after a great deal of soul searching. These men were generally among the first to experience frustration and dissatisfaction with CPS.

CPS men, with their rejection of violence, saw alternative service as an opportunity to establish a Christian community where everyone might live in harmony with God's law. This religious bond, however, was often not sufficient to overcome the deep divisions created within some camps by the diversity of the assignees and their differing assumptions about Civilian Public Service.

CPS men held an incredible variety of philosophical and political beliefs. The predominant religious fundamentalists were joined by the anarchists, absolutists, socialists, fascists, and atheists who had found their way into CPS, making the establishment of any kind of Christian community extremely difficult. Even members of the Historic Peace Churches had relatively little experience in working together; the 12 Mennonite denominations, for instance, disagreed on some issues of religious practice and belief. Under the best of circumstances, it would have been challenging to create a consensus among these CPSers about work attitudes, lifestyles, and the nature of a pacifist witness. Even a simple issue such as establishing when lights were to be turned out in the barracks at night could lead to lengthy and heated discussions. Camp meetings were held to resolve divisive problems, but their many differences made it difficult for the men to forge a common understanding. One man wryly recalled that "I had some of the most enjoyable fights in my life . . . with pacifists."[22]

The Mennonite camps had fewer divisions, but even they had some. The majority of Mennonites came from rural backgrounds. Many had not ventured too far from home, and for them the exposure to city boys who smoke, drank, and swore was an educational experience. They wondered about the sincerity and commitment of their more sophisticated comrades, often seeing them as antireligious.

An additional frustration came with the lengthening of the service obligation. The original year of service was extended by 18 months in August 1941, and then, after Pearl Harbor, continued until six months after the end of the war. Initial idealism flagged as years went by with no pay, dependency allowances, medical insurance, or workmen's compensation. During the course of the CPS program, 30 men died and 1,500 were discharged for physical disabilities without receiving any benefits.[23] Eight million days of largely uncompensated labor would be provided, with the Historic Peace Churches paying more than $7 million for camp operations and Selective Service providing $4,731,000 to cover administrative costs.[24] If the government had paid the COs for their work at the same rate it paid soldiers in the army, the expenditure would have been over $18 million.[25]

Not being paid was initially seen by most CPS assignees as additional proof of their pacifist commitment; General Hershey saw it as a deterrent to insincere men seeking CO status as well as effective public relations in sustaining congressional support for the program.[26] Moreover, after the Depression years, many men were unaccustomed to having much money and had few opportunities to spend it in their isolated CPS camps. Nevertheless, as one year's service was extended to four or five, attitudes toward pay changed, especially for the one-third of CPS men who had dependents.

Their family's response to the decision to join CPS had a significant influence on the men, and these reactions varied tremendously. For many, the decision reflected their family's values, giving the men a sense of shared vision. In other families, the parents had sons in the military as well as in CPS. Some parents were embarrassed over their sons' CO status. Many feared that future careers would be jeopardized by their son's CO stance. One Baptist minister chose to introduce his CO son's wife to his parishioners as the wife of his navy son rather than acknowledge that he had a pacifist in the family. Some of these same families, however, admitted to feeling relieved that at least their sons were safe in CPS. For conservative Mennonites, choosing to become a CO was often the expected commitment. Mennonites who chose to go into the military as combatants risked being disowned by their families or shunned by their church.

CPS wives experienced special difficulties. Some did not share their husbands' pacifist commitment and were chagrined at his decision not to serve in the military. Unlike their husbands, these women were not hidden away from the general public, and they had no protection against discrimination or harassment. Denied a dependency allotment, some were forced to live with their often disapproving families or in-laws. Most women worked to support themselves and their children, but finding a job was frequently difficult. Some teachers were fired when their school systems learned of their CO husbands, and others had their applications rejected. Even when they experienced little overt discrimination, wives often felt guilty because they felt they were not sacrificing to the same extent as those women whose husbands were in the military.[27]

As the war intensified, many men began to question the nature of their "work of national importance." When men were sacrificing their lives in the military, weeding seedling beds and clearing brush along trails in national parks did not seem to be making a significant contribution to the welfare of the country. Some CPS men complained, "My God, you're talking about planting trees and the world's on fire."[28]

The NSBRO began to lobby Selective Service for meaningful work projects, but the government feared public criticism if COs left the isolated CCC camps for more visible jobs. Those assignees with skills that were in short supply were particularly frustrated over their assignment to unskilled work projects. For example, Don DeVault, a research chemist and former Stanford University professor, was denied the opportunity to continue his penicillin research and instead was assigned to digging ditches.[29]

Initially, many of the men had hoped for assignments overseas in the area of relief and reconstruction. In fact, several special detached units had been established to provide the specific training necessary. One group of men was actually in the process of embarking for China when Democratic Congressman Joseph Starnes of Alabama attached an amendment to a War Department appropriation bill in January 1943 prohibiting the use of government funds to send COs overseas.[30] Denied the opportunity to engage in humanitarian service abroad, COs increasingly agitated for opportunities to do significant work at home that would address human needs and alleviate suffering.

Selective Service had already approved the assignment of COs as attendants in state mental hospitals and training schools, believing that not only was the work socially useful but it would continue to keep COs isolated from the public. Defense work opportunities had attracted many employees, and state mental hospitals desperately needed attendants. In June 1942, Eastern State Mental Hospital in Williamsburg, Virginia, received the first contingent of CO volunteers. Such assignments were so successful that mental hospital service rapidly expanded, and by the fall of 1943, one in six CPS men had volunteered for this work. By the close of CPS in 1947, over 3,000 men had served as attendants in state mental institutions. Although some men would volunteer for any detached service project simply to escape the monotony and futility of camp work projects, the majority were idealistic about their ability to change the inadequate and even primitive conditions that existed in many mental hospitals. Their idealism was soon tempered by the reality of working in these institutions.

At Williamsburg, a 19-year-old CO found himself in charge of a men's violent ward on the 12-hour night shift. He had received no training and was solely responsible for over 100 patients. Between 10 and 12 CPS men, one or two nurses, one unlicensed general physician, and a superintendent-psychiatrist composed the entire staff for this hospital with over 2,000 patients. The work was frightening and unpleasant, and the COs felt physically exhausted most of the time.[31]

Similar conditions at other mental hospitals and training schools led CO attendants at Byberry (Philadelphia State Hospital) in 1944 to develop the Mental Hygiene Program, which became the National Mental Health Foundation in 1947. Byberry had been constructed to house 2,500 patients, but 6,000 were in residence by 1943, with one attendant for every 300 patients.[32] The COs at Byberry, appalled by the quality of care, produced *The Attendant*, a publication dedicated to educating attendants, promoting the exchange of ideas, and detailing plans for the long-range reform of mental institutions. In its pages, CPS men discussed issues such as patients' living conditions and treatment as well as employee brutality.

The issue of nonviolent restraint of difficult patients concerned many of the COs, who were dismayed by the physical abuse some patients received from attendants. Some CPS men also opposed as too violent the use of electric shock therapy and hydrotherapy. They believed that even the most frenzied patients could be reasoned with and that, if necessary, four or five COs working together could peacefully restrain the most violent individuals. Other COs, however, did not hesitate to use force to control patients and protect themselves.

In addition to encouraging educational programs for attendants, some COs publicized atrocious hospital conditions in the hope of stimulating reforms. A 1946 *Life* feature article, complete with appalling photographs of Byberry, increased public awareness of the plight of mental hospital patients.[33] COs at Rosewood Training School in Maryland, Eastern State Mental Hospital in Williamsburg, and Cleveland State Hospital also publicized the barbarous conditions at their respective institutions. COs in the Friends CPS unit at Cleveland State leaked evidence to the *Cleveland Press* of "brutality, malnutrition and lack of proper treatment," leading to an investigation of the charges. The superintendent demanded the removal of the CPS men involved, and they in turn initiated a formal complaint against the hospital administration. This action led to the dismissal of the unit. A new superintendent was appointed, and later a Mennonite unit returned to the hospital.[34] Some of the tactics used by CPS men to reform patient care and treatment in mental institutions were not appreciated by Selective Service and the

NSBRO, but there is little doubt that the idealistic commitment demonstrated by the CO attendants led to increased public awareness and subsequent reforms.

Other CPS men, seeking to more fully express their beliefs, volunteered to serve as human guinea pigs in medical experiments. The Office of Scientific Research and Development and the Office of the Surgeon General of the Army had initiated a wide array of research and experimental programs designed to stave off the wartime threat of pandemic disease. Projects studying typhus, pneumonia, hepatitis, malaria, starvation, and other threatening, if less deadly, maladies were soon in need of human subjects.

The call for volunteers met with a quick response from the approximately 500 CPS men who took part in these experiments. For many of them, Civilian Public Service had offered only a limited witness of their beliefs. They had made a personal decision against killing but had had little opportunity to express their life-affirming commitments. Many saw their claim to conscientious objector status not as a sign of inner strength but as evidence of cowardice. Here was an opportunity to place oneself at risk, not by facing enemy armies but by encountering one of the dread diseases that plagued the human race. It was the type of risk that would not violate one's pacifist principles but would more fully express them.

The first involvement of CPS men in medical experiments took place not in a sterile research laboratory but in an isolated camp in New Hampshire's White Mountain Forest. In July 1942, 48 CPS men participated in a series of typhus control experiments. They wore lice-infested underwear while maintaining their forestry work schedule. After a two-week incubation period, various insecticide sprays and powders were applied during the third week, and their effectiveness analyzed. The experiment ran for two additional three-week cycles.

Other unpleasant, but necessary, experiments attracted CPS volunteers. An atypical pneumonia project involved inoculations with throat washings and sputa from infected persons. In a malaria experiment, a netted box with five mosquitos was placed on the volunteer's stomach; after the volunteer contracted malaria, he was treated with various drug therapies. For a hepatitis experiment at the University of Pennsylvania, 50 volunteers ingested or had introduced into their bodies through a gastric tube a suspension of feces in distilled water.

The medical experiment that won the deepest commitment from CPS men began in the fall of 1944. Five years of global war had caused massive devastation and produced millions of displaced persons. The task at war's end of restoring to health those survivors who had suffered from starvation and malnutrition seemed overwhelming. The first step was to gain a systematic understanding of the physiological and psychological process of starvation and the optimal strategy of reversing its effects.

On 15 November 1944, 36 CPS "guinea pigs," chosen from the many who volunteered, assembled in a test laboratory underneath the football stadium at the University of Minnesota. They began a yearlong starvation study that proved to be the most grueling of the CPS experiments. A minimal diet combined with a rigorous schedule produced powerful effects. The men grew withdrawn, listless, and apathetic. Because their body temperatures dropped, they "were always cold and slept under 3 or 4 blankets even in the heat of July."[35] Their prolonged encounter with hunger, even under controlled, clinical conditions, challenged them more deeply than they had anticipated. The official report of the experiment, despite its detached language, conveyed a sense of the ordeal they had gone through: "The great majority of the men now look back and are glad they participated in the experiment but are quite sure they would never have volunteered if they had been able, beforehand, to conceive the actuality."[36]

What was gained from their commitment to this experiment? The Minnesota study furnished the most sophisticated analysis of the process of starvation that had ever been made. It created a window through which to observe the physiology of starvation and its psychological manifestations, challenged certain assumptions about the nutritional strategies best suited to restoring famine-stricken populations, and offered strong evidence for alternative approaches. Its findings proved of great value to the public and private relief agencies that sought to heal the nutritional damage the war had inflicted.

The very nature of the experiment attracted wide public attention. The media, which often depicted the volunteers in heroic terms, provided the most favorable publicity the Civilian Public Service program received in the course of the war. More important, the extensive coverage of the experiment focused public attention on the responsibilities that would have to be faced after the war's end. With graphic photos of emaciated volunteers, their limbs swollen with edema, the *Life* account "Men Starve in Minnesota," which appeared the week before the United States dropped the atomic bomb on Hiroshima, furnished a compelling preview of the immense task of rehabilitating the war's victims.[37]

The starvation study was one of 41 medical experiments to which CPSers contributed 151,000 workdays. The NSBRO, refusing to participate in any experiment that had purely military implications, had evaluated each proposal. The determining criterion had been the experiment's "ultimate value to humanity."

CPS men became medical guinea pigs out of a commitment to service. In the midst of the war, when being "in the service" meant destroying the nation's enemies, they chose an arduous but life-affirming service. In accepting the onerous responsibility of this type of volunteer work, they finally achieved that elusive goal of "work of national importance."

By January 1944 more men were serving in special projects than in the camps. In addition to work as attendants and human guinea pigs, COs served as farm laborers and dairy herd testers, built privies for Florida communities plagued with hookworm, and provided health and educational services in Puerto Rico and the American Virgin Islands. Men looking for adventure and the opportunity to demonstrate their valor volunteered for the smoke-jumping unit. Created in the summer of 1943, the unit rigorously trained COs at a base camp in Missoula, Montana. They were then assigned to side camps in Montana, Idaho, and Oregon, where they parachuted into rugged, inaccessible country to put out forest fires. By the end of the war, 240 men had engaged in this dangerous work.[38] One CPS volunteer acknowledged the appeal of smoke jumping: "I felt I wasn't a coward, but I wanted a chance to demonstrate it in a very dramatic way."[39]

The almost 12,000 men who participated in CPS had as many differing perspectives on that experience. They brought varying assumptions and expectations to the camps. Their hopes of engaging in work of national importance, certainly in the first years, were usually frustrated. As opportunities expanded in CPS, other problems continued to emerge. The pressures created by the absence of pay worsened. Many in CPS, particularly those coming from outside the Historic Peace Church tradition, felt a deepening antagonism toward the NSBRO. Some claimed that it had become an agency for carrying out Selective Service's directives; others simply felt that it poorly represented the interests of those in CPS. The most deeply alienated COs voted with their feet, choosing government camps, opting for prison, or entering the military in a combatant or noncombatant capacity.

Most CPS men had a more positive sense of the experience. However disappointed their hopes were, they still saw it as a meaningful witness for peace in a nation mobilized for war.

What follows is an experiential history of CPS. CPS men—and two wives of CPS men—share their recollections and reflections on the program. Their different perspectives on Civilian Public Service bring us a richer understanding of this one exercise of conscience in wartime.

THE ORGANIZATION AND FUNCTIONING OF CPS
M. R. Zigler

"From that time on, I was never afraid of the military. I'm afraid of educators, college professors, historians. If I had to choose, I'd take the military to eliminate war."

Michael Robert Zigler played a pivotal role in the creation and direction of the National Service Board for Religious Objectors (NSBRO). Born on 9 November 1891 in Broadway, Virginia, Zigler studied at Bridgewater College and Vanderbilt University. Serving as a Church of the Brethren minister, he worked with the YMCA program at Parris Island, South Carolina, the Marine Corps training facility during World War I. This experience profoundly affected his pacifist commitment.

In the 1930s Zigler pressed for more collaboration among the Historic Peace Churches. That commitment to unified action was reflected in his work chairing the NSBRO throughout World War II. In the immediate postwar period, Zigler directed Brethren relief efforts in Europe, continuing through the late 1950s. He believed that peace issues were best pursued by a broad-based religious coalition, and he remained dedicated to such ecumenical activities until his death on 25 October 1985.

I was born a Brethren. I don't take any credit for that. I was born in 1891 at Broadway, Virginia, near Harrisonburg, Shenandoah Valley. And I stayed there till I was about 20 years old and went to Bridgewater College. I was a conscientious objector. Well, my colleagues didn't help me much on that issue, on the conscientious objector one. We didn't discuss it. We just took it for granted. Then I decided to be a missionary, and I went to Vanderbilt University School of Religion, and they didn't touch it either. They weren't bothered about conscientious objectors. It was irrelevant. Pacifism was irrelevant. And I didn't raise the issue too much in our discussions the year I was there, and in 1917 the call came for people to go into YMCA work in the army, and I thought of that as alternative service. They didn't call it that.

I was exempt because I was a theological student, but I thought if I didn't stay in the student body that perhaps I would have to go into the army or take a CO position in the army—that was the only alternative. But I decided that I would become a YMCA secretary. I went to Black Mountain, North Carolina, for training a couple of months, and I got assigned to Parris Island, South Carolina, United States Marines, and I was with them for three years. I was the youngest man on the force of 37 men, and I didn't know what my draft board would do. But they finally agreed that that would be the best place for me to be, and I didn't appear before a draft board. My brother went and told them what I was doing, and they said, just leave him down there, [it's] the best place he could be, way off on that island, and so I stayed there.

There I saw the training, and to my surprise, even though I was the youngest man on the force, I finally became the general secretary of the 37-man force, 10,000 Marines, about 300 coming in every night. And for one year I was at the reception center where the boys first came in. These are all volunteers, Marine volunteers. Sometimes a whole trainload would come from Yale University or something like that, that kind of combination, and I'd sit and talk with those kids. Boy, they were pure people. For the training of these men they brought sergeants and corporals from all over the world where the Marines had been, and boy, you could never find a tougher bunch of men than those men they collected to train those United States Marines for the First World War. Their language was sworn so beautifully, the swearing and everything else was just out of this world, and then to sit around in the evening and hear them tell each other what they had been doing, if I had had a recorder then, I would've had a best-seller, but who was looking for a best-seller then?

The commanding officer called me in and said, "I'm the most lonesome man on the island. I'd like for you to come to my house every Sunday night if you can." And they began to send a detail after me, and we'd talk. And he said, "I may not talk to you sometimes when you come in, but I just want you to come in and sit with me. And don't stop coming just because I don't speak to you." He had this swell place, leather cushions and everything, best place on the island, but he said, "Don't you preach to me." He used Marine language to tell that to me. Then one time he said, "Maybe you better pray for me." "Well," I said, "we religious people generally like to preach a little before we pray, so we know what to pray for, trying to get our minds made up together before we pray." Well, that hit him a little bit, and he thought it over and said, "Pray that I'll never have to throw my men into battle." Well, I thought that was a funny thing to hear a military man say, but he said, "If they do go to battle, pray they fight like hell and win." That night was the night that I found the other side of the Marines, and I found it in every Marine after that, and every military man, when I got with him long enough.

Then he began to use bad language against the church because he said the churches could have prevented the war. He said, "Nowhere in the New Testament does it say that Christians got to bring Jesus back by a war." That minute I turned pacifist. I was out to change the world to the power of the church. That's really when I started working. A conscientious objector doesn't work. He doesn't have a message of his own, but a pacifist does. There's where you got a conscience, and so I began working from then on. Later Lloyd George wrote a book in which he had a chapter [saying] that the church could've prevented the war. Ever since then I have been advocating the church to prevent the war. They can.

You base your pacifism on the Sermon on the Mount. Is that correct?

Well, "Thou shalt not kill" comes first, then the Crucifixion. I mean, they come and get you and then crucify you and take you. That's all. Just two things.

What do you say to people who attack your position as being too idealistic?

I go back to when I was talking to this general of the Marines. Get the churches to agree that they won't kill each other. Just that simple. To pin it down, I went to one pope, and I said, "You fight against abortion and birth control, but you get up to 18 or 19 and it's all right to kill people. How do you get that now?" I went to the head Lutheran man, Franklin Frye. I said, "You have Lutherans in America, Lutherans in Germany, enough to sway the life of both nations, and you killed each other. How did you justify that and you fight against abortion and birth control and things like that? How do you justify that?" And the pope and Franklin Frye answered exactly the same way. Either one of those two organizations could have prevented two world wars if the Catholics wouldn't have killed Catholics. I got that from a Marine general, I didn't get that out of a Bible, except that "Thou shalt not kill."

What about all the other people who aren't Christians?

Oh, you don't bother with those if the church is strong enough to handle the thing, and they are. There's enough Catholics to stop war anywhere they want to. I don't know why people skip the church, but they do.

When did you first meet General [Lewis B.] Hershey?

The first time I met with General Hershey was in October 1940 in Chicago in a Congregational church. I was chairman of the National Service Board for Religious Objectors, and this was the first public meeting I was in regarding the draft. And General Hershey came and met with this group. This was an open meeting, and the church was filled with people. There must have been 300 people there, people sitting in the windows. Arthur Holt of the theological seminary connected with Chicago University was presiding that night. And without saying anything to me about what he was going to do, he made a statement I shall never forget. He said, the Methodists and the Baptists, the Presbyterians and the Congregationalists, had carried the torch of Protestantism across the nation to the Pacific. But [that night], as we [faced] the world in the present dilemma of the war and the draft, he was turning the torch over to the Historic Peace Churches for the future. And he introduced me as the chairman of the National Service Board, that was hardly born at that time, and asked me to take the chair, with that mob of people that I didn't know. General Hershey was there that night, and I had to introduce him, that was my first contact. And he explained Selective Service and the rules and regulations as he understood them regarding conscientious objectors.

You were active in lobbying, were you not, in regard to the 1940 draft act?

I don't know whether I ever agreed that we "lobbied." I always felt that the Mennonites, Friends, and Brethren and the Fellowship of Reconciliation and all others, from a religious standpoint, had a working agreement somehow in the background of history that we didn't lobby. We interviewed each other and tried to come to some satisfactory agreement. Now, you might call it "lobbying"; I've always felt that it was just a little different. I never felt that we were trying to bring pressure. We were simply representing a group of people with which the government had to deal, and we were trying to negotiate how we go through a war period absolutely with the opposite positions.

But were you involved in going around to speak to senators and congressmen?

Oh my, yes. I think I interviewed half the senators and congressmen.

One particular issue in the air at that time was to allow provision for the "absolute objector." You recall the British act had allowed total exemption for

4

those who were opposed to any affiliation with the military. Weren't you trying to get that included in the American act?

We did not feel at the first that it was our responsibility to work for that group. However, we did not work against them on their position. We felt that they should organize themselves, as we were, and if the government granted them the privilege, okay.

But you weren't active in pressing their case?

Not at that time. See, this was all new to us. In fact, it was new to all of us working together.

What had you been doing prior to the draft act?

I guess my experiences in the First World War, as a member of the Church of the Brethren, made me act rather quickly and persistently to be ready for another war if and when it could come. And at that time we were beginning to feel something. I got the feeling of the nation from taxi drivers and working people more than I did college professors and preachers and government men about what was going to happen in the future. I felt something a-comin', and I had decided after the First World War that if I had a chance, that we ought to have a better arrangement with the government if another war would occur than we had in the First World War. But I did not have a chance to do anything about the peace business in the church until about the year 1935. I began to work for the preparation of youth for a war if it should occur, which in my mind was that you should be promoting peace and have an active program in peacemaking. Not so much that you were just against war, but you'd be actively engaged in peace.

The 1935 General Conference of the Church of the Brethren issued a strong statement opposing war, claiming that all war is sin, and the statement was then taken by a delegation to present to President Roosevelt and [Secretary of State] Cordell Hull. I believe you were part of that delegation?

We visited Mr. Hull, and he was very receptive. We had a 15-minute promise, and I think we stayed perhaps an hour, maybe longer. And he pulled the chair from behind his desk, and we sat in a circle. I think there were six of us or more, and [we] talked. And when we left, he walked out to the door at the street, and he said, "You don't know how important it is that people like you come. The pressure on one side is so heavy, unless somebody comes back on the other side to push you back up, you're bound to bend where the pressure is. And you need this other side." He was very congenial.

How many years were you head of the NSBRO?

From the time it was organized until 1948. I think it was about eight years.

Did you find General Hershey sympathetic to your group?

He was very sympathetic.

Why do you think Hershey was so sympathetic?

My own judgment, he's a good man. Very good man. He had been a head of Boy Scouts along with his military, which explains some things to me, and I feel personally that Mr. Hershey had a religious background, even though he didn't belong to any church, at least he claimed he didn't. He always said he was never washed. But on the question of religious liberty he was very strong. And I would say that perhaps he was the finest exponent of religious liberty that I've ever met, and certainly the best as far as any officials in American government are concerned. He had a deep respect for opposition and even wished that that could be the position of everybody. I mean, he didn't like war.

Did you ever have any points of conflict between the interests of the NSBRO and Selective Service?

Oh yes, we had some conflicts. But they were generally administrative, due to differences of interpretation. And I would say that, while government officials are hard to work with, the peace organizations are about the hardest people I know of to work with, to unite them.

Why is that so?

Well, that's one of the sad situations as I see it in the world as we face the elimination of war. And I regret it very, very much.

There seemed to be a feeling on the part of the Brethren and the Mennonites in 1940, when the NSBRO was being organized, that the Quakers wanted to take it over, wanted to run it. Do you recall that?

6

Well, if you'd like to know how the thing got organized, I think that would explain it. Well, how did NSBRO get started? To this day, I don't know who called the meeting, except that the United States government said to the Quakers, I think, that the peace organizations would have to get together, that they would not listen to all the different peace organizations in order to talk to them about Selective Service. So they decided then to call a meeting of the Mennonites, Friends, and Brethren. Now, the Mennonites were in on that somehow, because the meeting was held in the Mennonite Mission Church in Chicago. And I guess they came to Chicago so they'd be close to Elgin, to get the Brethren in on it.

So we had all the different branches of the Brethren and all the Mennonite branches there and all the Quaker branches. I think there were about six varieties of Quakers, five varieties of Brethren, and about seven varieties, I think, of Mennonites there. First time they'd ever met together. And Charles Boss of the Methodists came in on that. And who invited him I never found out. Well, the Quakers had been doing the major work on relationship to government, no doubt about that. The Mennonites didn't feel they had any business doing that, and the Brethren had not done very much along that line and depended upon the Quakers from the First World War until about 1936; we depended absolutely upon the Friends for our interpretation of peace and the leadership of the peace program and to do our relief work. We did all of our relief work through the American Friends Service Committee (AFSC).

But that's one thing I decided to take over about that time. And that was a difficult situation, to separate ourselves from the Quakers and be an independent organization. But the coming of Selective Service forced us to identify ourselves as Brethren, along with the Mennonites and Friends. I don't know what would have happened if this more or less legal thing would not have forced us. But anyhow, we had to really stand on our own feet. But who came to this meeting then with something in their hands to give us? Well, I never will forget Ray Newton of the Quakers. He pulled out of his pocket a whole plan. And the Quakers planned to be the representative to take over the Mennonites and the Brethren. [It] sounded very good—Brethren-style, let 'em do it.

That's the first time I ever ran into Orie Miller of the Mennonites in an official way. I'd met him in conferences before. I discovered that the Mennonites wanted to be absolutely independent, to have their own programs in relationship to the government, but would be willing to cooperate. I'd been appointed by my church to be the chairman of the committee to represent the Church of the Brethren with the government. So I had the authority. Why under heaven I was chosen chairman that day, I don't know. Because they didn't know me, and I didn't know them. Well, the question was, would we follow the Quaker plan? I saw the Mennonites weren't going along with

it. And I knew we didn't go along, but I was chairman and couldn't do anything. Charles Boss of the Methodists came in, and I finally said, "Well, Charles, what would you like?" He said, "We'd like to work independent." And that settled the issue. And we decided to organize our own board of directors, which finally was called the National Service Board for Religious Objectors.

Was Paul French [of the Society of Friends] involved?

Paul Comly French understood the situation clearly from the very beginning. From that meeting on, he saw what was in the minds of other than the Quakers and understood the Quakers. Well, the next day the decision was that each body should send a representative to Washington and organize. So we went to Washington and met in the Commodore Hotel around a bed. And we finally decided that we would organize. And I was elected chairman of the National Service Board for Religious Objectors in the process of formation at that time. Clarence Pickett [executive secretary of the AFSC] didn't like that. He got his hat and walked out. We elected Paul Comly French as executive secretary. And the Mennonites, Friends, and Brethren then assumed the total responsibility of financing the whole thing from then on and administering the program.

When you made that determination to assume the financial responsibility, did you have any idea what it would cost?

No, we didn't figure that out. We expected the Quakers to take care of their own, we'd take care of ours, and the Mennonites take care of theirs. We didn't know what would happen there, because if we'd known what was going to happen, we might've stalled along on that, because there's so many other people coming in that we didn't anticipate.

The financial responsibility you were thinking of assuming was basically the costs of running the camp?

Everything connected with the whole business.

Were you thinking of paying some kind of salary to the men in the camp?

No. See, the Brethren camps, as they were run, we had to take that financial obligation, and the Quakers theirs, and so on. So in a way, yes. But not collectively, we didn't. But what we did take collectively was the overhead

in Washington. And we settled our financial arrangement every month. We could've closed shop there every month and had no deficit or no money over. Every month we just took the cost that we owed to each other and cleared the deck. And we formed a pretty big organization there for a while.

Was there any thought of providing allowances for dependents?

That was discussed. But as I said, those things came day by day. We didn't know, when we started, we only thought of the Mennonites, Friends, and Brethren taking care of their own, you see. And when other people came in, we did not anticipate what that would be.

Were families of Brethren men in the camps taken care of during the war?

Well, in a way, our Brethren way, yes. We wouldn't have a stipend or anything, but if anybody was in need, of course we opened our gates and took care of the people. If you make a stipend, then everybody gets it, and they don't need it. And that's the way the Brethren were, I mean, if you need it, yes.

Was there any discussion or any consideration given to the possibility of persuading the government to pay the members of CPS a salary?

There might have been, but at that time you must remember very clearly the separation of church and state—what are you going to do to keep that line clear? Do you want the government to pay for this or not?

Many people did. I know that during the latter part of the war and after the war there was a backlash on the part of some who felt the NSBRO had overly accommodated itself to the government. You ended up having the military playing a much larger role in many of the camps.

Oh yes, we had that battle from the very beginning, and especially when these other people came in that didn't belong to the Historic Peace Churches. Here we had Jehovah's Witnesses and 137 different denominations, and when you add these outsiders, they couldn't understand the Brethren, Mennonites, and Friends. Now, the Mennonites and Friends barely could understand each other, but you get this other group in there, and how to run a thing was different.

So you believe that the persons who later were complaining about the fact that the government wasn't paying a salary and that perhaps the NSBRO had sold out were largely non-Brethren, non-Mennonites, and non-Quakers?

Well, I would say that the beginning of the discussion was that way. The Brethren, the Quakers, and the Mennonites later on may have got away from some idea of separation of church and state a little bit here and there.

When you began, did you have any figure in mind as to how many men would eventually be involved in the program?

No, we couldn't tell.

Was the final number more than you expected?

Oh yes! Of course, if we knew how many was coming in, we probably wouldn't have tried it, but we licked it. I mean, it's a good thing we didn't know. I think if we had gone to our churches and saw what was coming, I don't think they'd have voted for it. They couldn't have seen how we could do it, and to this day I can't understand how we raised the money to get it done, but we did. It's a tremendously interesting thing, from my point of view. It was far beyond any expectation that I ever had from my church.

How would you decide where to locate a camp? Did the government decide that with the church?

Well, at first we chose our own location and got it approved at a conference with the government, and the Brethren selected the first in Manistee, Michigan, but we never got that organized. The first one that really got started was in Maryland.

Would you look for communities where there would not be much antagonism toward COs?

Well, the aim, of course, was to do that, because there was no use to create a war by doing this, and it wasn't an easy thing to find a place where you'd be welcome.

Do you have any specific recollections of antagonism or of what the general public feeling about COs was?

Well, I can give you my own experience [from] when they began to go into the mental hospitals. I worked in Elgin. In Elgin we had a state hospital, and I worked with the hospital there, and they agreed to take a good number of COs. Everything worked so neatly, and I thought we'd be the first one to get into the mental hospital deal. Colonel [Lewis] Kosch [director of the Selective Service's Camp Operations Division] came out; he thought everything had worked out all right. The American Legion didn't like it, and when he came out there to finalize the program, he had to meet with the American Legion. And he called me at two o'clock in the morning and said he couldn't do a thing with them, and they'd just have to postpone working on the project then. That's just one sample in my hometown. And the next day two columns came out in the paper about it. I was humiliated to tears in my own hometown, which meant that we hadn't cleared it well enough, that's all. They came out there and wanted to run us out of town.

The camp at Crestview, Florida, was forced to move because of local political pressure. Do you remember anything about that?

No, I can't give you the details of that. Now, it might have been that this advertising the need for privies kind of lowers the image of the community, and you get run out for that more than the CO business, you see. There's many different things in this thing, and you get enthusiastic people eliminating hookworm. You just don't do this public stuff out in the open. I mean, people that's got the hookworm and gets free from it, they don't want to be told that they didn't have a place to go. I found this true of foreign missionaries. The people of India and China didn't like to be talked about as being a backward people, and this thing holds more true here in America than in foreign lands, and I think this is at the heart of the thing.

Did any of the mainstream churches express any antagonism toward any of the peace churches?

Now, you're touching a real spot, I think. I don't know how I ought to say this to sum it all up out of my own experience. I'll say this word: that even to today I would rather go to the Congress to get consideration for the conscientious objector on a religious basis than I would the National Council of Churches representing 32 major denominations. Or any national denomination, outside of the Historic Peace Churches.

They were antagonistic?

Terrible.

Why do you think that was so?

I came to the conclusion at the First World War that the churches could have prevented the war, and I got that from a general in the Marines. From that time on, I was never afraid of the military. I'm afraid of educators, college professors, historians. If I had to choose, I'd take the military to eliminate war.

Because they're afraid of war?

Well, take a policeman. He doesn't want a revolution just because he's dressed up to prevent it. He wishes the churches of the community would make it impossible to have crime in the streets. He doesn't want to get shot. Or if I gave you another case, take the fire department. They don't want a fire that's dangerous, but you're going to have them.

Well, I think the case of the policeman and the fireman might be different from that of the military. I think there are many military men who essentially don't want war, but war is their business.

I'm talking about when they take their uniform off, so to speak.

The 1940 draft act and the CO provision in that saying that you had to be opposed to all wars and you had to have come to that via religious training and belief—do you think that was a fair provision?

Well, of course, the Congress put that in, the churches didn't have any say much to that when it passed, and at that time it sounded pretty good, see?

The law has been changed since 1965, but from 1940 to 1965 you had to believe in a personal God, had to oppose all wars, and had to come to that determination by religious training and belief. Aren't there many people who have a very highly developed moral consciousness and who are not religious in the traditional sense?

I would fight for them to have their rights, yes. I did. But you can't fight for the rights of the guy who doesn't organize himself like we had to organize.

I think there were a number of individuals who weren't affiliated with organizations, who had an opposition to the war based on moral grounds, who were not entitled to CO status.

12

I think most of the guys had a clientele of a couple hundred people. They could have gone on to say they represented a group of people, and they should have organized and made an approach instead of putting us on the spot, you see.

It seems to me that the government felt much more at ease in dealing with the Historic Peace Churches than it did with others. They tended to dismiss other positions as simply political, or whatever, not religious.

Well, of course, Selective Service had the guidelines of the act, and therefore, until the Congress had changed, they were limited.

What is your sense of the newspaper treatment of the COs during World War II? Fair? Balanced?

I think, generally speaking, it was fair, better than I thought it would be.

Was the NSBRO involved in any public relations–type work, sending out press releases to newspapers?

Oh yes, we watched the area where there might be trouble. Paul French was the publicity man, public relations person, very gifted, and I would have to give Paul French a lot of credit for the way everything was handled with the government officials and with the locating of projects out in the field and the administration of the whole business. I requested the publicity for them.

Did you ever come across men who considered themselves political objectors rather than religious objectors? Do you think that a political objector or an economic objector is as sincere as a religious objector?

I think *sincerity* is a hard word, but on the other hand, I would say that I've seen many of these men, and I have thought that they've been as sincere as any religious people I've seen. In fact, they have a fervor and a commitment, they're willing to die for their point of view, and as far as I'm concerned that's when a man is sincere, when he's willing to die for what he believes. Now, when you come to the problem of eliminating war as a method of settling disputes—and that's my theory of peacemaking—I don't think that I'd go all out to settle all problems in my peace position. I fight for method— war is the wrong method of settling disputes, it does not solve the problems. Therefore I would say, let's eliminate war as a method of settling disputes

13

and have them take economic problems, whatever it is, and deal with it but don't go to fighting.

What books influenced your thinking on pacifism?

Well, you'd have to throw in Harry Emerson Fosdick there as one man that influenced my generation. Now, he didn't get into the movement so much, but he preached pacifist sermons and, of course, he was well known.

Can you think of any others?

Well, there had to be a lot of them, they don't come to me right now for some reason. Why don't they? Well, you had A. J. Muste [executive secretary of the Fellowship for Reconciliation], [John Nevin] Sayre of Fellowship of Reconciliation, but there weren't very many that did enough to stop a war, sorry to say, but the Friends and the [National] Council for Prevention of War [a broad based peace group] were the most honored ones. Put Kirby Page [social evangelist who preached a politically active pacifism] in there, Sherwood Eddy [pacifist leader stressing an international perspective] (now they're coming). Sherwood Eddy had tremendous influence on me.

Do you believe that Civilian Public Service was a successful enterprise? Were you disappointed in how it worked out?

Well, you have to judge things by comparison, and I would say it was a step compared with the First World War to the Second, it was a step in the right direction.

The 1940 act made it clear that the alternative service was to be performed under civilian direction. Do you feel that the CPS program was run by civilians?

As far as administration of the camps are concerned, we certainly had the responsibility to see that the camps were operated in accordance with the desires of the agencies: Mennonites, Friends, and Brethren. Now, when you're working with the government in a situation like this, they had to be sure that they were doing the right thing too. I mean, they were criticized heavily for being too lenient with us on certain elements, and they had to watch their step. Therefore, they had to know what was going on, and anybody that ever had anything to do with conscientious objectors knows they're not the easiest bunch to deal with. I think the government felt like General Hershey, that even though they gave us a lot of liberty, they still had to know what was going on. I think I would have to say that both the government and the representatives of NSBRO worked together. I'd like to put it that way: we knew what we were doing, it was a cooperative thing.

Now, to say that we were absolutely free of government, I would say no, and I don't know that we wanted to be absolutely free of the government. Now, there's where certain groups of conscientious objectors didn't agree. We had some of our own CPS people who thought we were too much for the government. So they walk out and go to jail, and I helped people get to jail. I'd help people get out of jail and come to CPS. I'd help them get out of our operation and go to the army. I'd help them get out of the army and come to CPS. I mean, I believe in religious liberty, you see. So I don't fall out when things don't go exactly like I want them to go. I'm an agency to help each fellow find a place he wants to be, and when he's in something he doesn't like, we find a place where he can go.

So it's your feeling that the relationship with the government worked fairly well?

Yes, but if we had a different man than General Hershey, who believed in religious liberty, I don't know what might have happened. I think that ought to be said.

Would you tell me a bit about your contacts with Victor Olson [part of the Camp Operations Section of the Selective Service System]?

Well, he was a little closer to the men; he did the visiting of the camps consistently. I mean, he really did, and he had a way with the men—they didn't like him, and yet he generally did something they'd all like when he visited the camp. And he knew how to give them the works, so to speak, from the government standpoint. Of course, when [government officials] visited the camps, the boys would ask them a lot of questions, and they made it just as hard for [Olson] as they could. That ought to be understood. I tell you, as I know pacifists, I don't know if I'd want to have been under a bunch of pacifists entirely or not. They're pretty tough. Not much flexibility. I think Selective Service allowed a lot of flexibility in it.

What are your feelings on the government camps?

That was an interesting episode. Some of the fellows began to petition for government camps, and the Methodist group did a good bit of that, and then when they came, they wouldn't go into it. Bishop [G. Bromley] Oxnam [Methodist who served on the NSBRO] worked very hard for that because he didn't want to raise the money to finance the conscientious objectors. I met him in Chicago in a hotel one night, and he sure went after me, because he thought that we had persuaded the Methodists not to go along and go into the government camps. But we did not persuade them. The Methodist boy said, "We appealed for the right to have a government camp, but we didn't want to go into them. We were only appealing for the rights of the guys that wanted it. We didn't want the government camps." That was embarrassing to Bishop Oxnam, and I felt sorry for him, but there wasn't anything we could do about that, and I never had a man talk to me as straight as Bishop Oxnam did.

The NSBRO established this program for members of the three Historic Peace Churches, and all of a sudden, after it began rolling along, all these other people you mentioned started coming in, the Jehovah's Witnesses and Methodists and political objectors and so forth. As an official of the NSBRO, what was your feeling about all these nonmembers of the Historic Peace Churches coming into the camps? Did that upset you?

Well, at first we didn't think there'd be so many, you know, and we said, "Come whosoever will." We divided them between the three groups, placed them in the camps, and we'd absorb them that way and take the responsibility. I mean, it was just that simple, it only took about five minutes to make that decision and we felt good about it.

Stephen Cary

"I would not do that now. I would not go into CPS, an alternative service program sponsored by religious agencies. I think it was a wrong concept, in retrospect, despite the fact that I profited from it a great deal, and despite the fact that, in my opinion, the government never did anything which was as fine a maker of pacifists as CPS was."

Stephen G. Cary, born in 1915 in Philadelphia, spent four years in CPS as both a camp assignee and a director of two camps. His career after CPS reflected his abiding commitment to Quaker values. From 1946 to 1969, Cary worked for the American Friends Service Committee, directing postwar relief efforts in Europe and then serving in various positions in the national office in Philadelphia. In 1969 he became a vice president at Haverford College; he retired from the college in 1981, having served for a year as acting president. From 1979 to 1991, he chaired the AFSC. He has received honorary degrees from Haverford and Swarthmore colleges.

What was your father's occupation?

He was the executive vice president of an electrical instrument firm, Legion Northrop Company. My father was a Quaker, and when Legion Northrop changed its product line because of the war, he quit, as a pacifist. And he said, as long as they kept making things that they always made and they sold some of them to the army, he would stay in. But they took a contract to manufacture a component of the Norden bombsight. He quit at that point.

What was your education at the time you went into CPS?

I'd been to Quaker schools, Germantown Friends School, and then came to Haverford and graduated in 1937.

You went into CPS in 1942. Between the time you finished Haverford and went into CPS, what kind of work did you do?

I worked for the General Electric Company in their accounting department and then got interested in something more socially useful, public housing, which at that time was a new venture, low-cost housing for the poor. I did work for a short time for the Philadelphia Housing Authority, but I got fired because I accused some of the important people of being in the employ of the real estate lobby. And then I couldn't find a job in housing, so I went to Johns Manville, which was in building materials, but it had nothing to do with social concern. I worked there until I was drafted.

Would you characterize your religious upbringing as strong or moderate?

I had a strong religious upbringing, although it didn't have much of an impact on me really until the war came along. But I certainly had a strong Quaker background, I went to Quaker school and college, and regularly went to Quaker meetings with my parents when I was growing up.

When you first filed for CO status, did your draft board pose any problems?

Not severe. I was living in Philadelphia, and the Philadelphia draft boards, especially out around Germantown where I was, it wasn't a case of they've never seen one before, which often is true, and they didn't have this policy that many draft boards had of refusing to recognize a CO as a kind of patriotic duty. The draft board situation, well, I suppose it's terribly difficult to devise any just system. It was a pretty vicious system. It depended an awful lot upon the prejudices of the local board what happened to you, whether you were half sick and were sent, whether you couldn't get a classification if you weren't a Quaker. They didn't pay any attention to the law. They were laws unto themselves, and it was very hard to deal with a local board in Peoria who had a bastard running the thing. My local board called me in for a hearing, and they tried to persuade me that my kind of person was needed in the army, that the kind of intelligence and concerns and ideas that I had could be helpful in making the army a better institution. But when they saw I wasn't going to buy that argument, they dismissed me and I got my classification. They, however, were damn sure I didn't jump ship. I had to report at a certain time; they took me to the train and put me on the train. But they didn't give me any static and hold up on my 4E.

What kind of work were you doing in your first camp?

Well, we were cutting wood and building reservoirs in the forest to provide a source of water in case of fire. And we were also fighting fires. And then I went into the office there as the camp accountant. And then the assistant director quit, so I became the assistant director of that camp [in Petersham, Massachusetts]. I went to camp in early 1942, and by about April or May I was in the office and was made assistant director. There was no resident director because there were two or three small camps, and they had one director for three camps.

I got chosen then to take this very interesting year at Columbia [University]. The navy was interested in training officers for governing occupied territories, which they then planned to retake from the Japanese in the Pacific. The university thought it would be an interesting experiment to put naval officers and conscientious objectors together. The COs were interested in studying relief administration, and the [American Friends] Service Committee was trying to develop a program where they could train their men who were assigned to CPS in relief administration. Columbia put the two together and put us in the same course with these naval officers because there was a lot of common ground between the problems of a governor and the problems of a relief administrator. So I had a year at Columbia studying relief administration and taking some courses, like the law of occupied territories, and the navy guys took some of our courses.

Did you live in the dorms at Columbia?

I lived at International House.

Were the navy people in the same place?

No, they had their own barracks at Columbia. But we had courses with them, and we met twice a week with them in the faculty club for dinner. Common program. Sometimes we had a naval officer talking about occupation problems, sometimes some relief administrator talking about relief, but we all went to every program. That lasted a year. Then I had a very brief time at Swarthmore because the Service Committee set up training units for men who were to go overseas and do relief work. And as a person who had a whole year's training, I was chosen to head up this unit at Swarthmore. But we only lasted two months, because this fellow, Congressman Starnes from Alabama, put a rider on one of the appropriation bills which said that no money under the Selective Service appropriation could be used to train any COs to go overseas. And while the programs were entirely financed by the churches, the officer signing the approval for the service was an army officer. His pay, therefore, was involved when he signed his name. So on a technicality, they threw us out, and we were then reassigned to the camps. So I went back up to West Campton, New Hampshire. They closed that in two or three months. The nearest Quaker camp was all the way in California at that point, and Colonel Kosch made his famous remark about the fact that he wasn't running a travel bureau, and we weren't allowed to go. So they sent us down to the Mennonites in Luray. I was down in Luray, Virginia, on the Blue Ridge for the winter of 1943, I guess.

What kind of work was that?

Well, it was stupid work. It was rebuilding the wall and opening up vistas on the Skyline Drive. Of course, there was no traffic because the cars never had gas, it was rationed. So it was just a make-work project, I thought. I worked up there in the winter, and then in the spring of 1944 I went to Big Flats [New York] as assistant director. Later I became director there and stayed until September 1945. Then I was sent as director to Elkton, Oregon, where I worked through the fall and early January of 1946. I came back and was discharged.

Did you have any sense that your discharge was unduly delayed?

I didn't. There was a lot of griping then about points. [CPS did not have a formal point system, such as the armed services did, but weighed age, length of service, and number of children in scheduling releases from service.] But I'd been in since early 1942 and therefore had accumulated a lot of points. The guys who came in later really got, I think, the short end of the stick on that. They did have to wait a long time. There was a lot of griping, I remember, at that period, even when I was being discharged, about undue delays. The war was over in August, and we weren't out yet.

On any of the assignments, did you ever experience harassment of any kind?

I did, [but] not personally, in the sense that I was a camp director [and] I did have difficulties, not in terms of people harassing me but in trying to work with some of the veterans' groups, for example, in Elmira and Corning, New York. They attacked the camp as a kind of hotbed of communism and immorality and so forth, without any basis of fact at all. And we were constantly under attack from American Legion sources for boondoggling and all kinds of sins. So I'd have to go in and deal with these people, and it was a tough job. They were irrational. But I was never physically abused. I never had any trouble myself. Some of the wives had problems with discrimination and abuse. But they would always treat me with some deference because I was the head of the camp, and they would always talk about the riffraff that I had to deal with, until I told them that I was also an assignee, and then there would be some difficulty, but I never had any personal abuse.

20

Were you at Big Flats when the work stoppages began?

No. I had left by that time. They had a government supervisor there named Elton Johnson, who had a lot of experience with the CCC boys and tried to deal with the COs on the same basis, and he had a very different kettle of fish. And he was constantly on my back as the camp director for not properly handling these men. He said, if he was running the camp he would be pretty quick, things would get done in a hurry, and if he needed to have the joint policed, he would just line them up in rows and have them march across and police the grounds. And I said, it wouldn't work with this crowd and I could handle them better than that. So I left, and within three months he had a strike. Less than that, I guess, within a month or two.

Was your overall sense of the CPS experience a positive one?

That's an interesting question. For me, it was. At an early age I had more responsibility than I'd ever dreamt I would have or that I was ready to take. In being a camp director and negotiating with Selective Service and trying to cope with all the problems, it was an experience which taxed every bit of ability that I had, which gave me tremendously valuable experience in all sorts of areas. CPS, because of the good fortune I had, both in the Columbia unit and in directing the camps, was really a very excellent experience.

But, several observations I'd make about it. One is, in concept, I believe it was completely unworkable. We were endeavoring to do social pioneering in harness with the government. You can't do that, in my opinion. You cannot be creative and flexible and experimental when you're locked into the embrace of Selective Service with a very different set of objectives. That's one problem. And I think for many men, a great many men, the no-pay, routine, often boondoggling nature of the work was a terribly deadening kind of thing over time. I think it hurt a great many people.

Another basic problem of the system was that you had in the camps (this was especially true of the Quaker camps) men of diametrically opposite philosophies in terms of work. You had some people who felt that the way in which you should deal with this forced labor was to give 200 percent and persuade the government by your industry. This was the Service Committee philosophy in the beginning, the "second-mile" philosophy. And you worked hard, and if you did a hell of a job, why, you'd get better opportunities, general hospitals or parachute units and exciting alternative service. There was another group of people, equally sincere and dedicated, who felt the whole thing was an outrage and the thing to do was refuse to work or do as little as you could in order to demonstrate the injustice of the situation. And these two were just pulling against each other. And complicating the fact that you have diametrically opposed philosophies is the fact that Selective Service was interested primarily in keeping these men out of sight, and they would throw into the camps guys who simply were unable to adjust. And you had up to 15 or 20 guys who were on permanent sick quarters, who were such a terrible drag on morale you couldn't get them out.

Physical difficulties?

Physical. I had guys carried into camp with arthritis so bad they couldn't get out of bed, and it took three months to get them out. Eventually you'd get a physical disability out. But the guys who in any compulsory situation couldn't adapt—they were reasonably adjusted on the outside, but within the narrow confines of CPS, living in the woods and only having a very limited type of work they could do, [they] would go to pieces. And you had eight or ten or twelve of these guys sitting around who'd seem to be healthy but wouldn't work or couldn't work and were depressed. You had to get a psychiatrist to state that he was suicidal because Selective Service just regarded them as malingerers.

When I was at Big Flats, for example, we had a psychiatrist over in Binghamton who would see these guys—they were depressed, had psychiatric problems of one kind or another—and he would recommend discharge. And he would get turndown after turndown after turndown. We had 15 of these guys, and he hadn't gotten a single one out. And he was just fit to be tied, because he thought all of them could not possibly adjust. So he said to me one day, when I took a patient over there, "What the hell am I going to do?" I said, "I know what you can do if you want to try it. You send me your diagnosis and your recommendation. Don't send it to Selective Service. Let me rewrite it in the language I know will get a guy out. I will send it back to you; you make a judgment whether I have in any way altered your professional diagnosis. I mean, I don't want to say anything that isn't your view as a professional." And he did that. And we got 12 guys out in a month, because I just knew the way that you got the poor devils out.

What was that?

You had to state the fellow was a danger to himself. That there was a real risk of suicide if he were kept on. You could not say that if he got out he would adjust reasonably well on the outside. You couldn't do that. You had to say that the problem was such, in the camp, that he was likely to be suicidal or a threat to others and—I can't remember all the things you had to say, but anyway I said them, and then he used to make modest changes on what I said and then send it down to Washington. We got almost all those guys out. And that changed the tone of the camp: if you've got 12, 15 guys sitting around here just not working, just moping all day long, week after week, month after month, and the guys who are working are sore because they can't see why Joe isn't working, that just dragged the hell out of morale. It was awful.

Were there any other points of friction among the CPS men, apart from different philosophies of work?

Well, yes. There were all kinds of views, you see, particularly in Quaker camps; they were the most diverse. The Mennonite tended to go to the Mennonite camps; they were the most homogeneous, and there was a docility in the Mennonite camps that there wasn't in the Quaker camps. The Brethren began to get quite a diverse group, and they stuck all the artists out in Waldport, Oregon; boy, they had their hands full out there. They had some problems. But the Quakers had the worst problems because they tended to be the most, shall I say, liberal of the peace churches, so that all the oddballs tended—an awful lot of them tended—to end up in the Quaker camps. And you'd have various kinds of frictions. People were there because they were religious fundamentalists and the Bible says, "Thou shalt not kill." And they used to sit and argue over biblical exegesis and all of that. And you had other guys who had almost no religion at all. They were supposed to have a belief in whatever it was, the supreme being, but guys would slide in there who were philosophical objectors, who had no religious values, and, of course, they got into friction and fights with the fundamentalists.

We had one guy in particular at the Flats who really was a Nazi. He was in favor of the Germans. He was an assistant to Gerald L. K. Smith, you know, the notorious racist and right-winger. And he was a real problem; everybody fought with him. In Big Flats we had a guy who won a Pulitzer Prize for biography, a Ph.D. and a college professor, we had a lot of college professors. We had some guys who were farmers, who were Maine woodsmen who were all muscles and short on brains, and there were frictions there. It was terribly difficult to build a community in that kind of an environment. And overall, there was the compulsion [and] no-pay feature. So to try to make that group function as any kind of a congenial or coherent whole was a terribly tough assignment. It was an exciting one, but it was difficult.

How did you resolve the dilemma of being both an assignee and an administrator?

Well, I took a position then that I wouldn't take now. I, after all, was very young when I was thrust into this, and I felt that men had various options, and if you chose to come to CPS, you accepted some of its inherent contradictions. And I was an administrator, and I was a good deal more troubled by having to put in reports on guys who were refusing to work, reporting guys who had left camp, AWOL. I did it, because I was loyal to the Service Committee's project; having gone into this, we had to see it through. But I would not do that now. I would not go into CPS, an alternative service program sponsored by religious agencies. I think it was a wrong concept, in retrospect, despite the fact that I profited from it a great deal, and despite the fact that, in my opinion, the government never did anything which was as fine a maker of pacifists as CPS was. From the standpoint of the government, it was a total failure in that you had nothing to do but argue and you were constantly discussing your own insights in terms of your war position. Either you were enormously strengthened and buttressed and became committed to a kind of lifetime concern in these areas, or you kind of quit and went into the navy, which some guys did. Or were burned out. It was a kind of hothouse environment.

I talked to one man who said that after CPS he never would go to a pacifist meeting.

That's true, there were some that did have that reaction. On the other hand, the peace churches have lived for 30 years on CPS men. I mean, the AFSC, its leadership, has absolutely; 90 percent of it came from that service.

But you say that, looking back, it was a mistake for the peace churches to make that kind of connection.

Yes, I think it was.

What would have been the desirable alternative—simply have government camps from the outset and men who could live with that would go there and other men would go to prison?

Yes. I feel, while it was terribly important for the peace churches to press the government, as they did, for some sort of alternative to get away from the problems they had in the First World War, there had to be some outlet for the CO, and they should have pressed for camps, they should have pressed for a rich variety of alternative service opportunities. But I don't think they should have run them themselves. I would have thought that the government had the responsibility to run them. And while I understand why they did it—and it certainly was in many ways a more attractive environment to have

Quaker camps with Quaker administrators—I think the compromise was too great.

Of the young men who had grown up with you, those you knew personally, how many went into CPS?

Well, I would have said of the young Friends that I knew, Germantown meeting where I went did better than most meetings. Some of my friends did go into military services; I would have said it was at least half or more who took a CO position in some form or another. Some went into the field service; they counted themselves COs, but in effect they were kind of 1A0 people. But if you include that group, who really weren't ready to go into the military, I'd say that better than 50 percent of the young members of that meeting were in that category. But there was an awful lot of soul searching, there certainly was. Many young Friends did not take a CO stand. It was a much more difficult war to be a CO in. I mean, Hitler was a pretty tough cookie, and there were a lot of terrible things happening, and you had to have a pretty deep conviction against killing. You recognized the fact that something had to be done, you were saying that this wasn't going to solve the problem. So it was a difficult kind of war because if ever there was a justified war, it was the war against Hitler.

Did you have any financial hardship while you were in CPS?

No, I came from a well-to-do family, and I used up all my resources, and I came out of CPS absolutely stone-cold broke. But I had resources back of me if I had needed them. So I did not have headaches. Plenty of guys did have real, real problems.

You weren't married at all during your CPS period.

No.

You mentioned that some of the wives suffered harassment up at Big Flats—in terms of getting jobs?

Well, they would get jobs, and then people would find out who they were and they'd be fired. There were several instances of people getting fired. On the other hand, there were some who worked at places like the Elmira hospital who, I think, had good work experiences. Some of the veterans' groups tried to get them fired. But sometimes the employer wouldn't fire them.

Did your family visit you at camp?

Yes. My father used to come up and visit once in a while. I don't remember the rest of my family coming. Although it could have been that they did. Yes, they came. At places like Big Flats there were quite a few visitors, because it was accessible. Up in Oregon, we were long gone. But Big Flats was quite accessible.

Had you considered at any point getting involved in any of the medical and scientific experiments?

Yes, indeed I did. I applied for the starvation experiment in Minnesota and also for the smoke jumping. But the [American] Friends Service Committee dissuaded me, asked me not to apply, to withdraw my application, because they were very short of camp directors, and since I was making out reasonably well as a camp director, they wanted to keep me where I was. So they asked me if I would cooperate by not applying for detached service.

Does the name Frieda Lazarus ring a bell with you?

She was a WRL [War Resisters League] person, I believe. And I didn't know her well, but I could identify who she was.

In one of her letters she mentions a case involving a CPS man in Big Flats who had been injured playing football and suffered brain damage, and I guess there was an attempt to have him released from camp, and that you were not helpful. Do you recall that?

No, I don't recall it. Often the camp director got blamed for everything; if you didn't get him out, it was your fault. And, you see, Frieda Lazarus, and the WRL wing generally, were terribly anti-CPS. They didn't believe in it. And while they were, I think, probably closer to being philosophically right than I was at the time, they generalized, or they made accusations without knowing what the hell they were talking about quite frequently. They were extremely annoying because they would accuse you of not being concerned about some poor devil when you were busting your tail to try to help the guy. And you're up against Selective Service. It's true that I wouldn't lie about some guy's condition, and she might have had a view of his health condition which I didn't share. In the first place, they didn't understand the religious motivation of the Service Committee in this thing, and they regarded that as pretty much poppycock. Philosophically, we were pretty far from the WRL, and I'm not surprised that she was accusing me of not caring about an individual. All I can say is, I did my best to care. As a matter of fact, I felt so much that I had had a break in the war that I went and did two years of service in Europe after the war as a contribution, to try and make a positive contribution.

What are your recollections of Corbett Bishop [one of the most resistant men in CPS]?

Well, I knew Corbett in his heyday, before he matured and deepened. I think the final experience he had in prison was a magnificent experience. But when I knew him, he was really finding his way. He had a great red flowing beard, and he looked like John Brown. When I first walked into West Campton, off the train from Swarthmore, I walked into the camp at lunchtime. And there was a guy outside the dining hall digging a ditch. I thought it was a broken water pipe or something, and I went up to the guy and asked what he was doing. And it was Corbett. And he said, "I'm digging my grave." Then I ran into him a little later. He was engaged in a fast at that time, and I went down to Boston on business, and I took that express back up to New Hampshire one night, late, and he was on the train. He was reading. I said, "Bishop, what are you reading?" and he said, "I'm reading a book on fasting. I really find that I have not been doing it properly at all. It's a great book. I recommend it to you. I really know a lot about fasting. Steve, just give me an issue, and I'll show you a real fast."

There were all kinds of tales that revolved around Corbett. And, of course, the most famous one grew out of that Colorado camp in the Rockies, Mancos, where he used to get up and give a word for the day at breakfast. And he got up one day, and he advised all assignees not to look out the window because it was beautiful out there, it might tend to raise their morale. He was wild. But anyway, later, he went into prison and went on a tremendous fast and really won over his jailers. He was a fantastic, devoted, and sweet guy. He got beyond his itchiness. In the end he won a release without any restrictions, and they finally opened the door and said, "Okay, you can go." It was a great triumph for him. And then, of course, the final tragedy was that he went back down and got murdered, of all things. Of all people to end up being murdered by a robber, I think Corbett was the most unjust.

Could you reflect a bit more on what kinds of changes CPS evoked in your life?

Well, I would say that I learned more about how to get on with difficult people in four years with CPS than I ever learned in any time before or since. I learned how to relate to very, very diverse people. I learned how to confront a system that you were against, and how to make something that was unworkable at least passably workable. I certainly have learned a tremendous lot about my own convictions about war, peace, and why I was a pacifist, and what that required of me. All those concepts grew enormously in CPS. I met some magnificent men in CPS whom I've continued to know all my life. Some of my greatest friendships were born there. And out of CPS, of course, because of my working so closely with the Friends Service Committee as a director, I became known to the committee. And they gave me, as a result of that, my great opportunity, which was to put me in charge of Quaker relief in Europe. And for two years I wandered over Europe in the immediate postwar period. I suppose I got as good an insight into the price men pay for war as anybody ever got. And to see the physical cost, the human cost, for war was a tremendously searing experience; [it] changed my whole life. I planned to go back into business when I got home. I never did. I stayed with the [American Friends Service] Committee for 25 years. My whole life was completely changed by CPS, in terms of what I was going to do and what I wanted to work for and what I thought was important. So it was, for me, for all its iniquity and evil, personally a very great learning experience.

Herman Will

*"And when they [the Urban Park Methodist Church in Chicago] had a
serviceman's flag with about 40 of their young men in military service, they
put a star on the flag for me in Civilian Service."*

*Herman Will, born in New Jersey in 1915, shaped his pacifist orientation while
working with the Methodist Commission on World Peace and the Fellowship of
Reconciliation (FOR). Married and an attorney when he entered CPS in June
1943, Will served at a camp in North Dakota and directed a camp in Puerto
Rico. Since CPS, he has continued his commitment to pacifist ideals, both in
the Methodist Church and the broader peace community.*

My family was somewhat of a churchgoing family, but not exceedingly
devout. We moved to Milwaukee, Wisconsin, for a couple of years, and then
to Chicago. I spent most of my later boyhood and adult life in the Chicago
area. I got into the whole peace field because of the United Methodist Church.
It was the Methodist Episcopal Church way back then and went through a
number of mergers.

Was your family Methodist too?

Yes, we were Methodist, although it was more or less my father's affiliation;
my mother had been Episcopalian. But they went to a Methodist church in
Chicago, and as a result, I got active in the youth work in the local church
and then the national denomination. From 1939 to 1941, I was president
of the youth work in the church nationally. The youth program was quite
progressive in its outlook. In a sense you could say that they were radical-
ized—in the Christian perspective, very definitely—by the Depression and
those difficult years of unemployment and youth's frustration with the whole
capitalist economy. And there was a good deal of Christian socialism in the
churches, the more liberal people in the churches, and in the United States.
I remember, in 1936, I was one of the members of the youth committee for
Norman Thomas, the presidential candidate of the Socialist party. The church
youth program had a heavy pacifist flavor, and many of the people, though
not all, took the pacifist viewpoint. The young people opposed strongly the

military draft that was enacted in 1940. We also took a strong stand on behalf of conscientious objectors.

Trying to get adequate provisions for conscientious objection written into the bill?

That's right. I had graduated from law school in 1937, and then did some graduate work in law school in 1938. I'd started getting interested in the Friends' emphasis on peace. I went to one of their institutes of international relations that lasted for two weeks the summer of 1937. And in 1938 I spent the summer in Flint, Michigan, in a Quaker work camp studying the United Automobile Workers' union and the auto industry. So with those contacts added on, I was asked by the Board of World Peace to become youth secretary. They had given me scholarships to go to these two programs of the Friends. I worked about six hours a day and took some more college work. I'd gone ahead with my law degree without finishing four years of liberal arts, so I went back and finished the liberal arts work. I never really practiced law, but I did do some writing of wills for friends and some real estate transactions.

I was able to counsel effectively the conscientious objectors and worked with the Commission on World Peace from 1938 to 1942; I counseled somewhere up to 500 conscientious objectors. Most of them were religious, but some not religious. The overwhelming majority were trying to comply with the law. A few faced jail because the law wouldn't cover their cases or wouldn't recognize their views, and a couple that felt really no obligation to society were going to try to escape by whatever means.

I visited a number of Civilian Public Service camps while I traveled around counseling. In February of 1942 (at this time I was engaged to be married), I decided to go over to the Fellowship of Reconciliation. A pacifist organization in wartime seemed to be even more challenging than working for a church, which supported pacifists but was not a pacifist body itself. So I worked with the Fellowship for about 16 months, or something like that, from February of 1942 to June of 1943. I was married in August, and my wife did some work with the World Student Service Fund and later with church agencies in Chicago.

How did you support yourself during this service both to the church and to the FOR? Obviously, you weren't being paid a good deal. You were used to "doing without" even before you went into CPS, weren't you?

Well, I got a munificent salary of $50 a month from the Commission on World Peace, and when I went to work full-time I went to $1,800 a year. With the FOR, since I was married, they raised me to $2,040 a year, so that's what I was making at the time I was drafted. My wife was earning on the side. Now, during that time, since I knew I was going to be drafted, my wife and I stayed with my parents. When I was drafted into Civilian Public Service, my wife accompanied me to the camp in North Dakota, stopped off just for the day to see what it was like, and then went on to the West Coast, where she stayed with her sisters and her aunt, her parents being missionaries in South America. She stayed with them for about three months, and then came back to Chicago, where she worked with the church agency until we went to Puerto Rico.

Can you tell me something about your FOR activities?

While I was in the Fellowship of Reconciliation, we had the problem of Japanese-American relocation, and the need to relocate people out of these concentration camps. I was vice-chairman of the Chicago committee on relocation, and we were in the midst of doing that at the time I was drafted. I remember going with a young Japanese woman, a student, taking her to a college in Chicago, which had agreed to accept her, and then having them say that, because of security—due to some classified contract with the navy or training navy students, I forget what it was—they really didn't feel they could take her in. So that was pretty frustrating. But my wife and I arranged with the FOR to get a young man [she'd known] out of a camp relocation center; [he] went to work as an interracial secretary for the FOR. He stayed in Chicago for a while in our home. And then I took him for his first field trip in downstate Illinois, which was interesting in wartime, and being with him in a church where he preached, and having three farmers call up afterwards and asking, "Could you get any Japanese-American farmers to help us with our farming?" They were short on farm labor in that area. Then also having the experience of seeing this young man go into theological seminary after the war, and then serve in Wisconsin as a strong pastoral leader in a number of large churches.

While I was working for the FOR, I visited the CPS camps at Cascade Locks, Oregon, and Lagro, Indiana. When I was at Cascade Locks, I met Lew Ayres, the movie actor. He was still in CPS at the time, but his position all along had been that he would be willing to serve in noncombative duty in the army if they would guarantee him medical service. At the beginning, they would put you to work driving a truck or doing any kind of noncombat work. He refused that, and the draft board accepted his refusal and assigned him to CPS. But his case got so much publicity about conscientious objection that Selective Service and the army decided they better do something, so they provided that persons would only be assigned to the medical corps, or maybe chaplains' assistants, unless they were willing to serve in some other kind of noncombat work.

So Ayres set a precedent.

He set a precedent, and he then went into the medical corps and later was a chaplain's assistant.

What was your family's response to your decision to enter CPS?

My family was supportive of me. They weren't enthusiastic about the war. I wouldn't say my father was a conscientious objector. He had not served in World War I. He was with the same company he had been with at the time of World War I; that was the Bristol Company, that made recording electrical control instruments of different types, and they were selling to defense factories. So he was related to it that way. But I had genuine support from my family and from the church. My local church was the Urban Park Methodist Church in Chicago, and they had even given some money when I made a trip with a youth group to Europe in 1939 to attend the World Conference of Christian Youth. The pastor asked from the pulpit for contributions. The cost was about $500, and one Sunday morning—this was a good sum of money in those days—people gave him $105 towards my expense. And when they had a serviceman's flag with about 40 of their young men in military service, they put a star on the flag for me in Civilian Service.

That was a rather enlightened attitude.

It was. It was a servicemen's committee with a newsletter, and I received a newsletter, and I was named in it, and it told about what I was doing. It was a fairly open church, which helped, but I think I had established myself so firmly that no one questioned my sincerity. I had been very active as head of the youth group in church.

Tell me about your first CPS assignment.

Trenton, North Dakota, which was a land reclamation project. After six weeks on camp cleanup, I was invited by the director of the camp to be his assistant in the office, and my responsibilities included keeping all the records of work performed. I also used to drive the lunches out to the men in the field crews, which gave me a good chance to get in touch with virtually all the men in the camp.

How many men were there?

About 130 or 140, something in that neighborhood. That was typical of these camps. In fact, it was an unusual camp because it had a large number of Catholics in it. The Catholics had operated a camp supported by the Catholic Workers, Dorothy Day's [leading Catholic pacifist] group, and they were basically a pacifist group, though some of them went noncombatant in the military. There were about 25 or 30 that had come from the Catholic camp, which was up in Warner, New Hampshire, [and] had closed for lack of money. They were sort of a bloc in terms of some common interest, and yet they weren't discriminating against other people, it was just that they had some sense of solidarity because they had come from one camp and had a common religious background. That made it a little more interesting than at other camps. It meant that, to some degree, because of different Catholic mores than peace churches and even some of the Protestant groups about drinking, there was more drinking in that camp than in some others. A large number of the Catholics were in the other half of the dormitory from my end. So about once a month, there would be a Saturday night blowout in the other end of the dorm from me, and we would be kept awake till about two or three in the morning by singing.

The Catholics were a mixed group. We had some Catholic Workers who were wonderfully radical Catholic Christians and dedicated people. You had others who may have just been objecting to the war in principle. But you also had some Father Coughlin followers who were antiwar because they looked upon the country as going toward communism or fighting alongside of Russia, and many of them [were] sympathetic to fascism, if not Nazism, a number of them being Irish Catholics. They were some interesting people. I remember one fellow named Bolton Morris. He was quite a sculptor, and he was sculpting a crucifix in wood for the local Catholic church.

The community nearby was heavily Indian at Trenton; it was an Indian reservation area. And living there wasn't too bad. At one time it had been bad. A North Dakota regiment was involved in the action at Guadalcanal and lost heavily, disproportionately, and after that time they broke up the National Guard regiments that were by states so they wouldn't have that repeated, so no one state would take unduly heavy casualties. And this had resulted in some strong feeling toward the camp and for COs there for awhile. By the time I was there in 1943, it had eased a little, and some of the men were received reasonably in the local churches. I worshiped in the Methodist church.

Did most men think they were accomplishing something positive?

I would say, to a degree, but in most cases it wasn't what they would have chosen. But some of this government land had flax on it or other crops, and there were two or three of the farming men who were quite content to work cultivating it and harvesting it. And potatoes were planted on other land, so during the potato harvest I was reassigned temporarily to oversee the picking of the potatoes. I was no farmer, but these farm fellows drove digging machines, and then Indian women from the nearby community were the pickers, and they would go down the field with sacks tied around their waists and would put about 80 pounds in a bag. That's hard work, and they would pick anywhere from 8 to 10 bags a day but get paid by the government. I used to keep the record on them, and I got to know some of them quite well.

When did you leave Trenton?

After about three months I applied for special assignment. The Church of the Brethren got in touch with me and asked me if I would consider going to Puerto Rico, and that was interesting to me. And they said yes, there would also be a place for my wife. And it turned out they were asking me to be director of a Brethren project. There was a large Brethren group, a large Mennonite group, and two smaller Quaker groups in Puerto Rico. The projects in Puerto Rico were established as a result of a trip by a very interesting member of the Church of the Brethren, Andrew Cordier. Cordier was executive assistant to the secretary general of the United Nations for a number of years. We had a 26-bed hospital with eight nursery accommodations. We used old CCC buildings and reconverted them. The men put new foundations under the buildings so the floors would be level. The work was all done by the time I got there, but they spent months doing that before they were able to even open up the hospital. The project had an obstetrician, and as a result of his interest, we performed quite a few postpartum sterilizations, maybe 400 in three years while this doctor was there.

He was in CPS?

No, he was not a CO. He volunteered to go as a missionary with the church and received a personal occupational deferment. The operation got so popular among women that we had to restrict it to women who were 30 or over, who had at least four children, and whose husbands as well as they signed the permit for the operation. Birth control technology wasn't that far along in World War II. They didn't have the pill or anything. Other methods were imperfect, and in the Catholic society, you had to confess your sins every time you practiced or used birth control devices. It's easier, I think, to have sterilization, to make your confession once and you're through. The bishop of the western part of the island, a continental American like we were, not a Puerto Rican, issued a pastoral letter to be read in all of the churches in his diocese, attacking us on the grounds that we sterilized virtually all the adult persons in the community. We had never sterilized a single man—their macho was a little too strong for that—and we had this policy of turning down many women, obviously. So it was a ridiculous statement in the first place, and it was interesting what happened. The mayor of Adjuntas and his wife had had eight children, and so, when she had her eighth, she had a postpartum sterilization. When he heard about the Catholic attack, he came to see us, and he said, "I will be chairman of the defense committee to defend you against this charge."

Could you describe some of your other projects?

We did, among other things, a patch test [for tuberculosis] program with 2,000 people in our immediate area and located positive reactions. We brought in all those people for X rays, and we located 30 to 55 active TB cases. And we had to try to isolate them, at least temporarily. There wasn't an island institution for everybody to get in. There was a waiting list, but TB at that time was five times as prevalent in Puerto Rico as in the States.

Another problem was the administration of worm medicine. You see, about 95 percent of the kids were infected with parasites. So they'd give them worm medicine, and you had to watch that the people didn't wander off, because that was the time you had to give them a laxative right afterwards to clean them out. But it wasn't as effective giving [the laxative] right away; you were supposed to wait an hour, but you didn't dare wait an hour, they may wander off, but it usually worked. If it didn't work the first time, you'd give it two or three more times. But that was a big job the lab had, testing all the stools for worms. Sometimes you'd get 100 worms out of one kid, literally. They would have big bellies sometimes, you know, and they were debilitated. We also worked to combat that by other means. We tried to get the people to wear shoes, and we had some success. And we worked on getting them to maintain their latrines properly and use them. And one of our men who married a Puerto Rican woman was in charge of checking out the latrines and working with people to move the latrines from another place if necessary, covering up the old hole. So we reached people.

We also had problems, we had no place to keep the cadavers when people died. We had about 16 people who died there a year on the average, and by Puerto Rican law, unless you had the body embalmed, they had to be buried within 24 hours. Well, if the family was standing by, that was fine, but there were instances where the family lived some distance away or couldn't for some reason be right there, and the person died. And two or three times they loaded a body in the back of a panel truck, and I had to drive up in the mountains hunting for that family. It was not a very pleasant experience, having to break the news. And what you do is park on the side of the road and start asking people, "Where is the family so-and-so," in Spanish, and they tell you, "Over this way." They would run and get the family, or I would have to go find them, and then I would tell them, "There's bad news, so-and-so died . . . ," you know, ". . . and I have the body."

We were an emergency hospital, so we came close to having 1,000 surgical operations, that includes some outpatients, and we had about 200 deliveries a year. And we would never take multiparas but only first children or complications, because we couldn't handle very much. There were midwives in the area, we worked with them and tried to give them training and help. It was a tremendous program really.

The U.S. Public Health Service was so impressed with what we were doing that they would send Latin American doctors studying at the school of tropical medicine out for two or three days to see what we did with what we had in Puerto Rico at Castaner, because they could see that, with very limited facilities, there was a lot they could do in their countries. One of the guys who came down there later became the dictator in Haiti, François Duvalier, Papa Doc.

We also visited public schools and gave immunizations in areas not reached by the island's public health department. The island health department gave us a lot of medicines free for our clinics, for our hospital, and so we got a lot of stuff free. The government also paid us for holding these clinics for them. We got so much a clinic. And then they had a *fundo*, which was like a workers' compensation: if you had people in your hospital, you got paid for them. These were nominal amounts, but still they stretched the money. The Brethren put in about $25,000 a year, the budget was around $42,000, so about $17,000 was income. Now, when we did the surgery on people that had enough money to pay, we would tell them about how much the surgery was worth and they would pay us. We never sent a bill. And the people whom we served would bring us chickens, and we would cook the chickens. There were times during the year when the avocados were just coming out of your ears. I'll never forget the time the kitchen tried making avocado ice cream. We were already so sick of eating avocados that when we saw that green-colored ice cream, we just didn't touch the stuff.

Another one of these special assignments was an interesting case. One of the men was assigned to work at Marine Hospital, which treated not only men in the marines but also working for the U.S. Merchant Marine. And his job was to deal with venereal disease cases. If they had contracted venereal disease, then he would work to try to gain the confidence of the men and get them to tell him who the women were who infected them so they could trace them and get the women to take treatment so they wouldn't spread the disease further. And he had quite a time with that, working in that kind of a context. They had a program for treating the women; they'd send them to camp for rehabilitation and treatment, like a CCC-type setting. But you had to get the confidence of the people. And I guess the government actually threatened them with prosecution at times, but most of the women would cooperate anyway because they realized it was for their own health.

It was great to work in Puerto Rico because, as I've said to people who talk about national service nowadays, never let it be compulsory because compulsion poisons the whole concept of service. If it isn't voluntary, if it's compulsory, you destroy a lot of the meaning of the service. And even while we were there, although it was good to be doing what we were doing, the sense of value of it and the meaning of it in your life was denigrated to a degree by your knowledge that it was under compulsion and you couldn't go home. You couldn't do something else, and the Brethren in Civilian Public Service had indicated in a poll that they were overwhelmingly in favor of the Church of the Brethren ending its administration by six months after the war was over. This was the idea at the time, that the war plus six months should be regarded as the end. It was a term that we picked up from other institutions of government who were using that as sort of a rule of thumb. And this was recommended, but the Church of the Brethren governing board, despite this recommendation from the men and from their own staff, decided they should finish it out. They had committed themselves to the government, so they should continue until it was over. But at any rate, when that happened, I had voted for withdrawal. I submitted my resignation as director, and I asked for a transfer. And I thought, conscientiously, "I've got to ask for a transfer to a government-operated camp." So I left them. I hated to leave it in a way. I'd much rather have stayed there doing that.

You felt that you could no longer work with any camp administered by the churches?

That's right, and I asked for a transfer, and they sent me to Big Flats, New York. The men in the camp decided to go on a work strike, so I went with them. And while we were on strike, the FBI came out and investigated it.

Why was the FBI involved?

Well, it was a federal offense, violation of the Selective Service law is what we were doing. Well, they came back the next Monday with warrants for the fellows they felt were the ringleaders, and they weren't the ringleaders at all. They were just individuals who had been moved by the spirit; you know how some people are, "I've had it, I am fed up, I am not going to do it anymore," and they had to tear up the warrants and go back and get new ones.

37

What finally happened?

Well, they were prosecuted and sent to prison, but we got them out on bond, so they didn't have to stay very long. As a result of that, they delayed my discharge. I got a discharge, if you can call it that, with "Discharge delayed due to refusal to work" typed in red typewriter ribbon on it.

Do any of your children share your pacifist philosophy?

Three of our sons faced the draft in one way or another. Our oldest son, Douglas, was at the University of Chicago. Had just graduated in physics and was starting graduate work in that field when he was drafted, and some of the professors at the school were interested in seeing him continue to be near the school and maybe take some courses if he could once in a while. So they helped him locate a job in the radiation research laboratory of the University of Chicago hospital, which did employ COs performing alternative service. Our second son, Donald, expected to be drafted, but it happened to be finally the year when they stopped just a few numbers short. It was the year when renewal of the draft was up. The third son, Alan, applied as a conscientious objector in the last stages of the draft when practically nobody was being called, and he asserted his claim as a conscientious objector but was put in this 1H category, which was sort of a holding category so they didn't have to do any more paperwork on the cases. So that's part of it. Our oldest daughter is a Methodist minister. She is a pacifist, and when she was at Bryn Mawr, she spent a day a week working as a volunteer in the afternoons and evenings for the Central Committee for Conscientious Objectors. Do you know about my relation to the National Service Board for Religious Objectors?

No.

When I finished with the war, I then did two months of traveling for the FOR. I went back to work with the Commission on World Peace. In my work, I was called administrative secretary, and I was assigned to work with conscientious objectors. And so, starting about 1947, I was elected a member of the National Service Board for Religious Objectors, and I've had, I guess, the longest tenure of anybody on that board.

Do you feel your CPS experience definitely led to your future commitment to this type of work?

It intensified it. I had it there before. But it was intensified, I think. Living in Puerto Rico gives one the experience of a different culture. Looking at the United States at least partly from the outside was helpful. It's not quite like a foreign country but still is different from living in the continental United States. But I have served on the National Service Board and was chairperson for about three years. I was the first person to be chairperson who is not a member of the Historic Peace Churches. One thing I think I played a role in doing was getting a Catholic priest on the board, and helping to get the first rabbi and the first woman on the National Service Board. And I also helped reorganize it. Now, instead of being called the National Service Board for Religious Objectors, it's called the National Interreligious Service Board for Conscientious Objectors.

Looking back, what was the most difficult aspect of CPS?

The thing that irked me most was the whole sense of compulsion. It wasn't present in your mind all the time, but it was present a good deal.

And it tended to negate some of the positive feelings that you had about what you were doing?

That's right. Exactly. I think that was the most adverse thing.

Do you think that CPS strengthened your marriage, or do you think it put new stresses and strains on it?

I never thought of it like that. It put some strains on it, but I don't know that it affected it. You see, there were a lot of things that affected it. The whole uncertainty of that period, the fact my wife and I weren't able to establish a home of our own right away. Even when we came back, we were so broke for a while, we really couldn't get out on our own, and housing was terribly tight. There were things like that that were disadvantages. So I would say it put strains upon it, but they were in a sense strains associated with the whole period which I am sure were typical of other families.

What was the most satisfying aspect of CPS?

The feeling that you were part of a team of people who were really doing a worthwhile service in Puerto Rico. We had good public relations. When we had these weddings, we used to have a roast pig and dance outside. We had a PA system, and we would use the radio or records. But everybody had a good feeling of identification.

Looking back now, would you do it all over again?

One, I am very much still a religious conscientious objector in the sense that I wouldn't be dissuaded by somebody trying to tell me that your point of view isn't practical—you know, it's not going to work, you can't resist Nazism by pacifist methods, or something like that. I just believe, as a religious person, I should not take human life, and it's that simple. And I usually put it that way. It's not my responsibility to decide how things work out. It's somebody else's job, maybe God's, who knows, but it certainly isn't mine. I am not going to dictate history by what I do, and there is a place for a witness, and the pacifists were witnesses and went to their death under Hitler. I always point out that it's curious that the Methodists, the Catholics, and the others weren't the great COs and resisters to Hitler in Germany. It was those very obnoxious Jehovah's Witnesses who stood up in the United States and made the government unhappy, all the way from their noncooperation in various ways to their fighting the cases to the Supreme Court and winning them very often. But they were imprisoned by the thousands in Hitler's Germany, and they used to go up and witness to the guards, telling them what they thought of Hitler. We used to hear during the war about a dozen a week were being shot. No question, there were hundreds and hundreds of them, maybe thousands, who lost their lives because of their witness. They were more consistent than the Methodists.

The other reason I was going to say I would do it again was not only because I was a religious conscientious objector, but also because I am not an absolutist really. I never have been. Maybe because I am a lawyer. I have a sense of trying to cooperate to a degree with the law, so far as I can, because I think the law is important in society. I see what happens to societies where men are above the law and take other peoples' lives into their hands, disregard their rights. So that's part of the picture. You have to have a certain degree of order.

Are you aware of any limitations that you experienced professionally or any other way as a result of your CPS experience?

In my work, it hasn't been a limitation. Possibly an asset. In a sense, I think—and I hope this is not taken in any sense as being an expression of pride on my part—but I think, and people tell me this, that I am thought of in the Methodist church as sort of Mr. Peace, because I am the person they think of when it comes to pure peace. I've been with it so long.

2

HISTORIC PEACE CHURCH MEMBERS ENCOUNTER CPS
Uriah Mast

*"I have to admit I enjoyed [being in CPS]. I wouldn't have told
my relatives that, I wouldn't have told my parents that I enjoyed it.
Because of the fact that it was supposed to be a hard thing,
an endurance thing that you go through."*

*Uriah Mast, one of 12 children of an Old Order Amish Mennonite farming
family, was born in Topeka, Indiana, on 12 October 1919. During his three and
a half years in CPS, he served at four camps in Virginia, Maryland, Iowa, and
California. For Mast, as well as many others in CPS, traveling thousands of
miles from his rural community proved one of the most influential parts of his
CPS experience. After the war, he moved to Florida to work as a cabinetmaker
and volunteer with the Mennonite Disaster Service.*

Would you say you had a strong religious upbringing?

Yes, I would say so.

Could you describe the considerations that led you to choose CPS?

Oh, I would say probably the knowledge I had of the teaching of the
church. We had a book on the conscientious objectors in the First [World]
War. I read that clear through, and there was a strong emphasis on the
wrongness of war and the need to take a stand against it, which is pretty
much the historical stand that the church has taken down through the years.
And then the parents' feeling that this was the right thing to do. I couldn't
say personally that it was a strong conviction on Bible teaching—here's what

the Bible says so and so—although that's the way I filled out my questionnaire, because that was pretty much the common way of filling out a questionnaire. But as far as having deep religious convictions from the Bible, I couldn't quite say that. It was mostly deep religious convictions which were embedded in my background of the family and the church really. I never was what you would call a rebellious type. I more or less took the attitude that if you belong to the Amish church, then you comply to the Amish rules.

So because of these convictions, going into the military was totally out.

That was out, that's right.

How about noncombatant military service?

That was pretty well out too.

And you didn't want to go to jail?

No, I didn't want to go to jail. I don't know what I would have done if the board would've refused me. I would have probably gone to jail. I don't know. They did refuse me the first time, and then we applied again.

You appealed?

Yes, they denied it, and then you had to appeal in front of the local board. My dad went along, and I kind of think that might have helped some.

Were there any pressures from any source other than those of your conscience to go into CPS?

Well, not particularly, although the church would have frowned on it very strongly on this matter of going to war.

You really didn't have any thoughts about not going into CPS? You knew about CPS, and that was your choice?

I was fairly well acquainted with it. Actually, I registered in the first registration, a lot of guys took off for camp, and I wasn't drafted. I don't know why, I never did know. But it was pretty near a year before I was drafted, from the time the first guys went. So I even had a chance to visit the camp before I went. So I knew pretty well what it was all about.

You had a brother who went into the military?

That's right.

Why did he go?

Well, he was always a little more rebellious, and he was not a member of the church. I was a member of the church and more or less accepted the fact that if you're not a member of the church, why, you really don't belong in CPS. Although from a technical point of view, I guess that would have been possible, because there was a lot of them didn't belong to any church were in CPS. But in our community, the whole idea was foreign, this idea of not belonging to the church and going to CPS. I don't even know of anybody that did get CPS in our community that didn't belong to the Mennonite church, or some other church. He didn't belong to any church. He was always sort of a little more rebellious concerning the matter of religious things.

Black sheep maybe?

Well, yes, a little more that way. He didn't stay with the rules and regulations of the family really. In the Amish community, you're more or less considered to be under the dominion and rulership of the family until you're 21. Then you go out on your own, and from then on your decisions are all your own pretty well, very little [is] done to persuade you, and, of course, he went out on his own when he was about 17. So when it came time for him to sign up, which was after I left, though he was very favorable towards my position, he himself didn't want to take it.

Did he survive the war?

Yes, he was injured with shrapnel in his leg.

He went into active combat duty?

Oh yes, naval.

How did you feel about that at the time?

Well, you see, my decision is the way I went, and his decision is the way he went.

How did your parents feel about that?

Well, they didn't approve of it, but they took it as his decision.

Did you have any other friends who went into the military?

Not close friends. Practically all my close friends went CO. You see, our community was pretty much isolated and close-knit. We didn't get out very far because we didn't have vehicles to go far. Now, my brother did. My brother had a car, and he went wherever he wanted to go. Well, you see in the Amish church you have horses and buggies, and you just don't go very far. The radius was smaller. When you get a car, then your radius gets bigger, see. I talked to other fellows that said in high school they had friends who went one way and they went the other way. I didn't have that problem. I didn't even go to high school. You see, the parents were opposed to higher education beyond eighth grade, so I really didn't have that problem. Most of my friends were from the church, the Amish. And the kids in town, like Topeka, they went to the army. But I really was not close to them. I knew them by name, and that was about all, because I didn't even go to school with them. The school that I went to was so heavily Amish that we hardly ever had anybody else, excepting once in a while a Mennonite boy.

You entered CPS in August 1942. Could you talk about the camps you were in and what you did there?

Well, I was in mostly soil conservation camps. I grew up on a farm, but I never liked farming. Part of it, because we did it the old-fashioned way with horses. If I could have used tractors, it would have probably been a different story. And soil conservation, I could see the value of it, but the way we went out to do the work was sort of old-fashioned. So much hand labor, and it seemed you weren't getting much accomplished. But you could see value in it, really, soil conservation, terracing, sod flumes, concrete flumes, great value in it, no question about it.

You started off in Denison, Iowa?

I was at Denison for about a year and a half. I was there when the Missouri River overflowed at Council Bluffs.

Did you spend time sandbagging the town?

Yes, I was on that gang.

I read that all the work the men put in had a decided effect on changing the community's attitude toward the camp.

Oh, that could be. I didn't know that. In fact, I went to camp and never left except to go to work.

You never went into town?

I never went into town. A lot of the others always had to ask for a leave on Saturday night—they had to go to town. They had to go up to see a movie, or they had to go up and watch the girls walk down the street, or something like that. I didn't. I was a little more conservative, I'd think, well, I don't have no business up there. Because I knew there was friction there, and I didn't like to see anything that would stir up friction.

So you basically just stayed in camp?

Stayed in camp. I'm a little more the type that was interested in education, but I didn't have the opportunity. So that is what I did, a lot of my spare time was read and take courses. Although I didn't take a course in typing, I took typing by going down to the soil conservation headquarters, which was right close to where we were. The night watchman was usually there, that was his headquarters, and I would go in there and use their typewriter. That's how I learned to type. And then they had courses in music and Mennonite history which I enjoyed. Later on I went to Clearspring [Maryland] with a group that was picked out to study community living. About a dozen applied, but two of us got to go to that. And they studied what makes a community tick and what tears down community life. We were still on soil conservation in daytime, but these were evening classes for four months. And then I took a course in bookkeeping, and these were all things that helped me in my education, which is something which I was denied when I was younger.

Why did you transfer to Luray?

Well, we had to get out: our training was over with for that school, and they wanted to start another one. I got to Luray in the fall, and then in May 1945 I went out to Three Rivers, California. My main job was to work with the park carpenter, a government employee, and I worked with him half the time and the other half I was on blister rust control. Blister rust was a disease that was affecting the pine trees up in Washington and Oregon, and it was moving south. The barberry plant was part of the cycle. It went from the pine tree down to the barberry plant, then back up again. If we eliminated the barberry plant, we eliminated the cycle. So we dug out all the barberry plants that they had in the area. And we did that by having 10 guys pacing about five feet apart, and the last guy pulled a string along so they'd know where they went. When you get to the end of the park (now Grant's Grove was a small park), you'd turn around and come back. And this we did, day after day.

You were discharged on 26 March 1946. Did you have any feelings that your discharge was unduly delayed?

No, I don't think so. It seemed like quite a long time, but at least you could see the end. But before that, you couldn't see the end. That was the gloomy part about it. You just don't know how long it's going to be. If you'd have known exactly how long it's going to be, why then you'd have just sort of prepared for it. Some fellows, they were really depressed about the whole thing; some of them were even affected mentally, I think, because of the fact that they had to go and leave their families. You take a person that's traveled a lot, has to go somewhere, why, he don't mind it too much, but a person that's in a small community and lives there, why it's a little hard on him.

For me, the whole thing that was depressing was the fact that you were going and you don't know when you're getting back. That was the worst part of it. I didn't feel that anybody was going to harm me, like they did through World War I, [or that] anybody was going to misuse me, any more than what they did at home. I mean, you had opposition there at home. I was going to town with my horse and buggy one Saturday night, and when I was coming back, about 10:30 P.M. when the stores closed down, some guy come along. As I met him, I heard something go "thump," and I didn't know what it was, and after he passed, I looked around, and here he'd thrown a rotten egg at me. Those are the things that were going on around home. Some of the kids from town didn't like these Amish boys, because they didn't go in the army. And when I went to camp, really the only opposition we had was when we'd go to work. We'd drive down the road, and we'd pass somebody, maybe a couple of guys, and they'd holler, "Hey, you yellowbellies." That's really the only opposition that we had. I really never did have much.

One problem I had before CPS was with my draft board. I wanted to know when I would be drafted so I could let my boss at the feed mill know. They really didn't know nothing about it; I thought they did. This guy at the draft board chewed me out because of the fact I'd gone CO. He was there the time we appeared to get the 4E, that was our classification, but he didn't say nothing, because the rest of the board were there. But when he was by himself, and I went up to talk to him, he really chewed me out. Evidently, he didn't feel it was the right thing to do when the rest of the board were there. The rest of the board were businessmen; all he was was sort of the secretary of the place, and he really chewed me out. Outside that, I really didn't have too much opposition.

Did you feel your CPS units were accepted by the local communities?

Well, they were fairly well accepted. In Denison, I think the farmers and the businessmen uptown accepted us, because of the fact that we're benefiting them. The rest of the people were not benefited, and they did not accept it too well. Now, in the other communities, up at Clearspring, it was pretty well accepted, because we were a little more rural. We were not right close to a town; Clearspring's just maybe 70 people, or 100 people, is all it was.

Several men have mentioned that they would go out and join local churches and choirs.

Some did, but I didn't. See, I was a stay-at-home guy.

Did you know many who would do such a thing?

In Clearspring, quite a few of them would go to church. We were a little more mountainous area there, and in one valley there was a Church of God, and they were pretty much like some of the hillbilly areas where they're all related to one another. The CPS men went down there on Sunday nights, and they seemed to get along real good with those people.

Your flood relief work must have improved your relations with that community?

Yes, the newspaper editor wanted to get a story, and they gave him a story. They told him what it was all about. Even the mayor came down and said, "Is there anything that we can do for you?" He said, "You're helping us, and we'd like to help you. How about some tickets to a movie?" Well, the man who was in charge said, "Well, our men don't go to movies." At that time the Mennonite church and also the Amish were pretty well opposed to movies. So he couldn't give them anything like that, so he said, "How about some aprons for your cooks?" "Okay, all right," so they got some aprons.

While you were in CPS, did you have a generally positive sense of your experience?

Oh, I think so, I think so. I seen some guys that were really emotionally affected by the whole thing, that it was maybe harmful to them. But I didn't feel it affected me that way. Personally, I enjoyed it. I have to admit I enjoyed it. I wouldn't have told my relatives that, I wouldn't have told my parents that I enjoyed it. Because of the fact that it was supposed to be a *hard* thing, an *endurance* thing that you go through.

But it really wasn't that way?

I enjoyed it. If I worked on the farm, which I did one summer, I'd work about ten, eleven hours a day. Out there, we'd go and we'd work eight hours. But the eight hours were from the time we left until the time we got back. Sometimes we're an hour on the road getting to our work, and then it took an hour to come back, so we only worked six hours. Then we'd have an hour for lunch, usually half-hour, or forty-five minutes, I don't remember how much it was, but anyway, that was quite a big difference from what I was used to working on a farm—and working hard, and working long hours. We'd work in the field maybe eight hours, and then we'd do the chores, see.

Some of the other fellows felt that it was such a depressing place that they'd do most anything to get out. And they did. Before I left Denison, they opened it up to go work on dairy farms in Wisconsin. Quite a number of them went that were very much interested in farming. But I knew that I was not exactly a born farmer, and I didn't see why they should call this such a depressing place. I didn't think it was. And they let these guys work on these dairy farms, and usually they were with that family, and that's all. There was nobody else involved, and time became quite a drag to them. Later on a lot of them said that if they'd had it to do over, they wouldn't have gone. Well, I thought that all along, because I thought we had it very exceptional nice where we were.

Did you all share a commitment to nonviolence?

Well, there would have been degrees of commitment, I would say. Degrees of it.

But by and large, it was a strong commitment?

It was a strong commitment that you don't kill. As far as nonviolent, I would say there's a variation in that.

Was this shared commitment to nonviolence, even with variations, a sufficient bond to develop a real sense of community within the camps?

Oh, I would say so, yes. Pretty much so, yes. Even Jehovah's Witnesses (a number of them were there in Denison)—our theology was so much different, but we still shared one thing in common.

Nonviolence.

Nonviolence. That's right.

Even having this shared commitment, were there any serious points of difference among the various segments of the unit?

I wouldn't call them serious, no, not too serious, I don't think. Not where I was. I think there was one place where the man who was put in charge, a Mennonite, was tarred and feathered because of strong feelings. But it wasn't at ours. CPS was a time when you learned to respect the other denominations and your own denomination. Mennonites are split up into about 12 separate groups, and this was a time when we learned to respect each other. Probably more than any time before or since. You learned to know what things to avoid to keep from making friction.

Were there any work slowdowns or protest?

No. Only the Molokans [a Russian pacifist sect], they were always protesting something. And they were not what I would call nonviolent; they simply didn't believe in killing, but they were not what you'd call nonviolent. So beating up wouldn't have hurt anybody, was their viewpoint. And the government man who was the superintendent of the camp isolated the Russians from the rest of the camp. They were in a side camp. I was in a side camp, but I wasn't put there because I was a troublemaker. They were put there because they were troublemakers. Of course, the government superintendent worked closely with the camp directors; when he went back there, a couple of times he took a gun with him. He knew that something could happen. He was not about to get beat up by a bunch of Russians. They wouldn't have killed him, they don't believe in killing, but you don't know what they would have done.

Could you describe the forms of church support given to the men?

Well, the Mennonite church provided money for the food, and later on they also started giving donations to the men, such as $10 a month.

Most of the other men have said that the church provided religious services.

Most of the churches had men coming around to visit.

Visiting ministers?

Visiting ministers, yes. But as far as having a minister there every time, no.

Would they provide you with Bibles or hymnals you would use in a service?

Well, most of our setups already had a chapel; that was part of the CCC program, but the songbooks the church supplied. The whole thing was very simple. There was just a little pulpit, and no benches, just religious chairs, and I think we had a piano. You had so many different groups coming together, some of them would have had pianos in their own church, some wouldn't.

I was told that the men would occasionally receive $25 or so, taken up in their home churches in a voluntary offering.

Yes, that happened occasionally. For me, it didn't quite happen that way. When I'd go home, maybe some of the people in the church, they'd say, "Well hey, I want to help you," and they'd hand me some money, and I'd stick it in my pocket, and later on I'd see what it was. Well, they had given me maybe $5, something like that. That's really the only help that I got outside of what my parents gave me. My parents sent old clothes; I'd tell them what I needed.

A couple of men have said that after they got out they received from the church a cash amount that had apparently been set aside in a fund at a rate of so much money per day that each man was in the service.

The Old Order Amish did that.

Did you receive a cash amount?

I was supposed to get that, and they had told us, do not take the money from the Mennonites. The Mennonites got an allowance of $10, and they said, "Don't take it, because we want to make up that amount, give it to you." Of course, they didn't do it right away. When you got home, then you were supposed to get that. Well, when I got home, I worked around Ligonier, Indiana, which was close to where I was born. In the fall, I came to Florida. I was still part of the Amish church. Well, in the meantime, they gave me $400. I was supposed to get about $800, something like that. See, $10 a month for so many months. When I came to Florida, I said, "Well, when spring comes, I'll either go back to the Amish church, or I'll stay down here." It so happened I got a job, and it worked out for me to stay down here, so I got a car, and, of course, then they heard about it, me getting a car. So I didn't get the rest of the money. I should actually have taken that $10 that [the Mennonites] offered to me.

Would you say your relationships with the non-Mennonites were good?

Yes. There really wasn't much trouble at all that I encountered with anybody. The majority of the people got along pretty good. While I was in Luray, new draftees came in from Kentucky or Tennessee, from the Church of God, a Pentecostal-type church. They were very strongly Pentecostal, and one morning, I remember, I went down to the woodworking shop, and one of these men was out there praying under the trees, praying, carrying on, I guess, Pentecostal-style. Of course, he was all emotionally worked up because that was about the second day he was there, one of those days before he went out to work. Really, nobody was against him, and he was all emotionally worked up, and he lived in a little world of his own. That's really what it was. Nobody had really done anything to him. Now, when I was up at the side camp at Grant's Grove, there was a colored man there from New York. He would've belonged to some Pentecostal church, I never heard of the church before. And he was very, very emotional, and in the evening, when we'd go to bed, he would kneel at the side of the bed and pray a long time. Sometimes I'd fall asleep, he'd still be there praying. His praying would be so that he would shake all over. And he wouldn't pray loud, he'd be shaking just like this, and I never could understand the whole thing, but that was some of the people you met up there.

Did you meet many blacks? Was he about the only one?

He was the only one in that side camp. Three Rivers might have had about two blacks. There were not many blacks in the whole camp program that I can remember. In fact, I don't believe I run across any of them until I got to Three Rivers.

Did you have much to do with either of the two black men there?

No, I really didn't. We were good friends, he slept right next to me, but we didn't work together or anything like that, and he sort of went his way and I went mine.

Had you dealt with blacks before?

No. Never seen black people until I went to Elkhart one time when my dad was in the hospital, I must have been about eight. First time I ever saw a black person.

Did you know any people who became disillusioned and left the camp to go into the army?

Yes, there were some that did; I was not close to any. They were more or less the persons not interested in going to the church, and a little more on the griping side.

Were they similar to your brother as far as religious beliefs were concerned?

Yes. I'd say so.

How did they get into CPS in the first place?

Well, I don't know. I think some of them actually belonged to church. But to them it was probably a matter of going through the motions more than anything else.

Did you have any financial difficulties during CPS?

It's funny about that financial part. I didn't get any money, except some gifts. I cut hair when I was in camp; I was a barber and got about 25¢ a hit. When I got out of camp, I had more money than I did when I went in.

I learned to live frugally. i learned to live without buying pop, without buying candy, and no going to town. Oh, maybe once a month, I might have eaten a candy bar. In other words, I was kind of tight, but I knew I had to be, otherwise I'd have to dig into what little savings I had. I had some savings. What did I need? My parents furnished me my clothes. You want to talk about living without any responsibilities, that was it. People ask the question, why do guys join communal groups? I can tell them mighty quick why they join communal groups, or some of the reasons: no responsibility, you don't worry. I thought to myself, when I get out, I'm going to have to go back there and have to worry about a job, and if I lose that job, I've got to worry about another job, and I've got to worry about where I'm going to live. What have I got here? I've got everything. No responsibility whatsoever. The only responsibility we had was what little we had in the camp, and, of course, I always assumed quite a bit because I usually ended up being a foreman on the job, and that involved a lot of responsibility.

Did you ever anticipate that the government would grant dependency allowances or pay?

Well, pay was always a matter of conflict and argument. Some said yes, and some said no. You know that the government should pay, because they drafted you, but I always took pretty much the attitude that I think Mennonite church leaders did, that we are not sacrificing much compared to what some are that go into the army. There was nothing wrong with us not getting any pay.

A little sacrifice never hurt?

Never hurt you. Whether you get paid or not has a lot to do with your image in the community. It's true that most people wouldn't believe you if you told them that you worked four years for nothing. People wouldn't believe you. But that's actually trivial.

Did your family have any sources of financial support other than the farm?

Well, that's a long story. I was a little boy during the Depression. We had 12 children in the family, and that's a heavy weight on a family. Many people lost their farms. And my parents had a lot of debts, and I remember hearing my mother say, "We'll never get out of debt, so long as we're here." Which wasn't true. And I remember when I was 12, 13, my dad went to my uncle, who was well-to-do. He was a man who people came to for advice. My dad said to him, "We just don't get very far. We pay the interest on what we owe, and we just don't get very far." And he said, "Well, where do you pay your interest?" "The bank, you have to pay 5 percent." "Well," he said, "that's too much. I'll loan you the money at 4 percent. Plus you got too many people eating food out of your house, you got too many mouths to feed. You get these boys out to work for the neighbors, and they'll bring in some money. In fact, I'll hire one of them." So my brother worked for him, and

I had to go to another place. I was just about in the sixth grade when I had to work for a neighbor. Of course then, on the weekends I'd come home.

Were you still going to school?

Still going to school. And all I got was board and room, until summer came, and then I got $15 a month.

Which went to your father?

That's right. And it wasn't hard work, but I was only 14 years old.

But by the time of World War II, were your parents in better financial condition?

Oh yes.

So that your absence really didn't hurt?

Didn't hurt them too much, no.

One man said that he was also on a farm, and that, on the whole, at the time he came out, his parents on the farm had actually prospered.

Yes. See, what I did, I stayed at home and worked and saved a lot of my money. So I had quite a bit of money saved up; I don't know how much, maybe $1,000 when I went to camp. So really, that's pretty well where it stayed; in fact, I increased that savings a little bit by the time I got out. You can always, if you're looking for something, find ways of picking up a little money here and there, even it might be digging a ditch. Mine ended up being cutting hair.

How did you maintain contact with your family during CPS?

About a weekly letter.

How often did you get home?

Oh, I guess about every year.

For how long?

About two weeks. Every year you got 28 days of furlough, something like that, and as I transferred from one camp to another, I'd usually stop at home and take some furlough days. Otherwise, I'd have to pay for it myself to go on a furlough.

Was leaving home for CPS difficult for you?

That wasn't hard for me; I don't know why. I guess part of it was because I was not the first one to go. Other guys had left quite a long time before I did, and I knew it was coming. I more or less felt I owed a responsibility to somebody, to the government, because of the fact that I'd been given the status of CO.

Or maybe the difficulty was in coming home after three-plus years away?

It was hardest to adjust to the community after you come back. Yes, that's right, that was a little hard.

Did any other members of your family go into CPS?

Yes, I have a brother that went in. He was physically not fit to go in, but it was at the point where they drafted everybody they could get their fingers on.

What was the most satisfying aspect of CPS service for you?

Well, I would think probably learning how to get along with people.

What was the least satisfying aspect of CPS?

You mean, the most frustrating? I guess probably the fact there was always griping; [it was] frustrating more than anything else. The guys complain, you know. Because I just didn't feel like that, and I disagreed with them. I didn't like all this complaining about everything.

Looking back a generation later, do you have any doubts about your decision to enter CPS?

I'd do it again.

No doubts at all?

No, no doubts about it. You can get through things a lot easier than you think you can. I mean, things look gloomy and dark, but they are not so bad. The thing that happens is not as bad as the imagination of the happening.

Do you feel your life was changed for having entered CPS?

I would say probably it has changed, yes. But then, you also have to think in terms of maturity, you know. As a person grows older, you look at things a little different, regardless whether you went into CPS or not. It was a beneficial learning experience. I think it gives you a little more appreciation for other people who have different religious views from what you do. It was quite a learning experience as far as the traveling. And then, what I appreciated quite a bit about it was the fact that I had educational opportunities. I guess even in prisons you'd have those.

Are you aware of any limitations that you have experienced as a result of having been a CO during the war?

Not in my field of work, no. I would have probably had some limitations maybe if I'd wanted to go in some other fields, without the GI bill for education.

Or maybe even politics?

Yes, right. No, it never really gave me any trouble that I was a CO. I don't think it ever came up as far as a job application.

What do you see as the effect on the church of having thousands of men in CPS?

I think it had a good effect. Many of the men came back and became active in the community, community builders. I think because of the fact that our church has so many different branches that it helped unite them together a little bit more than what they were before. I would also say CPS had a good spiritual effect on the church. They were tested a little bit more. Otherwise, you have something which you believe but you don't come to the point where it's really tested as to whether what you actually believe is serious.

Another thing that came out of it was the Voluntary Service Program in our church, which I think was an outgrowth of the CPS program. They've asked the young people, like the Mormons do, to serve a period of time in some service program without pay, or maybe with a small allowance. Another thing happening in CPS was that you mixed the educated and the uneducated together. The educated pretty well are on their side of the fence and the uneducated are on their side, but in CPS you mixed them together. In that sense, there was a breaking-down of the barriers, the walls that build up between those groups, which you wouldn't have had otherwise. I think it was a good thing for the church.

Do your CPS acquaintances generally look back on their service as a positive experience?

Yes, I would say so. Even a person who was quite a griper at Denison, I've talked to him since, and he looks at it quite positively. I was surprised.

How often do you think back about CPS?

Oh, I don't know. I guess a lot of times when we go to church, one of the guys who I met in CPS says, "Hey, did you see so-and-so?" Or when he goes up north, he says, "Hey, I seen so-and-so that was in camp." That kind of brings it back. Or when I go somewhere, maybe I see somebody that I was in CPS with. So we talk about it.

What memories about CPS are the strongest for you?

I would say the friends that you develop. When I went into a camp where there were about 125, 150 people, I tried to see how long it would take me to learn the names of all the persons. And some persons were there a year and they still didn't know all the names. I used to try to do it within about four months.

Robert Doak

*"I was a star football player at N.C. State. I was the starting quarterback,
and when one of those goes into Civilian Public Service rather than the army
at the time of war, it can get some rather good headlines."*

*Robert Renfrow Doak, born in Greensboro, North Carolina, in 1921, came
from a strong Quaker background. A football star at North Carolina State, Doak
entered CPS the evening after leading his team to victory over its archrival, the
University of North Carolina [at Chapel Hill]. Doak served four months in
CPS; he was discharged for medical reasons. After the war, Doak completed his
undergraduate degree, played professional baseball, and coached and taught in
North Carolina.*

What was your father's occupation?

He was a baseball coach and associate professor of physical education at
N.C. State College.

And did your mother work?

Yes, my mother was a political activist, and she was a secretary for many
years, and then worked for the Agriculture Department, just after the Depression, and she was also the first woman in North Carolina, and possibly in
the U.S., to ever have a radio program of her own.

Could you describe your formal education?

I went to the Raleigh public schools and then to one year at Westtown
Friends School in Pennsylvania and then came back and went to North
Carolina State and graduated in textiles. I did graduate work at the University
of North Carolina in physical education.

*Did your draft board give you a hard time when you said you wanted to go
into CPS?*

No, it was relatively easy for me, but not for a lot of young men. Since I was a Friend, it seemed to go much easier.

Did you have any financial support when you were in CPS?

Well, my brother went in, in the first draft, I guess it was 1941. And then I went in, in 1942. My sister, who was working in Washington, did, I understand, support the CPS program with something like $25 or $30 a month.

Did you have a strong religious upbringing?

Well, I don't know that you'd say it was strong; it was certainly meaningful to me. My family did not stress religion, nor did they let us go willy-nilly, we did have some guidance.

Do you think religious views are what led you to CPS?

Yes. At the time the Raleigh Friends meeting met with another church, the United Church, and this church was, if you want to use an outworn phrase, a liberal church. We were exposed to all points of view. I think the peace testimony of Friends such as Rufus Jones, as well as other people, had a definite effect on my feelings about war and peace.

What role did your family play in your decision to enter CPS?

I think probably my brother was the biggest influence on me; he was two years older than I was. When you were raised to despise war and the things that it brings with it and one comes along—it seemed to me at the time and ever since that some people say conscientious objectors are cowards, but I felt the opposite, that I would have been a coward had I taken up arms.

Was your family supportive?

Oh yes, Mother and Father were very supportive, [my] sister and brother too. I don't want to sound like I'm egotistical, but I was a star football player at N.C. State. I was the starting quarterback, and when one of those goes into Civilian Public Service rather than the army at the time of war, it can get some rather good headlines. I won't say they were necessarily good, but we didn't get a whole lot of flak. People seemed to accept that we were Friends and that I was living up to the tradition of my religious affiliation.

How much earlier did your brother go in?

The fall before Pearl Harbor. They sent these young men up to above Asheville, North Carolina, and they worked on the Blue Ridge Parkway as their project, and they got quite a lot of publicity about it. I can remember in the *[Raleigh] News and Observer* pictures of the men working on the parkway, and they were talking about their background, where they came from.

How many camps did you serve in?

I served in only one camp, at Powellsville, Maryland, where we worked on a drainage project for the government, draining farmland. I had requested at the time I was at Powellsville to go into the smoke jumpers, and I had been accepted, but in February I had a kidney removed at the hospital in Salisbury, Maryland. I came home to recuperate, then was discharged.

Did you know your wife at the time?

Yes, I knew her before, she's a Raleigh girl. We dated some before I went to camp.

How did she feel about you going in?

I really don't know, we didn't discuss it a great deal. She went into the navy, and she was a WAVE, and I guess she was in the navy for two years at least, possibly three. But she has been very supportive ever since.

Is she a Quaker too?

She is now.

Was your CPS unit accepted by the local community?

Oh, you could go on forever about that. One story was that here I am a football player and there was a big Jehovah's Witness in camp with us, and we went up to the local store there in Powellsville, which is just a little crossroads there in Maryland. There was a feisty little fellow with us, and we went up to the store to get some snacks. We had to walk about a mile up the dark road and back, and some of the guys had been harassed a bit from time to time going up to Powellsville, but it was not so bad that they ever stopped going up there. When we went in, this big coal miner and I, and I'm not all that big but at least this little fellow thought he had good company with him that night, because he went in, and when we got back to camp he starts yelling at the top of his voice, "Yeah, you should have seen me tonight," he said. "When I walked in the store, those guys sat back there and they didn't say a word, and here's this big coal miner and Doak there with me." And so, I suppose, from the early days that some of the people in Powellsville and other places didn't accept COs, but it wasn't really that bad.

How about here in town [Raleigh, North Carolina], with your father being a baseball coach?

I don't think anybody ever said anything much to Dad or Mother. I think they respected their views, and I think most of our friends thought that had the two Doak boys gone into the service, the people would have accepted that just as readily that we went as COs.

Did you have a generally positive sense of the CPS experience?

You couldn't help it! Being in the camp there with 100 or 200 fellows, and there were all shades of pacifism. Some of them wondered why they were there, some of them cursed the Quakers for starting CPS, some of them felt at home, others wanted to move to something more meaningful. One argument stuck in my mind. A fellow who later became a Presbyterian minister said, "Well, you Quakers started CPS, now they got us stuck off out here in the woods. Where's our voice? We're not saying anything, we're just dodging the war." Well, some felt that way and others didn't. I felt that I wanted to get into something a little more meaningful than just going out sawing down trees, digging a ditch; that's why I applied to the smoke jumpers. Then I would have felt a little bit better if there had been some sort of field service that I could have gotten into.

Were there any serious points of difference between the various segments of the CPS units?

Oh yes, there were good discussions every day out on the project. It seems strange to see fellows standing around with saws and axes in their hands discussing philosophy or whatever. Some of the government people, they weren't guards or anything like that, they were people who had expertise in cutting down trees. They were amazed, some of them would stand with their mouths open listening to these fellows talk, and it had a pretty good effect on some of them. They began to understand, and I think they were a pretty good liaison to the people by going back and telling them, you know, "These fellows are all right, they're not Communists or fascists or what have you, they're good boys."

Were there any work slowdowns or protests in camp?

Never.

Do you feel that the government ran the program efficiently?

Well, of course, the government didn't run it, the government spent no money on it at all, except for tools and that sort of thing, but it was up to the peace churches to finance it.

Did you think that you had a voice in what was happening in CPS?

There were shades of activists. I suppose if you wanted to have a voice you could. I don't know what effect it would have had.

But do you think everything was run fairly?

Yes.

Did you give any consideration to seeking 1AO status rather than CPS?

Only in the sense that I wanted to be of more help, and some of us had a hard time determining whether we were going to stay out in the woods and not have a voice, or whether we wanted to get into something that would further the cause of pacifism. Not that we wanted to become heroes. It was something that would be of more meaning to us. But 1AO, that never did just quite cut it.

Did you say that your brother-in-law was a pacifist?

I had a brother-in-law that went to jail.

Did he ever consider going into CPS?

I've never really discussed it to any great extent. He was influenced by his brother, who was a minister. He refused to sign up for the draft, and he went to prison. And then he was paroled and was working in Washington at the time he married my sister.

What was the most difficult aspect of CPS for you?

Initially, giving up my opportunity to finish college. Of course, I know that a lot of people would say, well, that wasn't much to give up, there were fellows that were going out and getting shot at and killed. They were giving their lives for their country. I've never bought that; there are very few people who give their lives for anything. These fellows that were in school with me, even ROTC people, they were deferred for other reasons to stay in college and finish. We had no recourse, at least in my case. I would have graduated by the end of that term.

And they took you out right in the middle of the term?

[There was a] great rivalry up there between the University of North Carolina and North Carolina State, and we had played six football games. Now, you have to realize that a young man who has played all his life, this is a big part of his life, and it was with me. I was an athlete then and continued to be one after school; I was a coach. We played Carolina on October 30th, and we beat them, I'm happy to say, and that night I left on the bus to go to Powellsville, Maryland.

But it had been touch-and-go all fall. Two weeks earlier they had said I was going, and we got a stay for two weeks while Congressman Harold Cooley looked into the situation. They found that there was no way in which they could allow me to finish that fall term. I would have finished in the middle of December.

You would have had your degree?

Yes. I don't know whether this was any harassment in that respect, but there was a definite factor, you're not going to get any deferments. I wasn't bitter that there were other boys on the campus and on the team that were getting deferments because of their position in the ROTC program. I didn't feel animosity towards them at all.

People that were drafted regularly, were they allowed to finish their terms?

There was an educational clause in there, that if you were in school, if you were not a conscientious objector. . . .

They would have let you finish?

. . . I think so. It was a waste of time and a waste of better than half of that term. So when I came back in 1943, after I'd had my operation and got back in school, I just had to do another term to graduate.

What do you think was the most satisfying aspect of CPS service?

Most satisfying thing about life in general is the people we meet as we go along. I met some great people in CPS.

What do you think was the least satisfying aspect of CPS?

It was inert, like the guy said one night to me, cursing the Quakers about putting CPS together—just felt like it's an easy way out. It wasn't necessarily easy; I suppose that would have to do with your degree of commitment. But I thought it was a step forward. I still agree with the philosophy of CPS, that the government did allow the peace churches to have some say in what would be done with their young men. Prior to that, there was no accommodation for COs, they went to jail, period. This is the first time conscience had really been recognized, that there was a place for men of conscience.

How did your CPS decision affect subsequent decisions by your children in regard to military service? How many children do you have?

Two boys. They've always accepted that Daddy did the right thing in the war.

What would you say if they wanted to go into the service?

I don't know that I have given my sons as much foundation as my parents gave me. I wish I felt better about it. But I really don't know if it came up today whether my boys would go in as COs or take some branch of the service. I would like to clear that up, talk about service to the country, there are other forms of service other than just that which they call military. I think service to mankind, trying to preserve some sanity on this planet, is better than the "rah, rah, shoot-em-up" type of service that gets all the headlines.

How would you feel if they did want to go into the military service? Would you try to discourage them?

64

I would talk to them, of course, and try to get them to understand better what Jesus meant when he died on the cross.

Looking back a generation later, do you have any doubts about your decision to enter CPS?

No. I think it could have been more meaningful, and in time it did work out a little bit better. I just wasn't around at the end to see the young men begin to go in working in mental hospitals and the impact that they had on the state institutions. Up until that time, the state hospitals had never seen this brand of individual who really cared about their patients, who wanted to see that they got better treatment, and they couldn't understand these people.

Did you feel left out when the war was over? All these people were talking about "I did this in the service and that in the service." How did you feel about that?

You ask me whether I missed the camaraderie of war stories and so forth. Never for one minute have I missed those stories. I had my own stories; had I stayed in CPS longer, I would have had more of them.

How do you feel when people say they were in the war? Do you just say that you didn't go?

Yes. I find most people that did anything in the war don't talk about it. Those that didn't do anything, they are the ones that won the war. It's bravado.

In what ways do you see your life being changed for having entered CPS?

I don't see that it changed one way or the other. I played professional baseball for seven or eight years after. Most of it was played right here in North Carolina, and I got some catcalls from time to time, but not very much. In fact, one night down here in—it was sort of a hotbed of redneckism, Ku Klux Klan people, I won't name the county, it's not too far from Raleigh—I heard some people talking as I came out of the dressing room after the game. I was walking away from them—these were guys who on certain nights that they didn't go to the ball game were probably out wearing Ku Klux Klan hoods—they said, "That's that Doak guy. He just told them he wouldn't go, that he just wasn't going to go into the army." And another fellow said, I forget exactly how he put it, but he was somewhat awed at the fact that I had been a conscientious objector, because maybe these people defy government entirely. And somebody that could say to the government, "Well, I'm not going to put on a military uniform and go fight," they might have some admiration for that person.

Are you aware of any limitations professionally as a result of being a conscientious objector?

I can only guess. I worked for the Carolina Cougars professional basketball team for the five years that they were in existence here in North Carolina, 1969 to 1974, as a business manager in Raleigh, and I put on games and saw that everything went off all right. After the Cougars franchise moved to St. Louis, I went back to the University of North Carolina and renewed my teacher's certificate, hoping that I would get a job in coaching close by, because I had established my home here for a long time and I didn't want to move. So I went to Carolina and renewed my certificate, and I went for this coaching job, and I didn't get it. I feel like I'm well qualified, and I see people getting jobs around here that I don't think have as much qualifications as I do to coach. And I think there might be one or two people in the Raleigh city system that kept me from getting in. I don't know for sure.

Do your CPS acquaintances generally look back positively on their CPS experiences?

I don't know of any of them who are going around wearing sackcloth and ashes. It was a fairly pleasant experience for me.

Ivan Amstutz

"I understand other people's points of view better because I've talked with many, many people I wouldn't have talked to from all walks of life. It just broadened your experience."

Ivan Amstutz was born on 8 January 1926 into an Old Mennonite farming family in Kidron, Ohio. He entered CPS at the age of 18 and served in five camps, including the smoke jumpers program. After his two years in CPS, he married, had two children, and worked in banking and insurance.

What considerations led you to choose CPS rather than the noncombatant option?

Well, [the noncombatant option] was really out of the question. That's kind of frowned on, although now I wouldn't think of it as being that bad. My thinking has been broadened. I'm not as narrow-minded as I was. Education and getting along with people has broadened my views. The original question—why didn't I take noncombatant—well, I associate that [with] the military, and I just didn't want anything to do with the military. I didn't think that was the right thing to do.

So CPS offered the best alternative?

It was sort of expected of me, and I felt that was what I wanted to do anyway. It all sort of tied together.

What did you know about CPS before you got in?

Well, I knew friends, people that had gone long before I did. The war had been on about two and a half years, I guess, before I went. I was quite familiar with it, because some of the guys would come home once in a while, and I talked to them. I knew pretty well what to expect.

Was your family supportive of your decision?

Oh yes. They were expecting me to do that. They'd have been disappointed if I'd done anything different.

Were there any problems in getting the CO status?

I had no problems. Wayne County pretty automatically took some of these without giving much of a hassle—I think especially if the background is solid Mennonite or Amish. There were exceptions, I know. For instance, somebody that didn't live a very consistent life as what the Amish and Mennonites believed, they might've had more of a problem in getting their status. But I didn't have any trouble. Just a very few were having problems.

You entered CPS on 4 July 1944, and you served until August 1946?

That's right. I first served at Sideling Hill, near Wells Tannery, Pennsylvania. It was what we considered a base camp. I think 300 fellows were there most of the time. Of course, they come and they go. Sometimes they'd be transferred out, for instance, to a mental hospital or other camps for various reasons. Some stayed there a good many years, three or four years I imagine, until it was closed.

What kind of work did you do there?

Well, one thing was [to] slope the banks along the turnpike, that was a tedious job. The more important job there was soil conservation. I did some of both, although I wasn't there very long [July to October 1944] because the camp closed down.

The crew that went out on soil conservation work did various things. It was also tedious work, such as digging ditches for drain tile, digging postholes in shale ground—that was work. And the toughest shale, you're lucky if you got one posthole dug in a day. That was tough digging! Stone, you might say. Then we would clean fence rows, set up contour strips, this type of thing. That was worthwhile. But there was an awful lot of poison ivy in some of those areas. Some of the fellows just couldn't work on the crew, they just got sick from poison ivy. I got a little bit of it, but I wanted to stay on that crew for several reasons. I liked to work, and I thought it worthwhile, and then we drove quite a bit of that time, and I didn't have to work all the time, only about six hours instead of eight!

That was a Mennonite camp?

Yes, it was administered by Mennonites. There was others there, too, besides Mennonites. But the majority were Mennonites.

Was there any antagonism among the members of the camp at all?

Oh, I don't think so. There was a lot of cooperation. There could've been isolated cases, but basically there was very good cooperation. They were there for the same reason, you know. And we sort of respected each other's views pretty much.

Did you receive a spending allotment for personal things, or did you have to rely on outside support for that?

Our church at Kidron was quite supportive. I believe we got $15 a month. A small amount, just enough to get soap and a few personal things. But it really wasn't enough to buy your clothes.

Was that church support important in helping the men and their families financially?

Oh, I don't think it was a major factor, although it may have made some difference for some people. I don't think that there was a whole lot of support given other than this minor token thing. But it was better than nothing. No, the parents or relatives would have to support them if there was any support to be given. My parents saw that I had enough clothes when I went, and that's about all. I was able to support myself one way or another. This $15, I got along with that pretty good. And then, not at Pennsylvania but at some of the other camps, I got work on the side, evenings. After a while we got Saturdays off. At first it was just a half a day, and then I think later on we got a full Saturday off, and I was able to earn a little bit.

What led you to choose Three Rivers, California?

There were basically three camps that they sent everybody to, and that was one of them. There were other minor considerations. There were sign-up sheets where the openings were, and I just wanted to get as far from home as I could, for the experience. So I took that rather than the other one in California, I don't know why really. Well, this one was further south and warmer, and I enjoyed warmer weather. It was Sequoia National Park.

What did you do?

Well, I went to side camp almost right away, which was up near two big sequoia trees out there, redwood trees—General Sherman and General Grant trees, you probably never heard of them. One of them you could walk through; probably the circumference was pretty near as big as this house—huge trees. We blacktopped various pads around the trees for the people visiting the park. That was great, living up in the mountains. I enjoyed my stay in California, but I wasn't there that long either, just for the winter.

You went there in October 1944?

Yes. Then the following spring, probably March, I went to Missoula, Montana.

What led you to choose Missoula?

Oh, adventure, I imagine. I just wanted to get into something more exciting. The government wanted permission from our parents before we got into this smoke-jumping project, and I sent this form to my parents, and my father signed it and my mother didn't. And time was getting short, so I didn't write back to ask why, I just had somebody else sign my mother's name. I was afraid it wouldn't go through with only my dad's signature, so I wanted to make sure. I wanted to get in there!

How did you find out about the smoke jumpers?

Well, I was aware of this even before I was drafted. I thought it sounded exciting, and it'd be nice if I could get into it, and I wanted this experience real badly.

What did you do?

Well, first of all you get training. They really built us up physically. We did all sorts of calisthenics. We'd do push-ups and run and get in shape physically. And we had to run through big culverts—well, not run, but crawl through and everything—just like the army did. In fact, we had ex-army personnel training us. And we had a lot of fun, don't get me wrong. We got along great. But that's where they got their training, and they trained us that way to get physically in shape. And we did an awful lot of hiking and walking, cutting wood, by hand with a saw. That was good exercise. Then we got fire-fighting training also. Then they got us in training to jump. There's some safety things; you have to know what you're doing. Then finally we got five test jumps, I believe it was. If you did them satisfactorily, then you were ready to go.

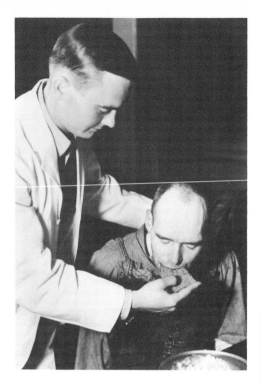

A CPS attendant feeding a patient at Philadelphia State Mental Hospital. More than 2,000 CPS men helped resolve the wartime shortages in state mental hospitals and training schools, significantly improving the quality of care. *Records of the American Friends Service Committee–Civilian Public Service. Swarthmore College Peace Collection, CPS Unit 49.*

A CPS assignee talking with a child at the state training school for boys in Cheltenham, Maryland. The CPS unit brought about the racial integration of the staff dining facility at this institution. *Records of the American Friends Service Committee–Civilian Public Service. Swarthmore College Peace Collection, CPS Unit 62.*

These men, part of CPS Unit 27F, worked in five Florida counties where there was massive infestation of hookworm. They built over 4,000 sanitary privies to alleviate this problem. *Records of the American Friends Service Committee–Civilian Public Service. Swarthmore College Peace Collection, CPS Unit 27F.*

A CPS man at Cheltenham explaining the physiology of speech to a hearing and speech impaired student. *Records of the American Friends Service Committee–Civilian Public Service. Swarthmore College Peace Collection, CPS Unit 62.*

Out of the plane . . .

. . . in the air . . .

. . . in the tree. More than 250 of the more adventurous and physically fit CPS men volunteered for smoke jumper assignments in Missoula, Montana. *Records of the American Friends Service Committee–Civilian Public Service. Swarthmore College Peace Collection, CPS Unit 103.*

In the first years of CPS, soil conservation and forestry projects were the predominant activities of assignees. Here, men at the camp in Royalston, Massachusetts, transport pumping equipment to a fire. *Records of the American Friends Service Committee– Civilian Public Service. Swarthmore College Peace Collection, CPS Unit 10.*

Outside speakers helped reduce the isolation of CPS camps. Pacifist leader A. J. Muste visits the men at the Powellsville, Maryland, CPS unit. *Records of the American Friends Service Committee–Civilian Public Service. Swarthmore College Peace Collection, CPS Unit 52.*

They took you up in the airplane for the test?

Oh yes. Of course, they had a mock-up plane we jumped out of too, at first. You learn where to put your hand and look straight out at the horizon and different things like this. And you have to know how to roll when you land. You don't take your shock with your feet or your legs—you break legs that way. You have to know what you're doing.

Was there more than one of these smoke-jumping outfits?

No, this was basic training camp in Missoula. Then half of them or so would be shipped out to various side camps. I went to McCall, Idaho. That was a side camp, and you did fire protection work there too. And that was all the U.S. Forest Service.

When did you go there? Summer of 1945?

Yes. That was a much smaller unit. I think there were only 37 fellows there. It was sort of a resort town; there was a big lake there. There were quite a few cabins, and people would go up there for the summer. I did babysitting on the side, and I made pretty good money doing that.

Did they give you any kind of hazard pay for what you were doing?

I don't recall ever getting any.

Did you get any type of compensation at all?

No.

Did you ever have to jump into fires?

Yes. Of course, when we got to Idaho, they flew us across several ranges of mountains, and it would take a long time. We went in these old Ford trimotor planes; there's only one or two left in the country. That's what we jumped out of, that was one kind of plane. We jumped right on the airport at McCall, so that was another jump we could rack up. That was another drawing point to go to a side camp: they usually flew us out, and then you'd get to jump again, so I had seven practice jumps. The fellows at base camp only got five. Then we jumped on six fires. We went out 40 miles from the nearest road one time—you know, in between fires, you have to do something. So they sent a few of us out there to enlarge a landing strip, and we were there several weeks. One Sunday I saw some smoke going up not too far from camp, maybe a mile or two, so we got to walk to that fire. We didn't even get to jump on that one. But we did, in enlarging this landing strip, walk in a little caterpillar tractor—a toy almost, but it did have a nice blade—and we leveled the strip off a little better, and we cut some trees so as to get a better approach to landing and also takeoff.

Wasn't there a danger of getting stuck in trees when you jumped into a forest fire?

Well, you might call it danger, but those are the softer landings. When you hit the ground, you hit something pretty solid. When you're hitting a tree, the branches give, so it's really softer, but there's more work in getting down to the ground. We carried 100 foot ropes. When we had practice, we were taught how to let ourselves down. And we left the chute there until the fires were extinguished, and then we'd get the chute later.

How big were the fires?

They were all sizes. Usually at the beginning of the season it would be small fires. The first one I jumped on, I went with an old seasoned fellow, and he was there, I guess, two seasons before I was. That's usually the way they team them up, an experienced man with a new guy.

Was he a CO?

Yes. I think he was a Quaker, if I'm not mistaken. He was an older fellow, he was pretty near 40 years old, single fellow, never got married. That was just a small fire. A lookout station spotted it, and they called in. We got to jump on that. It was right on the ridge, and it was really out in the sticks quite a ways because we were told there were mountain goats in the area; we even saw a few tracks, but we didn't see any goats. You know, that's kind of exciting too: lightning hit one tree, and it started burning what we called the turf buildup in needles around the tree. So we just built a little ditch around the whole tree, and we soon had it taken care of.

What about the bigger fires you fought?

The last fire I jumped on—that's, of course, towards the end of the season, when things are dryer and they spread faster generally, harder to control, and it gets windier too—that was a fire where I got to use my emergency chute. On a premeditated jump, you have to have two chutes, a backpack and a chestpack, and you're allowed to use your chestpack whenever your backpack malfunctions. And it so happened that one of the shroud lines through to the top of the canopy of the chute almost cut it in half—not literally cut it, but it spills the air out of both sides and you drop pretty fast. And so you're allowed to pull your emergency chute. Well, this is what I did, but I had trouble getting it fluffed out; it wouldn't take because I wasn't dropping that fast, I guess. I wasn't as heavy as some of the fellows either, I was only about 140 pounds, that was just above the minimum. So I finally got it out. Then I couldn't manipulate my guiding, so when I landed, I had two chutes open. And then I landed in a little bit of bush, it was the softest landing I ever had. That was fun. But I hit the opening I was supposed to hit—the little meadow with a few bushes.

Another fire, I landed into a great big fir tree, where I almost made it to the ground but not quite. But you know how these Christmas tree–type fir trees are—where there's nothing for the chute to hang on to and I just slid right down! I was a little worried, because I was afraid if I landed too high, I could fall quite a long ways; it was maybe 15 or 20 feet. And I was able to grab hold of the branches to slow the fall up.

Did you know anybody who ran into any accidents?

Most of the accidents, as I recall, happened in training even before they went aflight. Like one fellow, he just couldn't wait to jump, so he jumped off of a 10-foot roof near the camp there, and he broke his leg! Yes, it was stupid, but that's what happened!

You were telling me about a famous fire.

Yes, now, until we got it controlled, I don't think you could probably walk around the whole fire in a day's time, that's how big it was. They got a bunch of Mexicans in to help us too.

Was that a fairly normal thing?

On the large fires, yes.

Were they migrants?

Yes, migrant workers. Now, they would take them as close as they could with a truck, I believe, and then they'd have to walk in. They dropped quite a bit of food to us on that fire because we were on it for about a week or so.

How long would you work each day?

Well, just as long as you were able to stand it. You worked from morning to dark.

So you'd live out there until the fire was under control, then you'd come back in. How much free time did you have?

During that summer, we got Saturday afternoons off. And, of course, if you were in a fire during Saturday or Sunday, you got to take that time off later on or add it to your vacation, which was two weeks a year. But we got a chance for overtime, because if there's a fire, you've got to go. But at the base camps you never get that.

What did you do for your vacations?

I worked mostly. I think I did use part of it, and I came home. I hadn't been home for over a year. In fact, I had an opportunity to go to the state of Washington in the fall on my vacation—it was my earned time, we called it—and I worked for a wheat farmer. They had big wheat operations out there. We sowed wheat by the section. That was an experience too. It was really flat and dusty. Those were General Conference Mennonite communities out there. They wanted some help, and somehow we got the word. Then I transferred to Luray, Virginia, Shenandoah National Park. That was miserable weather down there. And, of course, the fellows from the West always got spoiled; they had better food, and the environment was better. In the East, they were so strict with everything, they had so many rules. Out there, we were more free to do as we pleased, within reason.

What kind of work were you doing?

During the winter months, several days we were sent to a natural tunnel along a highway, and there was water dripping through there, and we had to clip the ice off the roof. It was kind of a monotonous, useless thing, and they could've just as well put salt on there. And then, another thing we did, they'd take us out along that highway there, Skyline Drive, and we had to chop the little trees and brush that grew up along the banks in the cold, wet snow, and we did major work out there. Even if it snowed, you had to be out there. You get wet and cold.

It doesn't sound as exciting as what you were doing before.

No way! So I wanted to get into something more worthwhile. I don't know if I specifically requested this Florida unit. It was a health unit; they were working on hookworms. I think it was the Polk County Health Department. We worked on various projects. For a while we worked with the mosquito control program, and we built privies for the poor people—mostly blacks, there were some poor whites too. That wasn't very nice work, but the weather compensated for some of it. And that was very highly organized, I would say. You'd think there isn't much to [putting] four walls together, but we had different crews working. There were also cement pits we had to install. And that was all done in sections; we did it in advance, [and] we had to let the cement cure. They were even sawing their own lumber; I guess that was mostly for the cribbing. You see, the water level is so high in Florida, you dig a little bit and you get into water. We hit water between two and three feet. And then sometimes you hit this hardpan, and that was about as hard as rock in certain sections of that county, and that we didn't like.

How did the people of Polk County react? Were they pleased that this whole thing was going on?

I would say so. I imagine though that when they first opened the unit there was probably some opposition; as I recall, there were some comments. When I got down there, the public relations were going pretty well. We went in to a church in Lakeland regularly with a fine group of kids, mostly girls, so we had a good time.

Was that a Mennonite church?

No, Presbyterian. Well, we went to different churches. I chose the Presbyterian, and some of the others went to the Methodist church there.

This wasn't a church-sponsored camp?

Yes, it was administered by the Mennonite Central Committee. It was basically Mennonite, although I think it was done jointly to start with—the Quakers were in it too.

Were you in the Florida camp until you were discharged?

Yes. That was a smaller unit, too; I think there was 37 or 40 in it.

Did you ever get any type of hassles from people in the communities because of your status?

I didn't have much trouble. I remember one specific occasion, this was in Idaho. Again, I had an opportunity to earn some money, and, you know, flying gets to you, and I took some flying lessons during my off time. One time, a short time before I left there, I was out at the airport, and there was a couple other fellows there, and one fellow had a few too many drinks, and he was jealous of us taking flying lessons. He wished his son could take them. He was in the army and probably overseas, but he really gave us a good cussing.

How did you react to that?

Well, I just let it go in one ear and out the other, although I didn't forget it. But I understood the situation. I just didn't respond. We didn't talk back to him because we knew that he was not responsible for what he was saying. But I think he really was mad at us. And then on long weekends we tried to get out and see the country. We did a lot of hitchhiking. And hitchhiking, you meet all sorts of people. Some were very cooperative, and again, some didn't like us, especially in a town where the police would chase you out.

Where were you?

In the South; I don't remember if it was Florida or Alabama or where it was. I remember one weekend we got chased out by two young fellows. Of course, there was also a lot of service men hitchhiking, and we'd get rides together. It was very interesting. I remember in the South we got a ride on the back of a truck; I think there was a couple of service men on first, and they picked us up. We got talking in the back of the truck to a couple of navy fellows who didn't know why we weren't in the army or in the navy. So we explained our situation, and I guess we did pretty well. And a guy said, "I think I'd go for that too if I had it to do over." Then we told them, "Well, we're not getting any pay." "Oh well, that'd be all right; it would be better than this." It was very interesting.

Did you ever question why you chose a conscientious objector status?

"I wished I wouldn't have," you mean? Or something like that? No, I don't think I ever had second thoughts about it.

In looking back, do you see your life as being changed by this experience?

Well, I think I'm broader minded. I understand other people's points of view better because I've talked with many, many people I wouldn't have talked to from all walks of life. It just broadened your experience.

It sounds like you enjoyed your experience.

Yes, I did. That's part of my philosophy and outlook on life.

Do you think that a lot of other CPS men have the same attitude toward it?

Oh, I think so. There were some, of course, that were bitter and prone to failure and feeling sorry for themselves and this type of individual. I think I would say those were probably the minority.

3

CPS MEN FROM OUTSIDE THE HISTORIC PEACE TRADITION
Nathaniel Hoffman

"I think all of us from that kind of background thought we were going to point the way and change the world, and to a great extent we ourselves weakened and compromised when we saw that our coming in with shining faces wasn't going to change a lot of patients automatically or anything like that. I think that part was unsatisfactory, that we were not really skilled or trained, really didn't produce any long-lasting results, except for individuals."

Nathaniel Hoffman, born in New Rochelle, New York, in 1916, gained entry into CPS only after his rejection by his local draft board had been reversed. Hoffman's pacifism reflected the influences of the War Resisters League (WRL) and the Jewish Peace Fellowship. During the almost three years he served in CPS, Hoffman volunteered for medical experiments and served as an attendant in a mental hospital. After the war, Hoffman's accounting practice grew with many clients from the peace and social justice movements.

What was your father's occupation?

He was a dress designer, contractor, and manufacturer. Typical of the immigrant Jewish youths who came over prior to the First World War, he got into the garment industry.

Did your mother work?

She worked only to the extent that she would go to his shop and work there.

Do you have brothers and sisters?

I have one brother and two sisters. My brother had become familiar with the War Resisters League the same time I did, but he didn't feel as strongly, and he had an opportunity to get an accounting job at the Defense Department after 1939. He took that and got to rather large heights as an accountant. One sister's husband served overseas in England and India. The other one was supposed to be a naval officer, but his pulse was bad, and he wasn't accepted into the armed forces, but he did a lot of war work in his field.

What was your educational background?

I went to high school in New Rochelle and finished my last year when we moved to Brooklyn at the height of the Depression. And then went on to City College, all of our family being very thankful that at that time we all were able to get an education through the City College system. I studied accounting, and I wasn't drafted for several years because of back trouble [and] hay fever trouble, and I had already begun work in my field and passed my CPAs.

I had my first accounting job from 1939 until I was drafted in 1943.

Was your family strongly religious?

We came out of an Orthodox background. My father was more inclined to be somewhat agnostic, I guess. My mother came from a very religious family, and that was passed on to us. In New Rochelle we went through the conventional training for bar mitzvah and that sort of thing. But typically, at that point, there was a tremendous rebellion against immigrant parents, and so, as a single person, until the time that I was drafted, I can't say that being religious had much to do with going to synagogue on any regular kind of basis. When I was making my application to be a CO, I drew upon my grandfather, who died when I was born but who was a remarkably moral type of person, a teacher, who for years had a great influence.

Would you see the War Resisters League as the more important factor in your decision to seek CO status?

Joining the War Resisters League at that time, and the fact that many of them were Jewish—although they weren't drawing upon that necessarily— gave me a center which was actively opposed to war, actively helping COs. Without that, I don't know that I would have known how to or would have had the strength to push ahead on my own. I went to the meetings; we put out a CO newspaper at that time. Although I was Jewish and leaned heavily on all that, the War Resisters League also was a heavy influence on me.

Did you join when you were at City College?

By the time I graduated in 1939, I was already going to the War Resisters League, I'm sure I was.

What kind of role did your family play in your decision to be a CO? Were they supportive?

It was almost a total inability to understand how a Jewish person could not go along with what the country needed, or Jewish people needed, in terms of what Hitler was doing. I can't say that I was supported, but I was a favorite son, and they were embarrassed by it, quite embarrassed, but didn't take any active opposition.

I interviewed the wife of a man who was in CPS, and she worked in a settlement house in Chicago while he was in camp. She mentioned that there was a Jewish refugee family who lived there, and initially they were very, very antagonistic toward her because they simply could not see how anybody would refuse to fight against Hitler, why her husband would take such a stand. Eventually things worked out between them, and they became close.

Very often the wives took a terrible beating, working in the outside world and trying to support their husbands, getting a very unsympathetic reaction from the local public. They were under a tremendous strain.

One man who was engaged at the time he entered CPS showed me the letters from his fiancée, which were a kind of barometer of the pressure she was experiencing. Very poignant letters; at one point she wrote, "How could you do this to me? All of my girlfriends are engaged to military men." And then eventually she broke off the relationship. Many people in the military were, if not sympathetic, at least understanding of CPS, whereas people who were in neither often felt the need to be superpatriots.

It was difficult. I'm sure that my parents probably never acknowledged when they moved to this small town one of their sons was a CO. It's pretty hard when you come from a conservative community. New York City had a lot more anonymity for parents, but small towns, it was difficult.

Did you have much difficulty with your draft board in terms of getting the CO classification?

Yes, I did. I lived in a middle-class neighborhood in Brooklyn at that time. Our draft board, in dealing with CO applicants, tried to be fair, but there was just a type of turndown. We had the right of appeal to the state board. I won at that level.

You went into CPS in April 1943?

Yes. When I was drafted, I was assigned to a Quaker camp in New Hampshire. At that time, in the effort to show the government what good, sacrificing people we were, the Quakers tried to do it without any use of funds from the government at all. And the New Hampshire camp, Camp Campton, was rather typical, a former CCC camp, isolated. It served a good purpose in that most firefighters had gone and you needed competent firefighters in the area. So basically, it was a firefighting group.

At that time, there had been no victory yet in getting any real service work opened up. They saw that it wasn't going very well at all if everyone was just off in isolated camps in the woods. They succeeded, and Middletown, Connecticut, was one of the mental hospital units they opened up. It was 103 miles from New York, so I was permitted to go there; you had to be 100 miles away from your home. I was transferred after only being a firefighter some months. I really didn't have the proper physical equipment. I never had a strong back, and you really had to be pretty hearty. I did enter into medical experiments there that we did with the Harvard people. It was very important.

The medical experiments were at Cambridge?

Both. At New Hampshire we had medical experiments too. There was a great interest in dealing with the needs of the people of Europe at war's end who were suffering tremendously from lack of proper food. The Harvard fatigue lab people joined in with an experiment to see what lack of vitamin C and lack of proteins would do to one and then how to reverse that quickly, because they felt that this was going to be an affliction to a whole generation of people. And so we went on an experiment in which I was on vitamin C, some were on protein. All of our food had to be weighed. It was very poor food there, we were almost like refugees ourselves. Once a week this Dr. Johnson would come down and give us a pack test. We would step up, as if we were walking up a mountain with a heavy weight on our backs, and he'd measure the decrease in our flow of blood and take blood samples to see how we were doing when we were deprived of these things. I remember my gums getting to be awfully soft. So that was a type of medical experiment.

Do you remember the attempt to organize a CPS union?

You did have a rather substantial number of highly educated, liberal people who were active already in civil and human rights. When I went to Middletown, we elected a real union shop, in a certain sense. Middletown was not a usual unit, in that it was very close to major universities. An extraordinary number of the men were already Ph.Ds, maybe several dozen out of a hundred, just unbelievable.

Was Middletown a regular hospital or a mental hospital?

A mental hospital. Middletown was rather famous for the fact that it was the beginning of the whole modern concept of what mental hospitals should be like.

All kinds of conflicts arose concerning the units that were in mental hospitals. I don't know if there was much at Middletown, but, for example, at Cleveland State Hospital, the administration got so upset at CPS—in part because of reforms and changes they were asking for—that they removed the unit. Eventually they had to ask for them back, about a year and a half later. But that seemed to be a common pattern.

Yes, that happened. We had quite a few units, and there was conflict among guys who really were dedicated and went on to hospital work. Many were just doing whatever they had to, and some were doing it feeling that they were making extraordinary changes in the whole administration. I think we all came in with that idea. But many of us slipped, many of us weren't trained. It was three years, so it was really rather difficult, and finally it reached a point for me one day when I got up and said, I can't do this anymore, and I just refused to go on the ward. They discharged me thereafter as being neurasthenic. I think I know what it means, I've looked it up; in any event, I think it was probably the proper term at that time. So I did other things. We were doing a musical experiment on the wards. One guy, a musicologist, had developed the concept that had already been used elsewhere: that certain kinds of songs, when played one after the other, would build up moods, and if you played certain kinds of music (that was programmed for the morning music through the wards), that would give everyone a better spirit or attitude or make them happier. So I became the disc jockey.

You weren't discharged from CPS at that time because of the neurasthenia?

As the war came to a close, there were many threats, many statements that no COs would ever be discharged until everyone—and there were 12 million guys in the army—was discharged. I wasn't discharged until well after the war was over. I think that, really, I was suffering from what many did: you sort of had the strength and ability to carry on when everyone else was doing it, and when the war was over and there were all of these implied threats it would be a long time, it becomes much more difficult to take it. Another interesting thing is that I had a relative who all his life had been in a mental hospital, ever since he had arrived in this country. Although I was stationed nearby, my wife used to go visit, my sisters, everyone. I never would go to the hospital. Just to walk through a mental hospital, it leaves its. . . .

Were the conditions bad there in terms of patient care?

I think everything is relative. I'd say that, in the physical sense, the hospital at Middletown, Connecticut, as compared to hundreds of mental hospitals in the South and elsewhere, was relatively good. Doesn't mean there wasn't a certain amount of violence and untrained people. But the fact is that they weren't using drugs as heavily as they are now, and it was a very difficult, very nerve-wracking life. I don't think that the average patient there, especially if he was relatively inactive, suffered from physical threats so much. Food during the war was not good, but it wasn't good in many places. The states weren't able to really command good meats or anything like that. You were eating gruel, starchy things most of the time, but certainly people weren't dying from starvation. But in terms of anything more than mere custodial care, there wasn't too much. Many of the doctors were very old, or foreigners who couldn't practice elsewhere and had to get state jobs. But I'm not sure that we ever really succeeded in changing terribly much of it.

In some of the hospitals, the men were working incredible hours, 72 hours a week. Was that your case?

Well, it wasn't quite that bad. The regular employees didn't get the worst number of hours, and our unit wasn't going to do anything that their unit wouldn't do, as a matter of course. There were regular shifts, and the shifts might be all-night shifts. It's true that we got no compensation and no care whatsoever. Finally, one of the big victories was the state consented to give us $10 a month to buy toothpaste, things that one just had to have. And quite a few guys had no funds whatsoever, no means of getting any funds. My mother used to send me two or three dollars at a time; I had no monies to speak of. Some of us found jobs here and there. So money was a real problem. Middletown had built brand-new dormitories for married couples, and as a result of the fact that most other couples were gone, a lot of the apartments were filled with CPS couples. The wives—some got jobs, usually they would not just be orderlies, some were occupational therapists, some worked elsewhere.

Dietitians?

Yes. Generally it was that type of thing—they were already professionals—so that there was some cash income coming into the house. They had tremendous strains, and then if they had a baby, new difficulties arose.

You were at Middletown for three years, which was a long stretch.

I was drafted for, I guess, three years, the better part of which was at Middletown.

Did you get some time off?

We got the same time off as the regular employees did. I'm trying to think of what the schedule was, it's been so long. We probably worked the better part of six days a week, regular shifts. I think the night shifts, what time did we go on? Maybe it was 8:00 [P.M.] to 5:00 A.M. They were relatively long shifts, but they were not impossible.

Did you get a vacation? A stretch of a couple weeks?

After a while we worked up a kind of leave system. I remember going away, taking a week off for vacation.

In some of the units at the hospitals, there was a real antagonism between regular attendants and the CPS men, cases where they wouldn't sit with them in dining halls. Was there any of that in Middletown?

There wasn't any inclination to sit together at lunchtime. The natural tendency, under all the extreme conditions, was to be with your own COs, and I think they would have been uncomfortable to sit with you. I don't remember particularly, but the social stations from almost every point of view, the educational station, the reasons why we were there, tended not to

85

give you a social relationship as compared to a working relationship. Some, I think, were always antagonistic and some were very decent.

One of the interesting questions about the medical experiments is the whole issue of informed consent. Do you think that you were told fully in advance, so that when you said yes, you knew what you were getting into?

I think so. The doctors were treating their peers, in a way. Generally, in every one of the units, you had well-educated, competent people, so that I don't think that it was foisted upon us in any way. Wesleyan, like many other universities, was being used to do experiments that were useful to the army, and there was one experiment that was rationalized that would be useful to everyone. Seasickness and airsickness was a universal thing. They built a tower on the Wesleyan campus on which they placed an elevator in which you're strapped down, and you went up at a high speed, and the elevator was able to reverse its direction at a powerful speed. Wesleyan was completely across town from the mental hospital, and I remember getting out of that and walking all the way back to the hospital as if I were drunk. They didn't really understand what was happening physically and chemically in seasickness and airsickness, and they were trying to take measurements to determine what it was.

It seems to me that there were lots of pressures on people who were in CPS, psychological pressures.

Yes, there's no doubt about that; it was a way of showing you were making a contribution at some risk and discomfort. [The experiments] were publicized, people got to hear about it, so there's no doubt that part of it was an effort to make a positive image and to do something.

You mentioned at the beginning that there was literally no support from organized Jewish groups.

Generally speaking, the major Jewish organizations found it very difficult, didn't know quite how to handle this. Rabbi Hoffmann at Columbia—when I was first going over that maybe I was a CO, I had a long talk with him, got the feeling of how I related to being Jewish, the Jewish religion. He and several other fellows, graduate students mostly at Columbia, started something called the Jewish Peace Fellowship, which still exists, still a tiny organization which has had many members come and go through the years. So that was the only one that was specifically a Jewish pacifist organization.

I imagine it had very limited resources.

Very limited resources, but [it] was helpful to various people who were Jewish, who were COs, who were needful of sympathetic support.

When you were in Middletown, did you go to any Jewish services? Was there a congregation you were part of at all?

I didn't attempt to go to Middletown's because that was very middle-class, very conservative, and I think would have had no understanding. But I remember one particular occasion, I hitched up to Hartford and went to the services of a temple which had a very prominent rabbi. And I went up after the service and told him, and I think he was visibly embarrassed. In that area in West Hartford, there was a substantial Jewish community. There was a lot of war work being done; the Jewish people typically were all out for support of the war, support of their sons who were drafted right across the board. And I could see that he didn't want to really talk with me at any length. Just say hello and that was it. I'm not sure that that was terribly unusual in view of the fact that in his temple he had so many hundreds of men drafted.

To what extent would you say the unit at Middletown was a true community? What kinds of shared activities did you have?

There was, of course, the meeting. Not a Friends meeting, but there was occasion to have official meetings. Certain people would never attend the meetings, they weren't interested. There was no feeling that one absolutely had to be there, but there were a number of real crises, and most people would then tend to show. We were a community because we were all in the same boat. But I can't say that there was necessarily a tremendous warmth that we all belonged together. There were too many divergent types and too many different personalities and backgrounds.

Were there any serious crises in the group, any issues that became divisive?

The largest one was this: those who had a sense of independence finally reached a point where they proposed that the Quakers no longer be allowed to be the sponsors, that it was a false thing to rely on them, it was being childlike to have them be the sponsor, and we should be able to face all issues ourselves. This led to a tremendous crisis and vote, and the Quakers withdrew. Suddenly, the unit was isolated on its own, now having to contend with the state, the federal government, and everything else. That was one of the great crises, I'd say; for many, it was like removing their parents. I haven't really given it much thought in recent years. The fortunes of war were not good for a long time, and it would reflect itself in attitudes toward COs.

One of the things that emerged in many of the camps, in many of the men, was a growing sense of alienation from the National Service Board for Religious Objectors. There was a sense that the NSBRO and the man who was basically running it, Paul French, had been co-opted by Selective Service, by the government.

There was every possible reaction. It is true that Paul French and his personality and his way of doing things left all of those who came from more of the workers' circle, urban attitude, not feeling confident that he was really there servicing them. It was almost as if he were acting as a mediator. People did react. This was the amazing thing: many were not suited to be parts of groups, many had to be on their own to come to any decision. There was every possible attitude about it. It was one thing to act as if you were making your contribution and this was a nice way of doing it, volunteering. Then there was the opposite extreme, that while you weren't slave labor, you weren't really being treated as a free man. There were all sorts of threats if you didn't toe the line—aside from the fact that you weren't paid or anything like that—that you'd be sent off to one of the camps in an isolated area, that was pretty tough.

So you did have great conflicts all the time. Some guys were reasonably happy to have gotten off so easy, to live in a place like Middletown. Some had wives, they had their own stresses and strains, it was visible, and it was really tough. But for some it was relatively safe, money coming in, they were able to live with it more easily.

Did you develop any relationship with people in the community around there?

Some people did; I can't say that I did. I'd say, basically, the COs were the people I associated with and developed some friendships with. I don't think that I developed any community friendships in any way when I was there. The hours didn't lead to it, and it wasn't easy generally.

Once your decision was made to go into CPS, did it no longer pose a problem for you, or did you constantly rethink it?

I think, except for those who had come to it as a matter of course out of a total religious background, that there always were questions and alternatives. It didn't mean that one was going to do anything or felt strongly enough to go into the military, which I think would have been impossible. But I think that in view of everything that was happening, everything one read, everyone knew people that were changing to the military or to prison after being COs. I would say that various kinds of alternatives occurred to us, probably more about whether one could do this, or one ought to go to prison, more than to the military. But I think that was part of life.

The men you knew in the War Resisters League, how many of them honored that commitment, and how many rethought it and went into the military?

Those who were really working hard at the War Resisters League, I would think that very few ended up going into the military. Those were years of tremendous strain, they really were. I mean, lots of people will not recall it that way. I tend not to talk about it in general with people who do not have that background. It's not something I normally would raise, for very good reasons.

Do you have any children?

I have two daughters and a son. The son, interestingly enough, works for Raytheon in one of their groups that have to do with computers that relate to missiles. He's uncomfortable about it, but he never—I think partly as a reaction toward me—would never indicate that he was interested in being a CO. As a matter of fact, children don't want to hear about it particularly, just as they don't want to hear about one's military awards. My oldest daughter, at one point, borrowed my papers in order to give them to her friend who didn't want to go to Vietnam, [who] thought maybe he was a CO.

What was the most satisfying aspect of CPS for you?

That's an interesting question. I suppose it was a feeling of having carried out a principle that I genuinely felt that war didn't solve any problems and that we were trying to show there were possible alternatives. I suppose the failure with that thought is that we never really trained ourselves, although there were vast efforts to train in nonviolence. But as a movement, that never really took hold. But years later, in the anti-Vietnam and antinuclear days, there was quite a bit of training, march on Washington times, large numbers of units were being trained. We never quite reached that stage.

How about the least satisfying aspects of CPS?

I suppose anyone that's drafted would say that's not satisfying. I'm not sure that we were terribly successful, looking back at it all, in making any points of law that have a long-term basis. I think all of us from that kind of background thought we were going to point the way and change the world, and to a great extent we ourselves weakened and compromised when we saw that our coming in with shining faces wasn't going to change a lot of patients automatically, or anything like that. I think that part was unsatisfactory, that we were not really skilled or trained, really didn't produce any long-lasting results, except for individuals. Perhaps some patients appreciated us at times. Those of us who were physically assaulted and hurt, which happened, didn't at the moment think that we were too successful.

In what ways do you see your life as being changed for having gone into CPS?

Well, at the end of CPS, I had been deeply influenced by some of the Quakers and others who had conceived of organic farming and more natural ways of life, which was a great contrast to a middle-class, Jewish life in New York City. I went across the country going to one of these farms, giving it a great deal of thought, but then flew back, and coming back represented the fact that I really was not by nature willing to go that far.

There was another odd reward as a result of having been a CO. I thought that there was no way that I was ever going to be employed again in average middle-class circles, which generally meant maybe a small Jewish accounting firm. By placing an ad in the *Friends' Intelligencer* and some other papers and contacts, I got, when I was first starting out, this group of different people, all who came as a result of my being a CO; [they] gave me the nucleus of a practice which I have until this day. I have many of the Quaker organizations, the FOR, the WRL, they are all clients of mine, so that I may not go to meetings but at least I make a contribution, give them reduced rates. So all of these years—I think it's gradually now coming to a close with the ending of the generation I knew—but all of this meant that, whereas I had no connections whatsoever in any way, shape, or manner, I was able to build up a relatively successful and interesting life, a result of having been a CO, which seems an unfair thing since I contemplated just the opposite. I never would have made it, by the way, in competition with other accountants in the ordinary course of life. It was never the greatest interest to me. My practice was almost totally one which had come from my CPS experience.

Benjamin L. Reid

"This is what finally got under my skin more than anything else: the sense of not really sharing the fate of one's generation, but of sort of coasting alongside all of that; you couldn't feel that you were part of anything terribly significant in what you were doing."

Benjamin L. Reid was a distinguished professor of literature and a Pulitzer Prize recipient. Born on 3 May 1918 in Louisville, Kentucky, Reid was brought up not in one of the Historic Peace Churches, but in the Disciples of Christ, and he had largely moved away from that by the time he entered CPS. Reid spent the bulk of his service as an attendant in a mental hospital. He later went on to earn a Ph.D. in English from the University of Virginia and teach at Iowa State, Smith, Sweet Briar, Amherst, and Mount Holyoke. Reid wrote eight books, including The Man From New York: John Quinn and His Friends, *which received the Pulitzer Prize for Biography in 1969. Benjamin Reid died on 30 November 1990.*

What was your family's religious affiliation?

We belonged to a sect called the Disciples of Christ, which is mostly southern Protestant, offshoot Presbyterian Church. It was in that church that my father was a minister, my grandfather was a minister; I came from a long line of such people. There were 13 ministers on two sides of my family in the generations immediately preceding me, all in this same church.

Did you have a strong religious upbringing?

Well, it's queer. That's not a simple question. Oddly enough, we talked very little about religious matters in my house. By the time I was mature and earning a living, we had pretty much drifted away from the church. My father by that time hadn't had a job as a minister since 1930. So there's a period of about a dozen years in which we had been pretty much detached from the church, and he was simply hanging around the house, and we didn't have much to do with the church. But, you know, we were serious, moral folk, and that's about all it comes to.

When you entered CPS in 1943, did you share your family's religious views?

Such as they were, yes.

What considerations led you to choose CPS?

Well, that is a long, long story. My brother, Isaac, whom we always called Buddy, was two years older than I was and had declared himself a conscientious objector at the very outbreak of the war and had been swiftly inducted. He was doing pretty much the same sort of thing I was doing, going to college part-time and also driving a milk truck. But when the war broke and the draft started, he said, "I'm a CO," and persuaded the local draft board that he had a legitimate case. And they said, "Okay, you're a CO, and in you go." And so he was drafted in the very first months of the draft. And he went off to camp in North Carolina and stayed there for some time. He eventually moved out to California to another camp.

All of this time, I was working, going to college, and brooding the whole thing over and feeling very uneasy about it all on both sides. But fundamentally, I was the only breadwinner in the family. My father wasn't earning anything. I had a job. So it was a question of how to keep the family eating and get on with my education. But finally, the draft board ran me down, and I had to decide whether I was or was not a CO. And I dithered a great deal about this. I thought of saying, "I'm not a CO, and I'll go to the army if I have to." Or we had this sort of medial classification in which you could go into the army as a noncombatant, 1AO they called it. Or else you could say, point-blank, "I am a CO, and I can't and won't go in." And as I say, I dithered for a long time among those three choices, and the draft board was patient with me, remarkably patient, it seems to me, thinking back over it. But finally I decided, well, I am a CO.

The basic question, as far as I could see, was whether you were or were not willing to shoot a gun and take somebody else's life, and I decided I was not willing to do that. And the next question is, "Are you willing to be part of the war effort even if you don't shoot a gun?" and I decided, you couldn't really separate those two things. Once you go into military service, you are, in effect, shooting a gun, whether you're actually doing it or not, and I decided that I couldn't do that either. So then I said, "Okay, I'm a CO."

Then I had to persuade the draft board of all this. We didn't belong to the so-called Historic Peace Churches, and you had to persuade your local draft board that you were a CO on either religious or philosophical grounds, and I couldn't present myself as officially a religious CO, so I had to persuade them that I was philosophically a CO. And that's what I somehow managed to do—mostly all on just these very simpleminded grounds that I simply could not picture myself taking another man's life, although he was ostensibly an enemy. You know, I didn't hate the Germans really, the German people. I didn't hate the Japanese people, and my picture was that if I came up against a Japanese soldier or a German soldier, I was in effect dealing with a man very much like myself who had been told to go out and shoot me, and I didn't hate him any more than I suppose he really hated me. And so I said, "I won't do that." And they said, "You must," and I said, "I won't." And finally, they turned me down, first of all, and so I appealed it, and I was granted a CO classification after appeal. All of this had taken a lot of time. And that had been mostly used up by hardship deferments because I was earning the whole living for the family. I graduated from college in June of 1943, and I guess it was the following fall that I was actually inducted, so that would be late 1943.

What role, if any, did your wife play in your decision?

None that I can honestly specify. She supported me, but she didn't urge me in one direction or another. She accepted my decision. You understand, the ground had been prepared in a way by my brother.

Was your family supportive?

Well, certainly, they thought we should do what we felt was the right thing to do. This is our kind of puritanical Protestantism. There's no great deal about it and no great philosophical substructure under the whole thing. They thought we should do what we thought was right, and we thought this was right, and so that's the way it worked. And they went along and said, "God help you."

How many CPS camps did you serve in, and what was the basis for transfers?

Well, my history in CPS is comparatively short and comparatively simple. I went from Louisville, Kentucky, when I was first inducted to the nearest CPS camp, in Gatlinburg, Tennessee, where the CPS units were doing essentially the old-style sort of CCC work, maintenance in Smoky Mountains National Park, which meant all kinds of things. But I was only there for about three or four months. We worked all that late fall and winter on a heavy, dry stone wall supporting a road up above a big creek, and with a marvelous mountaineer foreman named Crow Hopkins.

But we finished up that job, and by this time there were options of other kinds of service. And we decided almost as a group to put in for transfer to work in a mental hospital. And we cast around for a place we wanted to go, which turned out to be mostly a question of what place would accept us as a group. Most of us were given a spot at Eastern State Hospital in Williamsburg, Virginia, and four or five of us moved there together. I actually worked at Williamsburg as a ward attendant in the hospital for the rest of my service, something like 15 months.

Then I decided to do another flip-flop. I decided what really made sense for me was to go ahead and go on into military service as 1AO. I still couldn't see myself shooting a gun, but I had begun to be very much bugged by the whole business of avoiding the whole responsibility and danger of the war. And there was a lot of pressure from my wife's family on her because of what I had done. This got on my nerves. And I decided, well, the heck with it, I'll give this up and I'll accept a 1AO classification and go on in as a noncombatant. And that's what I tried to do. I only tried; it didn't work. But I put in for this officially and told them, "I'm clearing out. I'm now 1AO, and you can take me when you're ready." So I then went back to Louisville, Kentucky, and sat around waiting for them to induct me as a noncombatant into military service. And my local board knew all about this, and they knew I was there ready to go and waiting to be called, but they did nothing about it. We finally went up to Pendle Hill, a Quaker establishment outside Philadelphia, and hung around there waiting to be called.

Were you by yourself?

No, my wife and my young daughter, Laurie, were with me. But that, too, hung on for several months, and actually what happened was that the war ended. They ran out of war. I never had to go in.

Were financial considerations a factor?

Well, I don't think so, no. I decided we just had to tough it out. My wife had a job at that time. She was working as a librarian at Louisville, Kentucky, and though her family gave her a very hard time about it, she could scrape by.

Was your family forced to change its living habits because of the financial stress during your tenure in CPS?

Yes, it certainly was. My parents were semistarving, and my wife and daughter had to move in with her parents, and that was a large part of the stress, you see. Her parents were good, straight, all-American patriots, and they gave her a very hard time because of the stand I had taken. I doubt that she suffered from her friends particularly. It was all a pretty quiet sort of thing. No great celebrity about it. People who knew us intimately knew what I was doing. Others didn't know. So that she would have suffered, I would think, primarily from her parents at home.

What was the most difficult aspect of CPS for you?

"The most"—you mean I've got to have a hierarchy? I suppose that must have been just the fact of separation from one's family, which meant at the same time from one's normal way of life, from any established pattern of living which one would like to get on with. A sense of marking time, doing nothing very significant and getting gradually older and getting nowhere with what I was doing.

Though if you were 1AO, you would have been in the same position.

Well, then one would have felt one was sharing in the fate of one's generation. This is what finally got under my skin more than anything else: the sense of not really sharing the fate of one's generation, but of sort of coasting alongside all of that; you couldn't feel that you were part of anything terribly significant in what you were doing. Not that what you were doing was useless, but it was not terribly useful. One would prefer to be doing something else with one's time, or to have felt, if one was kept from doing what one wanted to do with one's time, that the thing we were forced to do was in some sense significant and valuable.

Presumably one could adopt a philosophical position that would not make one feel that way.

I'm sure this was true. A lot of people felt that essentially what we were doing was saying we wouldn't do what everybody else was doing, and that we were doing this in terms of high principles. So that, sure, if one could comfort oneself that one was making a rather elaborate and valuable moral gesture, that got pretty old, pretty quick. It's hard to sustain oneself with that kind of high-mindedness very long. Though some people had to do it for five or six years. I was lucky in that I only had to do it for about two years.

I would think, though, that if you were part of a formal religious group, if you were all Quakers, for example, that the group would tend to be very supportive.

That is true, though I think there would be a dulling effect, see, of being part of a crowd. In a sense, what I was doing had more nerve in it, was more independent, superficially bolder, in that I had sort of set out on my own as a rebel. You have to talk to Quakers about how they felt about that sort of thing, but I observed it in them, that they were both comforted by being Quakers and bored by being a part of what was to their sect a sort of half-systematization of rebellious posture.

Do you think that the CPS experience strengthened your marriage or put particular strains upon it?

Both.

You already alluded to the problems with your in-laws. That obviously was a strain.

Well, at the same time one grew defensively closer together with one's spouse and would cling to her.

What changes did you witness in your wife during your term in CPS?

Well, she got older and tireder and more nervous and more persecuted. I think in many ways it was harder for her than it was for me, because, in a sense, I had a slot to fit into and she had none.

What was the most satisfying aspect of CPS service?

Well, that's simple. It was not really the philosophical one. It was that of meeting all these people who really were marvelous guys. I think, as a cluster of people, they were the most interesting and warm and intelligent and generally admirable people I've ever known. And I don't mean that there weren't a lot of klutzes among them. But as a spectrum of human beings, they were really fine, and I loved it with those guys.

What were the least satisfying aspects of CPS service?

Well, the least satisfying [aspects] were piddling sorts of jobs that I mostly avoided, but which other people suffered through, sometimes for years. The general sort of condescension or even contempt of the people who were in charge of you, who treated you as some sort of crazy person or malingerer or coward.

Looking back a generation later, do you have any doubts about your decision to enter CPS?

I suspect I would do it again, though I don't know. I might have been more strongly tempted by the 1AO business had I had the whole experience of CPS behind me. After all, that was the choice I made at the end of the war. But I still think I did the thing that was right for me at the time I did it.

In what ways do you see your life as being changed for having entered CPS?

More than anything else, I think it's been changed by the people I met there. Not just by knowing them, but by observing them as types of people, types of thinkers, types of workers. I think that's been very influential on me.

How would you characterize the types of men attracted to CPS?

It was a real mixture. There was the basic, old, hard-shell, unintellectual, countrified, rather stupid person who had simply grown up in the rural peace churches, particularly the Brethren and the Mennonites and Jehovah's Witnesses, who were a really queer bunch. And these people were fundamentally not only unintellectual but anti-intellectual. They really didn't know anything or care about anything except making their historic witness. You got a kind of urban intellectual who was basically not religious at all, who had talked his draft board into considering the thing he was doing religious but who was fundamentally philosophical, moral, ethical, but not in any traditional sense religious. And those people were often just brilliant, I mean, really high-powered, intelligent, and often very fine people. Then you had the intelligent wing of the peace churches, particularly the Quakers, and they were the people I knew more than anybody else. And I liked those very much, and they would often overlap with what I'm calling the intellectual class. Because they were usually pretty well educated, very bright, just nice people. Then there's a kind of gross middle ground that I don't know how to define, which was neither fish, flesh, nor fowl. And often you'd get some pretty crummy characters among that sort of people, people who, I think, were fundamentally just hiding out from the war in one way or another.

Any final thoughts on the CPS experience?

Somebody still ought to write a really good book from the inside out on being such a person. I don't think it's ever been done, though I know a number of attempts have been made. All kinds of crazy things went on. Some of them very funny, some very sad, some quite dramatic. But it's a queer kind of experience, because it's all out of the mainstream of life and it's all sort of reduced in scale from what other people recognize. I think you could treat it as comedy, for one thing. There was a lot that was very funny. For some people, it was more or less tragic, but for most of us, I think, it was dull, intermittently dull, often fascinating, very instructive. It's a peculiar kind of intimacy that one had there with people like oneself, living very close together, all sort of pariahs, all sort of tossed out on the edge of society and being both bored and fascinated by it [and] at the same time grieved and amused by it.

I think you could do a book or play or a sociological study or a set of poems or what-have-you about this kind of thing, and it would be very much like living in, let's say, a prisoner-of-war camp, that sort of marginal experience. Except that we weren't being required to suffer physically. But in a queer kind of way, this was a part of the psychology. We were being freed of the need to suffer physically, in terms of real pain or real danger to life. At the same time, we did a lot of dirty, hard work for no money, and that was the dullness and the frustration of it all. But the central fact of it was this tight, closed, common experience in small groups of a very interesting, small spectrum of psychological and moral types.

Gordon Zahn

*"I firmly believe that the COs were much more aggravating to the military
people than those who refused and went to prison. In a sense, the CO
position is a continuing rejection of the position they like, and it is a
continuing type of witness."*

*Gordon C. Zahn, born in Milwaukee, Wisconsin, on 7 August 1918, was
one of the relatively small number of Catholics in CPS. He received a Ph.D. in
sociology in 1952 and taught at Loyola University of Chicago and the University
of Massachusetts at Boston. His books, most of which illuminate the issues of
conscience and peace, include* German Catholics and Hitler's Wars *(1962),* In
Solitary Witness: The Life and Death of Franz Jaegerstaetter *(1964), and an
account of CPS,* Another Part of the War: The Camp Simon Story *(1979).
He cofounded the U.S. section of Pax Christi, the major international Catholic
peace movement.*

What was your family's religious affiliation?

My stepfather was Lutheran, nonpracticing, and my mother was Catholic,
also nonpracticing. I was nonpracticing until about the age of 16. A very
good friend of the family decided I had to be taken in charge and arranged
for instructions. I think my mother baptized me when I was born, if I'm not
mistaken, and then there was this conditional baptism at age 16 or 17, and
from that point on I was practicing.

So you certainly didn't have a strong religious upbringing?

No. I always considered myself a Catholic, though, because of that baptism
thing. I always talked about being Catholic. I'd go to the holiday masses and
things like that, but not [as] a regular churchgoer.

*What factors most strongly influenced the development of your pacifist philoso-
phy?*

I know it was basically reading. And I know also I was pacifist in high
school, because I was writing very bad pacifist poetry in the high school

paper. Now what kind of reading, I really don't know. When I was asked some time back, I thought and thought and thought. I've always been horrified—I guess it's sort of an emotional reaction against killings. I'd read all of the cowboy and Indian stories, but I don't think I ever really took the side of the cowboys as much as one should've. And there was a series of books, this I remember from childhood reading, Altscheler wrote several series of books. He did the French and Indian War series and the "Winning of the West" series, and the one I remember, the Civil War series. I read them all; the major battles of the Civil War were told from the standpoint of a young Confederate soldier and a young Union soldier. And I suspect that this may've been the thing that really got me going, how ridiculous it was. You'd identify with both sides. So I went over to the Boston library to read them again. I thought it might be interesting to check into Altscheler and find out if he was a Quaker or something like that and was doing this intentionally. They've got "The Winning of the West," but they don't have any of the Civil War ones. I suppose I'd have to go to the Library of Congress, or maybe out to Harvard, to see if I can find them there.

So all this reading that was so very critical in the development of your thought was self-directed?

Oh yes. I knew no one who took the same position or anything like that.

No one at all?

No. Some of these war movies may've scared me or something like that.

You'd never seen All Quiet on the Western Front *[1930]?*

That's it! I saw the thing on television recently, and I know I saw the movie, but I don't remember it being as much of a formative influence as it was for Lew Ayres and others. That was a good movie. I remember more *Four Sons* (1928), which was a very sentimental thing about a German woman who had two sons fighting on the Allied side and two sons fighting on the German side. I remember how moved I was by that. And again, it's the same theme of families divided that seemed to bother me.

What considerations led you to choose CPS?

I was bound and determined I wasn't going to accept military service, and I didn't expect to get the classification. I had sort of a martyr's picture in my mind about standing against everyone and doing this. But I decided to register for the CO position, and I got it on appeal. I knew very little about CPS.

Did you have any people that could speak for your religious commitment?

Not for religious commitment so much. Once I was involved in the antiwar thing, before the draft, I came in contact with the Women's International League for Peace and Freedom [WIL] people in Milwaukee. I never came in contact with the Catholic Worker people there, but the WIL, for the most part, was the contact. And this was, you should pardon the expression, through contacts in the America First Committee. I was one of their junior speakers at that time in the Milwaukee area. And the local unit of America First turned out to be riddled with pacifists when Pearl Harbor finally happened. I think we had about 10 young people going around talking to groups, and only one of them was not a pacifist, as it turned out. So it's a question of who's using whom. I could give a very good isolationist talk.

What was your family's reaction to all of this?

They were gone. My mother died the year before. Now, she was still alive when I registered and didn't approve or disapprove. I think she said, "Your father would've been scandalized had he lived," or something like this. And I think the German enemy was another factor that made her think that you couldn't really take that kind of a position. But she never argued against it.

She wasn't maintaining the traditional position of the church, for example, at that time?

No, she wouldn't have known what the traditional position of the church was. She wasn't that active in Catholicism at all. And my stepfather, as far as I know, didn't even know. It was one of these things where there was not good communication within the family, between stepfather and stepsons. Never talked it over with my brother, who was in high school at the time. I guess they just knew, and they made allowance for it and didn't get disturbed one way or the other. The cousins knew and were supportive, not that they were supportive that I should do it, but they were supportive personally. They weren't going to cut me off or anything like that.

There was always a sense of isolation, it seemed, for the Catholic who chose CPS at this point.

I'd been talking so much about it, already back in high school, long before this came up, that it wasn't anything new as far as they were concerned.

When did you first hear about Camp Simon and the Catholic Workers?

I don't know whether it was after I got the classification or when I was in the process of appealing. I was at one of these peace meetings in the apartment of the head of the WIL. I somehow expressed what I just took for granted, that I was the only Catholic who would take that stance. I knew that much about the traditional position of the church. I knew I'd be taking a stand against the church as much as against the government on that one. And she said, "Well, there's a camp for Catholics," and that kind of surprised me. And then she gave me a copy of the *Catholic Worker*. I had never heard of the Catholic Workers before, and even then I didn't know they had a Milwaukee group. Later, after the war, when I found out how active that Milwaukee group was, it's astonishing that I'd never run across them.

That says something about the way in which the Catholic Worker organization was viewed by the church.

Yes, because by this time I was involved in church activities, singing in church choir and things like that. But I would've been delighted to know about the Worker, not only for that but the general radicalism of something like that.

Do you recall when you heard about the Catholic Worker and the camp?

Well, the induction would not have been until after my brother died, and I think that was in July of 1942. Because up until that point I was supporting my stepfather. From the earliest days of the Depression, he had been unemployed; unemployment was a career, as far as he was concerned. When my mother died, we broke up the house, and I took my brother with me, so I was his sole support. He was going to high school at that time. But when he died, that ended my case for deferment.

And you went for a short period of time to Stoddard and then to Warner [CPS camps in New Hampshire]. What were your expectations?

Well, most of my expectations were unpleasant. I thought it would be more overtly incarceration than it was. Even with all the gripes I had about the camp, it was not as bad as I'd expected. The expectations of a religious nature—yes, I guess there was some looking forward to being with other Catholics and taking a Catholic position. But my CO position was a religious position. But not that much a formally organized religious position. I could cite all the scriptural passages and stuff like that that supported the case, but I would not have come out of a Catholic peace group. So that wasn't that much of an expectation. If anything, I wouldn't say I was turned off; I was made somewhat hesitant by the welcome letter's stress on religious activity, spiritual activity, that I had not been that much for. I went to mass regularly and sang in the choir, that was it.

Enough is enough.

Yes, that type of thing. I expected it to be much more religiously dominated than it was. I had no idea you would have such antireligious people in it, as it turned out. But I did not look forward with anticipation to that more religious tone.

How was the camp regarded by the surrounding community?

There wasn't much sign of acceptance. We kept ourselves pretty much apart, and we were kept apart, I guess. I don't remember any unpleasantness with any of the people in Warner.

I was intrigued, near the end of Another Part of the War: The Camp Simon Story, *when you talk about the controversies. The picture that emerges is of a basically unhappy group of men who did not feel as though they were really making a viable witness and doing something of national importance. And then you discuss Dorothy Day coming to the camp and sitting down and all these issues being tossed about. And you make the comment that, at the end, nothing really had been changed because she made no promises and she didn't say anything would get any better, but that somehow there was a greater acceptance of the situation for those last few weeks. Was this the first time you'd ever come in personal contact with Dorothy Day?*

Yes.

What impression did that visit make upon you?

Obviously by that time you had heard a lot about her, and so on a small scale it was like the pope visiting—"Dorothy is coming!" I think my first impression was she wasn't a very good-looking woman, a very plain-looking woman, but her manner, of course, was very impressive. I think this is what carried it off for the session she had that evening. People really couldn't criticize to any great extent anyone living her style of life.

So your sense of Dorothy Day was positive after that?

Those of us who thought the Catholic thing was important would've been already strongly favorable toward her when she came, even though she couldn't do anything.

Change the situation.

Yes.

A high proportion of Catholic Workers ended up going into the army.

All of them, I think.

Was this due to the extremely low morale in the camp itself?

Well, I think there's no question about it. I think the main thing was disillusion.

Draft boards appeared to have ignored many physical and mental disabilities in men applying for CPS. They were perfectly happy to have someone enter CPS who would never have been accepted by the army.

I don't think it was oversight necessarily. I think it was a way of getting out of a problem, at the very least. You could see a draft board just saying, "Well, we'll send 'em up there, and it won't make any difference." Also, you could see it as a punitive act. I think the draft board people probably had the same kind of idea about the CPS camps that I had, like a prison camp or something.

Out of sight, out of mind.

Yes, and not only that so much, but really a punitive situation, barbed wire, dogs, and things like that. And they would send people there rather than give them physical discharges.

I was interested in your comment that perhaps one reason why Paul French didn't push harder for pay for CPS men was that it was a lovely weapon that he had when it looked as though some adverse publicity might come out affecting CPS. He could always say, "Yes, but do you realize these people aren't even getting paid, so it isn't all that wonderful."

I think that's true. But I think he also believed that they shouldn't be paid. I think he was perfectly sincere in that position, and I think that most of the top peace church people were. It was kind of a weakness on the part of those who asked for pay.

How do you assess Dorothy Day's impact on Catholic pacifists when all of these people who felt most strongly about her movement and were closest to her went into the war?

I never talked to her about that. I'm sure she was disappointed when they went in, but she certainly wouldn't have held it against anyone.

What was your next CPS camp experience?

That would be the Oakland, [Maryland], camp. And that was mainly disillusionment, I guess, because we had these visions of the groaning board at Quaker camps or something like this. You had this impression the Quakers were living so high on the hog, and you get there and—well, certainly the meals were better, you have to grant that. You had meat more often than you did at Warner.

The only thing I remember about Oakland was the hassle over a black by the name of Stephenson. I imagine we brought problems upon the Quaker administration, because after mass, we went in [to town] for the usual cup of coffee, and they refused to serve Stephenson, and we all indignantly walked out expressing our opposition to this. Then Dick Leonard, [another CPS man], wrote a letter to the county attorney protesting this, and all of a sudden you had these things appearing in business windows, "We do not cater to COs," or something like this. And I guess we brought that down on the group more than anything else by raising a fuss over Stephenson.

Do you think it was mainly those from Warner who were most supportive of Stephenson?

Well, he was one of our group. We certainly started the row. Now, I think that the Quakers were certainly supportive, but they might not've liked the poor public relations. My impression was, public relations was very important to Quakers, always.

What was your next assignment?

Then I went to Rosewood. Rosewood [a training school] was something of a shock for the type of work that was being done, then you quickly adjusted to it. I adjusted more quickly than others because, after the first week of very dismal experiences, with a 12-hour day and two low-grade cottages, I became the medical secretary and typed up the clinic reports when they came in. So that was pretty good. That was a regular workday.

I electioneered myself into the assistant directorship at the camp, and I interpreted that as sort of the union steward more than anything else. Whenever any problems came up, I had to take them up with the administrator, and whenever they had a problem, they called me. I usually tried to cover for people who did violate the rules. The Rosewood unit was sort of a carryover of the dissident Catholic group at Warner. Now, the food, of course, was good there in comparison to what it had been. The living conditions were better in terms of buildings.

Were you one cohesive group?

Oh yes, we became a very cohesive group. The situation made it cohesive because I think from the third or fourth day that we were there, you could follow the path taken by one of the COs by listening to the shouts of "CO, CO, CO, CO" all along. Apparently, somebody had turned the kids on so that the kids—some of them in their sixties, they were all called children then, today they're called clients—and somebody had apparently got them to jeer at people as they went by and that made us more cohesive too. Definitely, here we were in a situation in which people we were working with did resent us, even though we brought the help they needed. I don't know how they were handling it before we got there. This was a big influx of labor. But they definitely made us feel unwanted, and only later did it sort of relax, and we got friendly with the people who were working there.

Was there also a sense of tension with the administrators?

Not so much tension as bureaucratic concern. They were worried about us getting away with something, and they'd be held responsible for violating the Selective Service law.

Was the work more satisfying? Was there a greater sense of doing something important?

Yes. There's no question that compared to the work that we were doing at Warner, one felt it was much more important when one was doing something worth something. It was a far heavier burden. Don't forget, at Warner we worked very little. And here you worked six 12-hour days. You were not particularly happy about that. You didn't have all the free time you'd had at Warner, but you felt you were accomplishing more. And Dorothy Day came to visit us there too, and she was quite taken by it. The idea was, as she saw it, you made this beautiful contrast. Instead of going out and destroying lives, you were devoting your time to these helpless, useless inmates. I think she wrote a couple of pieces about it. And then we took the patients' side on things too. We felt that we were really doing something for the patients. When we left, I wrote a rather lengthy exposé of Rosewood.

Was this for the Catholic Worker?

They published it later. We sent it first to the Board of Visitors, and somehow somebody on the Board of Visitors gave it to the *Baltimore Sun*, and the *Baltimore Sun* ran a feature. Then I wrote three columns about it for the *Catholic Worker*. And I think it worked, it changed things quite a bit.

Did this work at Rosewood have an impact on what you chose to do later?

I think my whole inclination, before I got to Rosewood, was to get into college after CPS and get into social interests. That's why I was interested in sociology, to see what I could do and always to utilize it for the peace movement.

How long were you at Rosewood?

A little over three years.

And you left CPS from Rosewood?

Yes.

Was your discharge unduly delayed? Did you get a little frustrated at the slowness?

Once the point system was established, I was willing to go along with it. Essentially, I guess, I'm a cooperative-type person, even though I speak a good revolution.

Watch out! A second-miler?

No, I felt that it seemed to be a fair enough arrangement, that those who got in first—although I would not have opposed those who felt that they should just all be released.

Did you ever consider going 1AO?

No.

If the same situation existed, and if you had to make the decision all over again, would you still choose CPS?

Yes, no problem. Become a CO and chosen CPS, or refused altogether. I still think I would've taken CPS—partly prudential judgment. But when I was counseling kids during the Vietnam thing, I'd make the same point, that I firmly believe that the COs were much more aggravating to the military people than those who refused and went to prison. In a sense, the CO position is a continuing rejection of the position they like, and it is a continuing type of witness. I always told the kids that if they became COs and had alternative service and still felt they weren't doing enough, then they could always terminate.

Take the absolute.

Take the prison witness. But I still feel that the CO position is a more effective opposition to war than the prison witness.

You indicate in your book [Another Part of the War] that there is that sense of continuity between what happened at Warner and what happened in the 1960s, with the Berrigans and so on.

And it would be, I imagine, not too easy to trace. Some of us remained active in the sense of writing and speaking and doing things like that. And that establishes a continuity. Dan Berrigan said that he and his brother had never given any thought to the question of war until they had read my book on German Catholics. And certainly, the Jaegerstaetter book has stirred an awful lot of people, so that makes a continuity, although not a direct one.

In a sense, you personally show that continuity through your work. Do you know many of the men who were at Warner who then continued to be active in pacifist organizations and groups?

One of the criticisms I make is that more could've. Now we have Pax Christi. When that was restored, I was able to get in touch with several people, and they attended this rejuvenation meeting of Pax Christi, but they haven't been active in it since. They haven't done anything of that nature. Well, they weren't active before they got into CPS, and they haven't been active since. No, this is unfortunate. I think the same thing is true of the Vietnam generation.

Were you aware of any limitations professionally or socially that you've experienced because of your CO stand during World War II?

No, I don't think so. I've never attempted to hide it. In fact, I probably make the mistake of forcing it on people too much. The priests at St. John's [a small Catholic institution in Collegeville, Minnesota] were supportive. There was a split between the former chaplains, who wanted us out, and the others, who were supportive of us, not necessarily the CO position. But we got the scholarships at St. John's that first year *because* of the CPS factor. We wrote letters to them pointing out that there was no GI "bill of rights" for us, that we had taken that position, and that we were looking for scholarships. The two Franciscan colleges in New York never answered, but St. John's did answer and offered tuition for scholarship, and that's how we got out there. So in that sense, CPS was an aid rather than an obstacle.

What was the least satisfying aspect of CPS?

I imagine it would be the feeling of uselessness. Honestly, I think I would've enjoyed the change in situation, being out in the woods and something of this nature. And I certainly enjoyed the companionship with people I would never have known or met otherwise. So the camp, as such, wasn't such a horrendous experience, and yet there was this awful frustration of, what's the thing in *Death of a Salesman*, "not having attention paid." That was the thing that bothered me more, the feeling of being shoved aside, put there, and given whatever had to be done to keep us busy.

What was the most satisfying aspect of CPS?

I would imagine the associations. One man told me that he was there for so short a time and yet he made some of the closest friendships of his entire lifetime. And he went on to say it was not the sense of solidarity in an unpopular position—that he's been in unpopular positions with groups ever since—but he's never felt that kind of friendship.

4

FROM CPS TO PRISON
Bent Andresen

"I think I made the same mistake in supposition that a lot of other people did: that because we were opposed to killing we were therefore, ipso facto, of a higher stripe, and therefore we should have made that [a] community of Christian love . . . and it wasn't so."

Bent Andresen, born in Copenhagen, Denmark, on 14 January 1907, came to the United States as an infant. His pacifist orientation represented a blend of spiritual and political values. Andresen, 37 years old when he entered CPS in March 1944, served at a camp in Pennsylvania, participated in a medical experiment at Cornell, and went to the government camp at Germfask, Michigan, before walking out of CPS after the bombing of Hiroshima. He went on a prolonged hunger strike while in prison. Andresen sustained his antiwar commitment with his continuing involvement with the War Resisters League and the Central Committee for Conscientious Objectors. He died on 11 February 1991.

Could you describe your formal education?

Four years of high school, graduated in 1925, went to work, and in 1931 got to New York City looking for a progressive social activist cause to work in and found that, without a college education, nobody but no one was going to take any chance. First of all, it was 1931, and it was already bad times. So [at] none of the places I went was there any possibility.

So I applied for admission to Columbia University, and they looked my credits over, and they said, "When you have another year of math and two years of a foreign language, come back and we will talk to you." So I went to New York Evening High School while I was working and got that in one year and got into Columbia in 1932 and was there for two years. And I joined the Socialist party and the War Resisters League. So I was a peace and socialist activist on the Columbia campus those two years, and in spite

111

of that, I managed to get some scholarship help. But when I flunked the dean's course in trigonometry, I was told, no more scholarship, which wasn't unreasonable. So I spent the summer in a private, progressive labor-oriented school in Dutchess County, New York, and met my wife there.

What school was that?

Manumit School at Pawling. Founded by Bill Fink, who also had founded the Brookwood Labor College in Katonah.

Where A. J. Muste was?

Exactly. I have much that same background as A. J.

Was there much interest in the War Resisters League at Columbia when you were there?

Oh, you know, it's always been a minority. There was that time when it wasn't hard, between the wars, to get people to sign that they would never participate in another war. Imperialism was on everybody's shit list, and so it was easy to say that they would never fight for king or country again, that kind of thing. But as you got closer to the war, the bulk of people very readily forgot it. You know, this is different, this is a war for peace and democracy, to end fascism.

What kind of work were you doing after you left Columbia?

I spent one year [at Manumit] as a counselor. Obviously, I couldn't be a teacher, and as a counselor I did the sports with the older boys. I knew very shortly that I had not the patience for working with kids. And then the husband of one of the permanent staff there was head of the International Ladies Garment Workers' Union [ILGWU] in Fall River, Massachusetts, Bill Ross, and he got to know my interest in the labor movement. So when it was obvious to me that I had no future there, and when Bill was there, I asked him about working as an organizer for the ILGWU. So he took me on. Within weeks I was busted by the local [Fall River] police at the instigation of a forelady who falsely accused me of threatening her. A general organizer for the Pocketbook Workers' Union came through and asked Bill Ross, for whom I was working, did he have anybody to lend him for a quick look-see whether Fall River-New Bedford had any possibilities for organizing pocketbook workers. So I was loaned to them, and that lasted two and a half years. And incidentally, a year later the superior court in New Bedford threw out my convictions, so that one didn't stick.

When did you leave Fall River?

Well, 1936. We were married in 1936, and I went to work for the Pocketbook Workers, 1936 to 1938. My father, who had then, by steps, moved from Minneapolis to Cleveland to Philadelphia, was working at S. S. White, [which was his company]. He was second from the top, but on account of the circumstances there, he supported the rank and file when they wanted to make a union, and that cost him his job. He wrote me, "CIO's going great guns in Philadelphia." He knew I was dissatisfied with certain aspects of the job I had, and so he urged me to come to Philadelphia and gave me names and all.

I thought he was more conversant with the actual circumstances in Philadelphia and the CIO than it turned out. I came down, and there wasn't a thing, not the slightest thing, excepting at my own expense I could try to organize the used-car salesmen on the little lots in Philadelphia. And what was their issue? Primarily, having to work on Sunday. They were completely at the mercy of the bosses, the owners, and so they wanted that. So after not many months, I got the men to shut down Philadelphia. And then they made a private deal, they reopened on Sunday and the thing went up the flue. So I was out some money.

Then for a year I tried to sell products door to door; it was the worst year of my life. Then I got a job in Rohm and Haas [a chemical company], and two years or so there, and meanwhile I had developed an interest in cooperatives and there was a co-op store here in New Hope [Pennsylvania]. And so, from the other end of the county, we came up there to shop, and I got on the executive committee. And in 1940 the manager's assistant quit, and after two board meetings where we couldn't find a replacement, I said, "I'll give you a year." I went to work there to salvage a small co-op in Medford, Mass[achusetts]. They were bankrupt, they owed more than their shares were worth, and in a year's time we earned enough to make their share capital valid, and stock was on the shelves. And then I was drafted in 1944. I went into Camp Kane in March of 1944.

What was your family's religious affiliation?

My parents went to a Presbyterian church in Minneapolis. When the United States got into the war, the minister got up in his pulpit and preached a sermon of hatred against the Germans. My father promptly wrote him a letter and said that he had served his apprenticeship in Germany, he had

German relatives, and this was a lot of hogwash. He didn't think it was proper for a minister of the Gospel to get up and preach a sermon of hate. He resigned, and the minister came to the house and tried to talk him out of it.

Would you describe your own religious upbringing as strong or moderate?

Varied, extremely varied. From the Presbyterian church, a lot of little splinter churches, Wee Wisdom from Kansas City, a succession of them. My brother had a wonderful tenor voice and sang in choirs according to where he made the best deal. So I actually held membership in the Presbyterian and Methodist churches. I attended the Christian Science church conscientiously and studied it for two years, Baptist church for a year, and a Hindu philosopher came through Minneapolis in 1925, and again in 1929. I would say that I always had an interest in the ideas of religion. I did not join the Society of Friends in the forties because I didn't want to be looking as if I joined them to get under their umbrella for CO classification. I joined the local Society of Friends about 1952, when I came back.

Well, I'm not getting clipped until 1944. I'd had enough time to know about nonregistration and other types of resistance, so that I had to make up my own mind. I registered in 1940 with a guilty conscience. I figured I had no business registering, the government had no right to make that demand on me, but I did. And from the time I was involved in the system I thought, well, it's just a matter of time until they push me too hard or too far and I'll be out. And so that's essentially what happened.

After six months at Kane, which was a project of the Forest Service, selected cutting, piling in cord wood, I had no sooner gotten there than some of those who had been there a while already and were on the fringes, socialist and other fringes, were making the point that, here this was supposed to be to get as far away from the war effort as possible, and yet here we were cutting wood, piling it, and then twice a year they had an auction, and who would pay the highest price for cord wood in those days but the steel mills to make coke. So we were indirectly supporting the war effort. Those of us who made this very clear to the rest of the camp were very unpopular. It was a Brethren camp, with predominantly Brethren boys from Ohio and Indiana who had their cars there and who had weekend passes home and were really on the gravy train. I wouldn't characterize all of them as, you know, just "playing it cozy" for their own easiest out. But they came from Brethren churches where they would have been expelled had they gone in the army. And some of them married, and one of them had kids. There was certainly an element of Brethren young men there who were taking the easy way out, and when we talked about closing the camp down, they really hated our guts for that.

114

What role did your wife play in your decision to go into CPS?

Well, I would just say that she was supportive, but other than that, I can't say that she played much role. But she gave me no hard time, neither then, nor prison, nor since.

And how about your family? Were they supportive of the decision?

No, not too much. But neither did they give me a hard time.

When you filed for CO, did your draft board give you any difficulty?

No, because it was Newtown, and there's a big Friends meeting in New-town, the biggest one around, 400 members. And so the local board there was quite accustomed to handing out CO classifications. And I'd gone to New York, trying to get work with a magazine called *World Tomorrow*, a pacifist paper. I was selling advertising in the magazine, and boy, that was rough. So I could indicate fairly well that I had never taken a job in my life to make money but always tried to do something to leave the world better than I found it. So I had no problem getting the classification.

Did your draft board at any point try to persuade you to go 1AO?

No, no.

That was a common practice.

I was 36 and vocal, and they had that background of COs, and so they might with others, but they wouldn't waste their time.

Did you go into the medical experiments after you left Camp Kane?

Well, I don't call it medical. It was "guinea pig" at Cornell, and it was one month at 60 degrees, one month at 40 degrees, one month at 20 degrees, and one month at 0 degrees. They had a room inside of which was a smaller refrigerated or insulated room where the four of us slept and ate. In the larger room, we exercised on a treadmill. This was the Office of Scientific Research and Development, OSRD. They had us on a high-protein diet. [They were studying] the relation of diet to cold temperatures. The military, with their foresight, was looking ahead to after the war was over, when they might have to tangle with Russia, which would include the Arctic. So that's what this program was.

How long would you be in the larger room? Did you stay for a full month in there, or did you get out periodically?

Well, after a while we did get furlough on the street and went to some dances and some games, sports, on the campus. I'm very foggy now on what the routine was, but we were exposed a certain amount of time in the day or in the week to these temperatures, and working at dawn, from starting at 60 degrees. A month [at] each [temperature], and then the weekend between for going down.

What led you to volunteer for that?

Oh, anything to get out of the camp. There's guinea pig projects, there's the camp projects, there's government camp, and there's the mental hospitals, and I had sort of in mind getting a quick crack at all of them before something happens and I bust loose. So I got three out of the four. I got camp, and the guinea pig, and then government camp. And the only thing that I really missed was where you put your health on the line.

In a sense, I put my health on the line with what I did, and I'll tell you one thing I got out of it was hemorrhoids. I never told anybody else, but I think it's time for it to be made part of the record. We were given this carefully controlled diet, all four eating the same thing, and they took our breath on the treadmill. They did other things, blood pressure, all kinds of things. They made up our lunches and then they put a like one in the freezer, and later on, after the project was over, then this was to be analyzed by the panel. Well, they had one man in charge and two helpers who were running the thing. They were all guys who would trap animals and study their habitat, and they would at times cut them up to see what was in their stomachs. They were used to working with animals, small animals. They were interested in deer and wildlife; that was their background and training, and they didn't know the first thing about dealing with human beings. And so we were allowed out, and I don't remember how far we were into this program when another fellow and I started eating on the outside. And at the time I'll admit that I hadn't yet figured out what the hell this was all about. When I later came to the conclusion that they were laying the groundwork for a diet to fight the Russians on, then I was glad that I had sabotaged their program. Wasn't nice, and I have qualms about it, you know, but I did. I heard indirectly that they wondered what had screwed them up so badly. They knew that the whole thing was a fiasco.

Did you consult with your wife before you volunteered for this program? Did you inform her?

No, I don't really recollect. I more likely told her the best.

What was she doing to support herself while you were in CPS?

She had a background of teaching in arts and crafts, so she got a job painting scarves in a studio in New York. It really was piecework. And she did very well.

Did you contribute anything to the cost of your maintenance in CPS?

When I applied, I applied for a Friends' camp, even though I wasn't a Quaker yet, and it was at that one short period when they were in transit. They had been taking anybody, and then they found the burden considerable financing it, and if you had it you were expected to pay your own way. I didn't have it, or wasn't going to do it. At the time I asked for it, I was sent to a Brethren camp, and I let them foot the bill, and in retrospect, I have no second thoughts on that. I think the government should have paid it, but the church used to make it easier for their young men and want[ed] to pay it.

When you left the experiment then, you chose to go to a government camp?

That's right.

Tell me about Germfask.

Well, of course, I helped close it by the escapade with Dick Lazarus and Danny Dingman. The government camps were essentially for what they like to think of as the troublemakers. There were people there who didn't belong there because somebody goofed in their understanding of what the guy was trying to say or do at some camp. But the ones that I came to associate with and know the best were the rebels, and I think no one exemplified it better than Dick Lazarus. I understood him to want to create all the disruption and discord that he could short of going to jail. And I think he ended up doing exactly that. Danny Dingman wanted to create all the resistance that he could and ended up in jail. But by that time any number of the fellows had refused to work or walked out or done these things, and then when they went to court, they were represented by somebody, sometimes a sympathetic lawyer, but they were represented by a lawyer who accepted the bounds and constrictions of the court, and they weren't allowed to say and make their own case the way they wanted it. And so Dingman wanted, when he went to court, to be there on his own, all alone, and talk for himself, and no compromises with anybody else. I thought when we walked out and went to Easter sunrise service, that was a beautiful, beautiful opportunity to put the government and the war system and everything on trial. That three men could be arrested and tried for going to Easter sunrise service.

So you anticipated being arrested when you went?

Oh sure.

I've read some reports of people who were not unsympathetic with the resistance, but said Germfask was kind of a . . .

Pure anarchism.

. . . kind of an uncivilized place. What comes up a number of times is the table manners. A lot of people comment that it had an almost brutish quality. Is that fair?

That I don't remember, and I'm not as sensitive to some of that as some others would [be]. The guys just went their own way, and the authority was not respected, and I say in many cases, with good reason. I was there so very briefly, and then came Easter, and then Dick and I walked those 20 miles, and while we were having breakfast, the state police picked us up and threw us in the can. I'll always remember that, because we were in there when Roosevelt died. And you never heard such cries of elation. Why, I never quite figured out.

From the prisoners?

Yes.

This was a county prison you were in?

County jail, right. So anyway, we were locked up for five days, and then Frieda Lazarus [Dick's mother and an attorney with the War Resisters League] got us out.

What kind of woman was she?

Oh, I don't know. I liked Frieda, a lot of people didn't, but I loved her. She was doing what she thought she should be doing. And when she helped, for instance, get somebody off the hook who maybe really didn't want to be off the hook, they wanted to have their confrontation and get it over with. So there was some criticism of her for the deals that she made. She made the deal for us three, and I had no objection. I would've preferred to have stood trial, because I thought it was such a beautiful thing to stand trial on. What's-his-name from the Methodist church, visited there . . .

Carl Soule?

. . . Carl Soule came there. I don't know whether he sensed that our interest in Easter sunrise service could conceivably have been more to create a confrontation than it was to go to Easter sunrise service for the significance of Easter in the Christian church.

So the deal was struck by Frieda Lazarus?

Yes. In return for each of us reporting to a new assignment, the charges would be dropped.

All of Germfask closed down not too long after that.

They were all scattered. It was a confession of failure; they couldn't run a camp with the assortment of men that they had there.

So you went from Germfask to Minersville.

I barely got there, I hadn't really gotten settled in, when they dropped the bomb on Hiroshima, and I walked out August 10. It took that long to get a statement written and mimeographed.

You had informed the U.S. attorney that you were going out?

No, I just walked out and hitchhiked across the country, giving out my statement in various towns and giving one to every person who gave me a ride. The first confrontation I had hitchhiking was in Rochester. I was giving out my leaflets, and a cop read one and asked if this walkout wasn't against the law. I said, "Yeah, eventually the FBI will be after me, and I'll go to court." Well, first he let me go, and then apparently he went and either got on the phone or reported in, and he came back and took me in. This was a Friday, and I had to appear back in court on Monday, so I hitchhiked into New York and then went back on the bus. I wasn't even AWOL from Minersville, because I had so many days furlough time coming, and until that was expired and I was ten days overdue, I wouldn't even be reported absent.

When I got to New York the second time, I went down to Foley Square and told the U.S. district attorney where I was. When he wanted me, he had only to telephone and send somebody out. And so, when he did and I went in, he wanted me to appear for trial in Sacramento on such and such a date. I said, "Okay, where's the ticket?" He said, "No ticket." I said, "No ticket? You provide the ticket." So I was locked up in West Street for a week to 10 days until they got a couple of marshals scheduled, stupid horses' asses that they are. Here I had turned myself in and everything else. They knew they could have handed me the ticket, and I would have appeared out there. They had two marshals, and we had fare for three men on the train, and they put me in leg irons every night.

I got to San Francisco just in time for Sunday dinner. It was chile con carne—slushy, sloppy, wet, you know, terrible—two pieces of white bread and a cup of tea, no sugar and no lemon. And so I was still green, and I forget whether I put it all down the toilet or what, but this was unforgivable. No matter how lousy the food is, there's always somebody else who will eat it. I learned that real quickly. I knew about the hunger strikes that had taken place already, and I knew about Corbett Bishop, and so I went on a hunger strike then and there.

A day or so later, I was moved up to Sacramento, and I was lucky, there was an upper berth available, and I knew that I wanted to stay by myself and not do a lot of circulating. I didn't shave, eat, take water, nothing. So these three guys came in, and they wanted to rape me. I couldn't tell you to this day what I said or what, because certainly I was no match for them physically, [even] if I had been eating I wouldn't have been. I'm not a physical person. But one way or the other, I talked them out of it. I didn't have that indignity for an experience. No. Then finally somebody told, "This guy isn't eating," and so the guy came and took a look and asked me if it was true. A day or so later, I was in court, and the judge committed me to the county hospital for forced feeding and mental observation. So the doctor—and just as I had felt that these three men at Cornell were using their availability to run this guinea pig project for the army, were thereby escaping their own service, this doctor was there in the hospital very glad not to be [on the] front line. He belabored me, saying he would like to bash my head in for what I was doing. I was requiring this special service and other people were being denied, because he had to put a tube up my nose and feed me intravenously. But the shrink came three, four times and we had a good nice chat. When I went back into court, the shrink was there to say that I was as sane as he was.

What happened in the trial?

There really wasn't any trial. I didn't plead. "Had I walked out?" Sure I had walked out. All I wanted now was to say why, and I had a reasonable opportunity to say why. And this was a "two-year" judge. They tended to fall into patterns, and this was a guy who just threw two years at everybody. And the marshals came around and tried to talk me into eating for the duration of the trip. "Why not make it easy for yourself?" "Make it easy for me" is what they meant. So that trip was by car.

Were you assigned at that point to Springfield?

Yes, right.

Because of the fast?

I suppose, yes. Because there they would have the facilities. But I never had a day of discomfort, 10 days without food and water. One day or two and your mouth gets dry, and then you know you're making adjustments, you start living off your own fat.

Did you know what the physiological implications of this were? Did you know that you could go x number of days without water, or were you just working from faith?

All I knew—and I remembered this from my youth—was that MacSwiney, the lord mayor of Cork, died in a British prison after 60 days or so. So I never told anybody, I'm going to fast to the death. I never made any pronunciamentos on that. Anything I had to say was about the war, and at no other time did I say, I'm going to do this or that. And I always thought that those guys in prison who said that they were going to "do something until . . ." were very foolish, because almost invariably you end up for one reason or another changing your plans. You can look awfully silly. So I was prepared. I have no death wish, then or since. I had no thought whatever of hurting or harming myself.

So when you got to Springfield, you continued to fast?

I fasted for eight months. The first month was consumed by San Francisco to Sacramento to trial to the hospital and to Springfield. Actually, if they count the time in jail, I did seven months on a two-year sentence. And the significance of that is that you're not eligible for parole until eight months. But add the seven months at Springfield to the one month before that and that gives you eight months that I did not voluntarily open my mouth for food or water.

What was sustaining you? Were you on intravenous fluids?

Oh yes. The intravenous was to restore the body fluid, so immediately, the first thing in the hospital was intravenous. The second was a tube down the nose into the stomach, and that is a milk, egg, and other vitamins and nourishment. It's a balanced diet, because at one time I was annoyed that I wasn't creating any disturbance there at Springfield. So after the feeding, I went into the shower and tried to bring it up, and I couldn't. I tried swallowing part of the towel, my finger, nothing, I couldn't bring it up.

Were you just trying to push it a notch further?

Yes, why not. I wanted to get in their hair. They weighed me periodically, and they knew they were feeding me adequately because they had stabilized my weight and I looked well.

They released you after seven months?

I was put on a train, and I think I had my first meal in Kansas City, scrambled eggs. I figured soft something, and I had no problem, and I went right back to eating.

I guess one of the hopes at the beginning of CPS was that the units would become communities, that a sense of connection would evolve, and it appears in most cases that didn't happen. What the men had in common was an opposition to violence.

Yes.

But the more men I've talked to, the more complex it becomes, because there were just so many different types of men and different values and different attitudes.

You couldn't say it any better than that. There were a couple of Christadelphians at Kane who asked, "What have you done?" "I organized for a pocketbook workers' union." The Bible says, "Be satisfied with your station in life." Friends, of course, were on the whole more liberal. There was a small coterie of liberals among the Brethren. I had very little contact with any Mennonites.

Who was the most interesting CPS man you met?

A dozen faces popped up in front of me, and I'd have a hard time giving the top billing.

Who were some of them?

Roy Kepler. He came east and ran the War Resisters League for a year or two.

What was striking about Kepler?

Well, general competence and intelligence. He did more to help me write my walkout statement. There were a few others. I'm not really an intellectual myself, but I gravitate that way entirely. I relate to people on the head level much more than the heart level.

Were there men at Germfask who were opposed to the disruption?

Oh yes. "Work jerks" we called them. I can understand it. I'd rather be busy versus [going] out on a work project and sit there. If I couldn't bring something to read, I'd go crazy. So I'd rather swing an ax and be physically busy or work on the bridges or break rocks on the road. So that I've got to be highly motivated to be a slow-downer. And there were others, we obviously had to be everlastingly grateful to some of these guys, because they ran the kitchens and the other absolute minimum maintenance. Without some of those, we would have been in one hell of a fix. Each one would have had to do it for himself.

Do you have any doubts about having gone into CPS? Do you think it might have been wiser to go to prison right off the bat?

I just accept the fact that I knew that the more clear-cut thing would have been not registering, clear opposition from the very beginning. But no, the very slight contribution that I made for six months at Kane to the war effort doesn't lay heavily on my heart. It doesn't make me feel that I shouldn't have gone the route of CPS. And because I feel so strongly that the cardinal sin was the bombing of Hiroshima and Nagasaki, I'm really very happy that that is what triggered my walkout. I'm proud of the fact that that's what did it, not some incident with an employee of the government in the camps.

What was the least satisfying aspect of CPS?

Well, I think I made the same mistake in supposition that a lot of other people did: that because we were opposed to killing we were therefore, ipso facto, of a higher stripe, and therefore we should have made that [a] community of Christian love or however you want to describe it philosophically, religiously, and it wasn't so.

Do you think there was a realistic possibility of creating those kinds of community?

Really no, because the point is, the men came from all these different backgrounds. You had the sophisticates of New York and others from the radical movement, the semisocialists, some anarchists, and you had the super-religious, the second-milers, and really, there's too scant a bond. Then you've got a system where some people, I'm sure, went in—and I did to a certain extent—with higher hopes and aspirations for the whole thing, that it would be an elevating experience. But it wasn't, for various reasons, including the people that were in it as well as the people who were running it. And then the inherent contradictions in being government-run, church-operated. The churches would like to have thought that they were running it, and they damn soon found out when they tried to do some decent things that the government was running it, and yet the government wasn't even footing the bill, and this also bugged me.

Can you think of any specific ways in which your life was changed by the whole experience?

Not [directly], no, because I don't think that this was the high point of my life in that everything else has hung on it. When somebody finds out about it or wants to talk about it, I can always talk about it, but I don't push it.

Did you experience any kind of limitations afterwards in terms of work or something you might have wanted to do?

No, and I have ignored the fact that I'm a felon, a convicted felon, and I register, and I vote, and do so as I damn please. What I haven't done is run for public office. And that is not so much because that history would likely come out, but because the public office that I might have run for, city commissioner here, you've got to go to all these flag-waving things and you've got to kiss babies and all that crap. And your telephone is public information, and people call up when their sewers don't work. Nuts.

How much contact do you have with CPS men?

Well, after prison, I came out, and I worked for the War Resisters League in New York for a year, and then, with Dave Dellinger and Ralph DiGia and Bill Kenning, we formed an intentional community at Glen Gardner. After three years there, my wife said, "Well that's enough of this," because I'm something of a workaholic, and I worked hard there, and some of the others liked to sleep late in the morning. I didn't care if they wanted to sleep late, but the night before we'd said, "Now we're going to get up and be on the road or in the garden at 10 o'clock, let's be there," and they would show up two and three hours late. I bitched, and then my wife got tired of my bitching, and so we left.

What did you do after you left Glen Gardner?

Seven years as a carpenter and mason, that was 1950 to 1957. Five years and I went into the factory, and I learned to run a Swiss screw machine here in town. And having learned it, I taught it to others, and I became head of a department and had three to four men working two shifts on this screw machine and a dozen women assembling these parts. But this was miniaturization, and these things were going into satellites and all, and here this was 1957 to 1962, and the world situation was sufficiently unstable. I was always nervous about the fact that I was too close to defense work, and had a crisis developed, I would have been out of there on my ass, right away, because the minute they found out what my history was, I would have been suspect.

So meanwhile, the Central Committee for Conscientious Objectors advertised for an administrative assistant in Philadelphia, and I applied and got the job. And I was there for seven years, from 1962 to 1969. And the thing grew; when I went, there were three of us and we had a budget of $30,000. At the top, it was 22 on the staff and $300,000—all contributions, all the nickels and dimes from people in the mail. That was fantastic. So then in 1969, I retired for the first time, and after six months I went back to work as a shipping clerk. That was heavy physical work, and I did that for two years. And then I retired again. Been part-timing it since then, because you can't live on Social Security.

Edward Burrows

"Prison is very hard on people. The whole point of prison is to break you of any individuality, to make you conform to a set pattern, and there is very little rhyme or reason to it. . . . Most of the people in the prison were little fish. I saw real injustice."

Edward Burrows, born in Sumter County, South Carolina, on 17 August 1917, graduated from Washington and Lee University in 1939. While teaching high school, he received an M.A. degree in history from Duke University. He entered CPS in the summer of 1941. Burrows grew disillusioned with CPS, left camp in February 1943, and served two years in federal prison. After the war he undertook graduate studies in American history, working under Prof. Merle Curti, and received his Ph.D. from the University of Wisconsin in 1955. He began teaching in the History Department at Guilford College in 1948 and remained there until his retirement in 1979. He has been active since in peace campaigns, voter registration, and AIDS support groups.

How did you become a pacifist?

My background was Episcopal and Presbyterian; I became a pacifist when I was at college at Washington and Lee.

So it wasn't really because of family upbringing or religious training?

Well, indirectly. My mother was very religious, and I had a traditional religious training, and I guess I take things very much literally; from very early, when they said you're supposed to love your enemies and so on, I took them at face value. So that when I went to college—it was during the thirties, and you know, there was a widespread antiwar movement, and a large number of young men at Washington and Lee organized "Veterans of Future Wars." It was never really any organization, but there was a myth around, and we had meetings and studied the whole question of the alternatives. I became acquainted with Gandhi for the first time and read books on pacifism. I don't know how it got started, I don't have any recollection at all. But when I got through, I was convinced, and two or three of my closest friends were very strong pacifists, although they ended up in the service. Then when I got out of Washington and Lee and went to Duke, in the fall of 1939, that's where I for the first time got acquainted with the FOR [Fellowship of Reconciliation], and that just reinforced my pacifist convictions. And when the draft went into effect in October of 1940, I was sure that I was a conscientious objector, but there was no provision in the draft act for registering as a CO. I was teaching school in a rural South Carolina community, and I had my master's from Duke at that time. The registrations had to take place, in South Carolina, in the schools. We suspended school for a day. And I went to my principal and told him that I could not register for the draft and that I couldn't participate in this. He said, "Okay, but you will have to register, because if you don't, you're going to have trouble." So I went ahead and registered but wrote on the card that I was opposed to military service. I spent the day cleaning up the latrine; this was an old school, and they had no inside toilets. So I spent the day giving that a thorough cleaning, because I refused to help with the registration. I think that might have had something to do with the fact . . .

That you were accepted?

. . . Yes. I don't know, it was a peculiar community. Clarendon County later became famous because it was one of the counties involved in the Supreme Court case about race. It was about 75 percent black, and the whites in the community were drafted very rapidly because many of the blacks were illiterate and diseased or had problems of various kinds, with a high incidence of syphilis. So that the whites were just wiped out very quickly. The ones that had very high numbers found themselves being drafted, and within that first year, almost all the white young men within the community had gone to war. But they never, never discriminated against me in any way, and in fact, ironically, many of the young men in the community came to me for help in filling out questionnaires when they got them, and I would do it. But there were never any questions, and the next year I was drafted.

My draft board was very nice. I only had one unpleasant experience. They sent me a card, so they said, to appear for a physical. I never got it. So then, after some time passed, I got a letter, a very nice letter, saying, "We realize that you are opposed to going to war, but you have to have a physical, because you may not be physically fit to do anything, so please report to the doctor." Well, when I got to the doctor's office, he was very irate. He said, "Why didn't you come when you were supposed to?" And I told him I didn't get the letter. He said, "You don't expect me to believe that!" "Well, I'm sorry, I didn't get it. I would have come, because I realize that it's to my advantage." So I was given a physical, and then I was drafted and went to Buck Creek, [North Carolina]. But the clerk of the draft board was a very nice man, because he even sent me an article which came out in the *Saturday Evening Post*, which I had not seen, about Civilian Public Service. And then, of course, the South Carolina newspaper came out with a headline that there were only two conscientious objectors registered in the whole state of South Carolina. My family was horrified.

Were they supportive or not?

Yes and no. In a traditional southern family, it was their duty, no matter what I did, to accept me, they had to support me. But at the same time, they were horrified. They thought I was committing some really terrible mistake. And as a matter of fact, my family reacted so strongly that when I first discussed it with them and told them I wasn't going to register, they said, "Do register as a CO, for heaven's sake, but register." Actually, if I had done what I felt strongly I should have done, I would *not* have registered, because I eventually ended up in prison.

Was it family pressure that led you to register?

Yes. To make it easier for them, I went ahead and did what I just described.

Once you were registered, did you decide on CPS over 1AO as the lesser of two evils?

Yes, definitely. I never considered 1AO, as that was being in the army. I went to CPS. And the other guy that had been listed, he had better sense than I did. When he saw there were only two of us, and they listed our draft boards but they didn't give our names, he wrote to my draft board, and the draft board passed it on to me, so he and I communicated. When I reported, they put me on the bus and sent me up to Buck Creek [North Carolina], August of 1941.

Didn't you experience a shock financially when you went into CPS? You were earning, what, probably $2,000 a year?

No, $90 a month teaching. I was a member of the Episcopal Pacifist Fellowship at that time, which I joined through the FOR, and so the Episcopal church agreed to pay my costs, my $35 a month, and I signed a note that I would pay it back eventually. And then at the end of the first year, they wrote and told me that they released me from that note, so I never had to pay a cent, and I would get, as I recall, $2.50 a month.

So they maintained you for those two years?

Yes. I stayed at Buck Creek until April of 1942, and I had become concerned, particularly after Pearl Harbor, that we were really not doing work of national importance. The work was interesting, it was outdoors, and I really thoroughly enjoyed it, but I felt that, when people were dying, it was not the most significant thing to do. So I applied for a transfer. Now I realize that what really was bothering me was the whole idea of conscription in the back of my mind. And I was one of the first transferred out of the camp down to Crestview, Florida, a joint camp of the three peace churches. It was a small project; we had 20 people. We worked with the public health service, and I was there from April until the next February.

What did you do specifically?

We built outdoor toilets, privies. We did all the work. And it was a pretty congenial group, and it was very, very satisfying, because you could really see that you were doing something significant, because we were helping human beings. We would go out to homes which never had any kind of sanitary sewage system, and we would dig a pit, build the toilet for them, and you could feel that in this county where 85 percent of the children had hookworm, you were really doing something to help these kids. And we also did pump projects. I didn't work on that very much, but we would put in wells, pumps, so they could get clean water.

But it was in the middle of feeling that you were doing something that was very positive and productive that you made the decision that CPS was not for you. How did you come to that decision?

Sometime after I got there in April, I began to question whether I really was doing what was right. And I wrote to people like A. J. Muste and debated it all fall. I went home at Christmas intending not to come back, but when I got home, circumstances were such that, when I told my family, my father, who had just lost his oldest brother, just got so terribly upset—and my mother also, but not quite as much—that they persuaded me to go back to camp and rethink the whole thing, which I did. They persuaded me, which I did willingly, to again engage in correspondence with various people. I wrote to the Episcopal bishop, and I talked to others, and for about six weeks I tried to rethink the whole thing, but I came back to the same conclusion. And so in February I left camp and went back to South Carolina.

130

Did you notify someone in the camp?

Oh yes. The camp director took me into town to catch the bus. I wrote my family that I would not come home. What I was concerned about was the making of a stand against conscription, because I think conscription is evil. I don't think we have the right to conscript anyone—for good or bad, for that matter. And also, I really felt that in the South we needed to begin the process of working on race relations, and I wanted to dedicate my life to that. So I wrote my family and told them I would not come home, I would try to find something else. But they insisted I come home, and I did, and I was there for a few weeks and then was arrested. I wrote to the attorney general, and I wrote to my draft board and told them what I was doing and where I was going and sent them back my draft card, which later caused me trouble.

Why?

Because when I was in prison, I made parole, I got a job, and just as I was going to get it, they handed me a draft card. This officer, who had never liked me anyway, I told him, "I didn't bring a draft card in here, and I'm opposed to the draft, and it would be ridiculous for me to take one now." And he handed me a form to sign, and I said, "I'm not going to take the draft card," and before I could sign the form, he grabbed it back. It meant I would have to spend another year in prison, because I didn't get paroled.

Going back, the officers actually came to your home in South Carolina and took you in hand. Then where did you go?

Well, I went to the county jail, and it was rather funny, because my father was a county commissioner, and his responsibility was supervision of the county jail. And it was almost like something from the Bible anyway, because the jailer was the father of one of my close friends in high school. So I was arrested late, I think it was Washington's birthday. I was cutting brush on a ditch bank, and I came in, and I was all dirty, and the FBI man was sitting there, and he told me he had come to arrest me, and we'd expected it. And I said, "Well, can I go upstairs and take a quick bath and get something to read?" And he said, "Well, I'm not supposed to let you out of my sight." And I said, "Well, that's the only staircase upstairs. And if you sit right here, there is no way I can get out of your sight without going out on a roof, and I'm not going to do that." So he permitted it. He said, "It's against the law, but I'll let you do it," so I went up. He sat there and talked to my father.

And I took the *Testament of Devotion*, I believe, and a Bible, and some other pacifist literature. So by the time we got to jail, he was very nice. He said, "Don't say anything, because anything you say can be held against you," and I said, "That's okay, I don't care." And he checked me into the jail. Well, the jailer was up in his own quarters and told some other official to check me in. I was put in a cell block. There was nobody else in there. It was very clean. During the night, a drunk came and was put into that block. And then, the next morning, it appeared in the paper that I had been arrested. My father was fairly prominent, and I had a lot of relatives in the neighborhood, and they began to call the jail, and the jailer got terribly upset. I had already eaten the regular jail food, but he came up and brought me breakfast from his table, and he said it was all a mistake putting me in here, that federal prisoners were put in a special cell. I don't think that's the truth, but there was a suite up on top, a penthouse that had a private bath.

You started off well.

I started off well. It shows you something about justice in the South really. But I was put up there, and I stayed in jail two days until they could arrange bond, and I was fed from the jailer's table and I read and I didn't suffer. It bothered me in a way, because it shows me how, because of my family connections, I was treated differently. But then I got out on bond and went back to work on the farm until May, when I was ordered to appear in a Florida court.

What kind of a trial did you have?

Well, it was very simple, because they asked if I had left camp, and I pleaded nolo contendere, which meant, in effect, guilty. There was a long docket, and I sat. I was arraigned that morning, and they asked if we wanted a lawyer, and I said no.

Was it just a judge, or was there a jury?

Well, he had a jury, but it wasn't a jury case, he was hearing the nonjury cases first. He told me to come back at 2:00 P.M. I went out and had this very nice picnic—it was in May and it was very pleasant—and then I went back to court. When we got there, the cases had gone very rapidly, and my case was being called just as we walked in. The judge read out the charges against me, and they made multiple charges that I'd left camp without permission, and I think there were about four or five charges. And then there was a letter that somehow my father had gotten the head of the draft board in

132

my hometown to write, which was saying that I'd been misled by my college professors and all that stuff. And the judge got very angry, quite angry. Up until that time he had been very reasonable, I thought. He'd heard a lot of cases, and he'd given suspended sentences and probation and stuff. But he got very angry.

Angry at you?

He gave us a lecture, and he asked the prosecutor, "What is the maximum?" Oh, my heart sank when he did that! And the man was sensible enough to realize the judge was mad, and he said he'd have to go look it up. I'm sure he'd already looked it up, but he left and was gone for about 10 minutes, during which the judge lectured me and asked if I had anything to say. I told him that I was doing what I thought was right, and I had prepared a statement, which I think I read. And then he sentenced me to three years.

What prison were you sent to?

I was sent to Federal Correctional Institution in Tallahassee, Florida. It was just being built at the time, and we never had more than about 600 prisoners.

You were just thrown in with all of them?

Oh yeah, federal prison is quite a cross-section, and it was quite an educational experience. I consider it one of the most valuable parts of my education. I wouldn't want to repeat it, but I don't think I'd want to repeat much of my education.

It must have been staggering initially, and terribly depressing.

I was exceedingly fortunate, because I had an opportunity to work in the prison hospital and, within two months after I got there, the prison doctors changed and a very fine doctor came. He was a Jewish refugee from Czechoslovakia, a brilliant man and just a very fine man, and working with him was a real privilege. He and I became close friends.

What was the reaction on the part of the other prisoners when they found out why you were there?

I had problems with officers but not with prisoners. I don't remember ever any difficulty with any prisoners. It was shocking, because the first night I got there, we were put in a county jail, which was an awful experience. It was dirty and unbelievable, and we were there for six days, and then we were taken to prison on Saturday. And the first night we came to isolation, but then the next day I was put in just a regular cell block where they kept the new prisoners. And I found, to my amazement, that probably out of the 12 or 15 men that were in my cell block, almost half of them were illiterate, so I spent the first Sunday afternoon writing letters for them.

Were there many blacks there?

The blacks had separate quarters. They were entirely segregated. We ate in the same dining room, but the blacks ate on one side and whites on the other.

Did you feel called upon when you were in prison to make your feelings known about that situation too?

Yes. In fact, I asked to live in a black dormitory and, of course, was refused. But I made friends and later wrote letters for a lot of them; I was a secretary for them.

You were there a year before the attempt was made to release you?

Yes, I was given parole at the end of the first year. It took some time to work out all the details. But they were finally worked out, and I was getting ready to leave in August of 1944. I entered in May of 1943 and would have left in August of 1944, but then when that happened, I had to stay until August of 1945. I got out right after the end of the war. And, of course, the same guard told me, "You'll be back in here in a few days," because I wouldn't take the draft card then. What is interesting, as a postscript, is we had a meeting here at Guilford a few years ago, talking about this. And our president, Ramsey Hobbs, a Quaker, took the position of 1A0 during the war and so did an economics professor. When we were talking on this panel, he said, if he had to do it over again, he would probably become a 4E. Another professor who was a 4E, if he had had it to do over again, he would probably have refused to register. I said, "I don't know what you all are going to push me into, I guess I would have to burn myself. I don't have anywhere left to go to go further than what I did."

If you had to do it over again, would you simply not have registered and just taken the jail route?

Right.

Did you get a sense at Buck Creek and Crestview that the commitment to nonviolence was a bond, or were there many differences among the men?

There were many differences, I thought. There was some bond, particularly at first at Buck Creek, because we were a small number, but even then there were differences on interpretation. It was difficult. A lot of people had subscribed to nonviolence, and I suppose I was one of them, partly out of a deep sense of religious convictions and partly intellectually working it out. But they came from a lot of different backgrounds, and I remember there were some men in the camp who considered themselves atheists, and the whole commitment to nonviolence had not become totally a way of life, as I saw it. So that there was evidence actually of violence within the camps, not in the sense of physically attacking each other, but just a lack of consideration. We had problems, for example, with noise. I know one guy played the drums. And dealing with this was a very difficult experience.

Were there any open confrontations between groups in either of the two camps?

I remember long discussions about how we solved this problem. I don't recall any open confrontations. I remember, for example, one guy, he was the only Jehovah's Witness at Buck Creek. He took a car or had a car or borrowed somebody's car, but I remember the discussion was whether we should take his keys away from him. The director of the camp wanted to take his keys away, and some of us were concerned that was a form of violence. We had to convince *him* that it was undesirable. There was a lot of this, because the community was not friendly. Some people were, but on the whole the community was not. And there were times that there were rumors that we were going to be invaded. Other camps were invaded by the local community. And some of us went into town and drank beer and stuff like this, and they would get into discussions and begin to get into trouble. I know one group came back, and they were being threatened and there was a sense of tension. There was this feeling that we had to be extra careful not to jeopardize the movement, not to jeopardize the camp. But some people felt this was an unfair restraint on their freedom.

I had one experience in Florida like that. There was a small group on the edge of this little tiny town of Crestview. And I was the only Episcopalian in the group, although I had come under Quaker auspices. But there was a remarkable lady living in the community, and I began to go there because she would have Episcopal services. A priest would come once a month, and a few people gathered for services in her home. Well, one Sunday I was walking back from her home to the camp when a car drove up and stopped and asked me if I was going to the camp. It had several men and at least one woman, I remember, because she came to my aid, but they were very belligerent. They had been drinking, I think, and were very threatening and said they were going to kill me. They insisted I get into the car, and they would show me what it was like. Well, I tried to not show any fear, and I stood on the sidewalk talking to them, and I said, "Well, why don't you come out to the camp and see what it is like? We are not threatening anybody, and we believe this is a better way to solve problems," and tried to talk without further antagonizing them. And finally, the woman in the car said, "Oh, you all don't want to hurt him." And I said, "Why don't you really come out to camp?" So finally, the next day I believe it was, a couple of them did come out to camp. And I showed them all around. And they saw there was nothing dangerous there, but that was one time I really was frightened and I felt very much threatened.

Was there much moonlighting in the camps? We know some men who got their Ph.D.s when they were in CPS and others that took jobs on the side to earn money to support their families.

See, I was in in the early years, and in those camps I don't think there was any moonlighting. There were individuals who went out and did volunteer work. That was encouraged.

Were you able to establish any positive relationships with any people in the community while you were in CPS?

Not in Buck Creek. Some of the others did. I didn't. In Florida, with this lady I just mentioned, she and I had a very good relationship, kept in touch afterwards. There were a few other neighbors that we had pretty good times with.

Did you feel any pressure from your family?

Very little. Again, you see, my family was really very considerate. They didn't understand, and on occasion it would come out. I remember once, I had been in prison, and I came directly home from prison, and the sister older than I am was married and had a little child who had never seen his father because his father was in service and had left before the boy was born.

And she asked me to drive down with her to visit her in-laws so that I could do the driving and she could take care of the child. And we went and spent the day, and they were just as cordial and pleasant. And on the way back, she asked me rather pathetically, she said, "Would you mind just trying to explain to me again *why* you did this?" And it was that that made me realize [*very emotional*] how much what I had done had affected everybody. But they never complained. One brother one time did, but other than that— even cousins, I had a cousin who was in the legislature, and politically it would have been very harmful, but he did come over and offered to see if there was anything he could do. He wanted to support me.

Looking back at both CPS and your time in prison, was there a satisfying aspect of the experience?

Well, I don't know. In CPS I guess there was a real satisfaction in knowing there were some other people who held the same views, because I had been very isolated in South Carolina. In addition, I enjoyed the kind of things we were doing. I enjoyed the outdoors. I was healthy. Then I began to get this uneasy feeling, which eventually led to my being transferred. The Florida experience was a very good one. I felt we were really doing something worthwhile, and while I agonized over my own decision, I never felt particularly unhappy.

And how about prison?

Prison was both positive and negative. It was very difficult in prison to see what was happening to people. Prison is very hard on people. The whole point of prison is to break you of any individuality, to make you conform to a set pattern, and there is very little rhyme or reason to it. And there were just so many illogical things and so much unnecessary pain and the injustice of the whole system. Most of the people in the prison were little fish. I saw real injustice. A black man I became very close to, a fine, really hard-working, unsophisticated miner, or bootlegger—I'm not sure what he was in prison for. He worked in the hospital. He and I had become very close friends. And we had something that approached a riot, and he was totally innocent. He was not really a violent person, but one of the guards remembered him being there, and so he pointed at him and said, "He caused the trouble," and then later that same guard came to him and said, "Well, I had to have somebody," and said, "I didn't know whether it was you or not," and yet he had gotten on the stand and testified. And this man was going to be released just a few months after I got there. Of course, he lost all of his good time, and he was given an additional sentence, and he had done nothing to deserve this. And it was that kind of thing that was really hard to take. On the other hand, because I worked at the hospital, I was freed from a lot of the petty routines.

Did you become interested in prison reform as a result of this experience?

Yes, I did, very much interested, but I haven't done anything in that area because, emotionally, it's very difficult. I found it too unsettling to go into a prison. I feel guilty about it. I considered working in various ways, but I don't really trust myself.

Did you feel you went through any kind of a personality change?

Oh yes. There are scars. Some of them are pretty deep, but again, I would say I was very lucky, because the work in the hospital was really quite satisfying. I could see I was helping people. And this doctor, he was just unbelievable. Because, occasionally, he would see I was getting tense, and he would call me in, and we would just talk about all kinds of things, talk about what we read. He had a grand sense of humor, and our relationship was just one of really close friends.

Really a sustaining relationship for you.

Very, very sustaining. I remember one night that, because of our responsibilities—for a while I was the only so-called nurse, I think we were without a trained nurse at least two or three months, but we had to go on, so I did all the sterilizing of equipment. And I remember one night we had a series of things, and I was totally out of sterile operating room materials. And so I was there working all night trying to get ready in case we had an emergency. The doctor came to see some sick patient, and he came by and sat for several hours talking to me. I remember we talked about atheism, and we talked about evolution, and we talked about astronomy and things of this kind. It was that kind of relationship. I think he valued the relationship, because the general personnel were the kind that he found very little in common with. In fact, most of them probably had not had much education. I had a master's degree in history by that time.

In what ways do you see your life as being altered by CPS or prison or both?

I don't know really. CPS definitely reinforced my whole interest in the field of race relations, because I know from CPS I had the first real interracial experience. Although I had grown up in South Carolina and had been surrounded by blacks, it had always been a superior/inferior relationship. And I didn't feel it then, although I had many black friends as children and we worked together. I had, from quite early, questions about them, and I had asked my mother why it was that we had better school facilities than they did and why we went to different schools, but it was all intellectual. I had really never thought of associating with blacks as equals until I got to CPS, and then I remember going to a meeting and eating with blacks for the first time as equals.

Was this at Buck Creek?

This is at Buck Creek. We went into Asheville to a meeting. I think it might have been an NAACP meeting, I'm not sure. And it reinforced that, and it reinforced my pacifism. Other than that, I don't know. I was very fortunate after I got out of prison. I went out to this community and was there for several months while I was on good time from prison. I had to report regularly to a parole officer. This was isolated, and we were trying to get a school started and were raising our own food. I was also tutoring two boys, and I enjoyed the year there with them, but I became concerned that I wasn't being true to my race relations commitment, and so I applied to Dr. Charles Johnson out at Fisk, a well-known sociologist. I wrote to him and asked for some advice. And he invited me to come out and offered me a year of working with him, which I did for $75 a month, and I spent that year and lived as a black on the Fisk University campus in 1946–47.

Were you accepted?

Yes, by the black community. In fact, it was sort of a game, because a group of us ate together in a small little restaurant which gave us a special deal. For a flat rate, once a month we would eat there and she would feed us. And there was one other in the group who was technically classified as black who really was quite as light as I was. And when some stranger would come in, they would ask, "Is there somebody in here not a black person?" And they would say, "Well there is one of us who is not," and it was about 50-50, sometimes they'd guess him, and sometimes me. But they never showed any—well, occasionally, there would be a little bit of some, but never any real unpleasantness. I was accepted.

What did you do after that?

Well, while I was there, Dr. Johnson helped me get a Rosenwald fellowship. Rosenwald left something like $25 million to be used as fellowships for blacks and for white southerners. The man who used to be head of the *Atlanta Constitution* got one of them. Anyway, I got one of those, and with that I was able to go to the University of Wisconsin. I wrote to Merle Curti there and told him I was very interested in interracial studies. And so he welcomed me there.

So you worked with him?

I worked with him, a tremendous experience, and I wrote my dissertation on the Interracial Commission in Atlanta. So I spent that year, 1947–48, at Wisconsin. I spent the summer of 1948 in Atlanta doing research, and then I was getting ready to go back to Wisconsin, although, because of family situations, I felt I really should be getting a job and trying to help financially. Then, by accident, a man who was supposed to teach history at Guilford resigned late in the summer, and the president was talking to a former Duke friend who that day had gotten a card from me. I had written, "Well, it looks like I am going back to the university to finish up my Ph.D., because I can't get a job"—so I got a job. Then two years later, Guilford very generously gave me $100 a month, and I went back to the University of Wisconsin and finished.

So really, CPS and the experience with blacks in prison had a strong effect on you.

Yes, it reinforced the direction I was going. The only other area I can see that it might have affected is my social life. I went to an all-male school, and then I went to CPS and then into prison, and I always thought I would get married. But it was always a problem when I started becoming very fond of someone, then I would always get bothered. How much do I need to tell them about my background, and when? I don't think it's the sole reason why I never got married, but I think having been in prison affected my ability to really work through that, and I haven't solved that completely myself.

There were certainly women who had strong pacifist backgrounds too, but you just weren't fortunate enough . . . ?

Well, I kept hoping I would find one, but I never could. I remember meeting one and hoping it would work, but it didn't.

Obviously, getting the job here at Guilford, you never have really experienced any limitations professionally because of CPS and prison.

Precisely.

I am sure this was one of the things that your family worried about.

Oh, definitely. My father, when I first told him that I couldn't register, said, "Oh, if I had only known that, we'd have never bothered about your going to college. You've just wasted that money and time. You're just throwing away your life." I am sure that he believed that. But I really never suffered. When I came to be interviewed here, I told the president right away, "There are three things you need to know: one is that I am a pacifist, I do not believe in war. And the second is that I believe there is no distinction between blacks and whites, and we've got to work in that direction. And thirdly, that I have been in prison." And he said, "Well, I know all those things. Just so long as you don't get up on the housetop and say that everybody else has to do it, there won't be any problem," and I never have.

In fact, I had an interesting experience in class. We had this freshman course, and I taught one section, and we were talking about how we accept a lot of things without even thinking about it. And I mentioned that, when I was in college, we were taught in sociology classes that you could identify a criminal type and that, when I went to prison, I found this was not true. And I noticed some of the looks on the faces, and I said, "I told you last time, didn't I, that I had spent some time in prison?" and they said, "No, what were you doing in prison?" And I said, "Oh, well, I was in prison during World War II because I refused to go fight." "Why did you refuse to go to fight?" And so they began to ask me questions, and I said, "Look, that is not dealing with what we are supposed to be talking about. I don't mind answering your questions." Really, they were very cute about it, very interested in how that happened. And when they realized, I think, that I had made that decision when I was about [their] age, it had some impact.

I was going to ask you if you thought much about CPS and prison. Obviously, you do. It comes back.

Oh yes. CPS not so much. I have been back, tried to find Buck Creek. It's now just a grown-up place. I went back to Tallahassee once after 20 years.

It must have been traumatic.

Well, it was more interesting. Of course, it had changed a lot. The warden had changed. They have added to the prison. There were still a few guards that were there, and I saw a couple of them and talked to them. They remembered me. I think of that more often. For example, I never hear a train whistle that I don't think of prison. There was a train track very near, and the object was to escape when there was a train going by. Because you could get on the train and get away, and we had a number of escapes while I was there. It was a medium-custody prison, and the prisoners would always know who was gone. The guards wouldn't, and it was a game. It was interesting, because I found myself really on the side of the lawbreaker, again and again. Fundamentally, I believe in the idea of law. [But] we would hope they'd make it, even though you knew their chances were slim. They shouldn't be out there legally. But I never hear a freight train that I don't . . .

Just brings back the whole experience.

. . . and one other experience that hits me is a new moon. This man that I told you was treated so unjustly: he was placed in solitary confinement for 28 days. When he got out, he was very bitter. And the doctor came to me and said, "Burrows, is there any way we can do anything to help him?" And we asked him to come work in the hospital, and he refused. He had worked in the hospital before. He said no, he didn't want to have anything to do with white people. And they put him on just the nastiest job, it was the lowest job they had. It was the punishment detail, they had to clean out septic tanks, and they had to shovel coal and do anything that was just . . .

The most demeaning jobs?

. . . yes, he had to do that, for I don't know how long. And then, finally, the doctor asked them to assign him to the hospital. And so he came back up there, and he was very, very withdrawn. He would barely answer a question. He would do his work but would have nothing to do with the rest of us. But gradually he came back around, and he and I became very close again. And I wrote letters. I thought it was to his sister, but it turned out to be his mistress, or his girlfriend, who was married. But finally, his time gave out, and I had made parole and was expected to be released at any minute. And he was expected to be released. We had an emergency in the operating room, and it was quite late. We had worked until maybe one o'clock or so. We did all kinds of things, but this night we had an appendix. After the operation was over, I had to clean up the operating room, because it had to be ready, we were always having people get hurt, people in fights, and just normal emergencies like appendectomies. And I remember opening the door of the operating room, and there was my black friend. And I said, "What in the world are you doing sitting here?" He said, "Well, Burrows, you're here." So he helped me clean up.

We got all through, and when we were being taken back to our respective cells—the blacks were, of course, kept in one cell block, which was, again, just a barracks. There was a cell block where you were kept temporarily, or if you were kept in maximum custody you were kept in a cell, but most of the prisoners slept in these four big barrackslike buildings with no partitions in them, just glass-enclosed bathrooms. So if you took a shower or went to the toilet or anything, you were just there.

Always on view?

Yes, no privacy whatsoever. But most of the officers were really very nice. So that night, after we got through, the guard had to take us back because we weren't allowed to wander around after dark, even though the barracks were locked. He said, "Burrows, do you mind if I go over to this guy's dorm first, and then we will come back by yours?" And I said no. And we were walking along, and there was a beautiful new moon, just a crescent, and my friend said, "Burrows, the next time we see that moon, you and I both will be out of here." And so when I see a new moon now, I frequently think of prison.

Were you out?

No, that is when I lost my parole. He was out. I was in over a year. I saw 12 new moons there.

Have your religious convictions changed?

As I have grown older, my religious convictions are very deep, but they have changed. I have become much less satisfied with the conventional expression of religion and much more concerned about some kind of ecumenical religion, some way in which we can reconcile the various religions of the world, and that could be more of a personal thing rather than an outward social expression. The last years I have not been very active in a conventional religion setting, but I would still feel myself as being basically religious.

5

THE SEARCH FOR WORK OF NATIONAL IMPORTANCE
Human Guinea Pig in Medical Experiments
George Granger

*"I think the only satisfaction that anyone could take from such an experience
was that you made a witness, however small it might have been, and that
really, in my judgment, was my satisfaction."*

*George Granger, born on a Wisconsin farm on 29 January 1912, became one
of the 673 Methodists to enter CPS, the largest contingent outside the Historic
Peace Churches. Granger's CPS stint included participation in two medical
experiments conducted at Welfare Island in New York City. He later served,
until retirement, on the Methodist church's Board of Church and Society.*

My father died about the time I was 10. We moved to Chicago, and our
family was active in church. I was married in Chicago, and when the draft
came, I applied for a CO classification and was assigned to Big Flats. I
remained there for about a year and a half.

Our job was working in the Department of Agriculture nursery, and there
were two jobs that were done. One was to plant pine tree seedlings, and the
other was to cut lumber in the wintertime. I didn't do too much of that.
Because of my accounting background, I worked in the office part of the
time, but did get out into the forest and cut trees and planted seedlings.

From there I volunteered for a project at Welfare Island in New York in
1944. This was a high-altitude experiment, and the purpose of it was to
determine the best method of treating shock. The doctors were trying to
determine how to administer oxygen to shock patients, the absorption of
oxygen in the blood, and the psychological effect on individuals. One of the
things we did was to work in the decompression chamber. By reducing

atmospheric pressure in the chamber, you can simulate any altitude you want. And we would sit in the chamber, and they would reduce the temperature and take us to maybe 15,000–20,000 feet, and then, during the ascent, we would be given certain mathematical problems, and the object was to see what effect it would have on the ability of the individuals to concentrate and perform. We would sometimes go up as high as 50,000–52,000 feet.

Then we did another experiment with a French doctor who received a Nobel Prize as a result of his work in this field. We submitted ourselves to a surgical operation which involved the insertion of a catheter into an artery. This was done from various parts of the body, from the femoral artery, from an artery in the arm, to see how rapidly oxygen would travel through the blood and what effect it had on the rate of circulation. This was done not only at sea level in the hospital but also at high altitudes. And, of course, they discovered that at high altitudes the blood didn't circulate very fast. We never knew what the technical results were.

One of the other projects at Welfare Island was the life raft experiment. This particular experiment was to discover how long people could survive without eating and to develop the kind of rations that could be provided in life rafts that would sustain persons for a long period of time. During the starvation periods, our blood pressure and blood were checked a couple of times a day and we were not allowed out of the hospital. We were really patients in the hospital and were given maybe six ounces of water a day, and then, in addition, we were given a package of candy Charms a day. Now that's heavy concentrated sugar. As I recall, the starvation period was some-where around 14 or 15 days. Then I worked as an orderly at the hospital on the island.

Were you informed, before you volunteered, of the exact nature of the experiment?

Well, we had a pretty general idea of what the purpose of the experiment was and what we would be subjected to. Now, I believe the first one was the life raft experiment, and then we were asked if we wanted to volunteer for the high-altitude experiment. We had the doctor who was going to do the surgery come in and explain to us precisely the procedures, and what we would be subjected to, the risks involved. There weren't too many risks. Some of them backed out because they felt the risk would be great.

We had quite a bit of freedom, as far as our schedule was concerned, at Welfare Island, and when we finished the experiment for the day, we were free to do whatever we wished. But then when the experiments were over, we had a choice of either being reassigned to a camp or doing work at the hospital.

Which was more regimented than what you had been doing?

Yes, and I felt that working at the hospital was a little more rewarding than pulling weeds or chopping down trees, because there was a shortage of hospital attendants, and most of the fellows who were stationed on Welfare Island worked in the hospital.

Do you think you made the right decision, looking back now, to volunteer for these experiments? Have you had any long-range physical or psychological repercussions?

I don't think so. It's hard to say, but I kind of believe so. I still have the scars.

Before you went into CPS, was your wife working?

Yes.

And you had been married for how long?

About three years.

Was her job essential to your being able to survive while you were in CPS?

Oh, absolutely.

Since you were receiving no pay, if she hadn't been working, you would have been in dire straits.

That's right. If we had had small children, that would have been an entirely different problem. I would have felt obliged to take noncombatant service in the army, because I didn't have relatives who were either supportive or who could afford to help. She might have been able to live with her folks, but that would have been a burden to them. We didn't want to ask them unless they volunteered.

Looking back at the way your CPS experience affected you and your wife, did it strengthen your relationship or did it produce certain stresses and strains?

There is no question about it, it did strain the relationship during that period.

Why?

Well, I don't think she was fully supportive of the position I took; I would say she more accepted and went along with me.

Did you discuss it with her before you did it?

Oh yes.

She was not wholeheartedly behind you?

I think the physical separation, I think that would probably be a major factor.

Did you see changes taking place in her during this period, as a result of your being in CPS?

Well, that's hard. It's a long time ago. Of course, whatever happened during that period has been forgotten. There were strains, there's no question about it, but once we established a normal family relationship, things fell into place, and we went on from there.

Did you experience any pressure from either your wife or parents or her parents to perhaps go 1AO?

Yes, of course, there was some pressure, but it was more just the understanding that they didn't share my views, and her parents felt that this was placing a burden on her that she would not have had to bear if I had gone into the army.

Do you think she experienced any social stigma or sense of discrimination because of the position you took?

No, and this is an interesting thing. We belonged to a church group for some 20 years before and since, and there was never any attempt on the part of any one of them to argue the point or to be critical. They just seemed to accept it as my choice. I think in the business world, however, this was a little different. But I didn't feel the pressure nearly as much as I thought I would.

Did you provide any of your own maintenance?

I provided my own clothes and personal items, but I did not contribute to the maintenance of camp.

As you look back, what do you think was the most satisfying aspect of CPS?

I am not sure that I would say there was any aspect that was really satisfying in the same sense that what I am doing now is satisfying. I think the only satisfaction that anyone could take from such an experience was that you made a witness, however small it might have been, and that really, in my judgment, was my satisfaction. The reason I went into the experiments at Welfare Island was basically so I could get away from Big Flats, and that's why I think quite a lot of them volunteered.

Do you think the fact that you were less regimented while on these experiments was a factor in volunteering?

Yes, and we were in New York City, and you had opportunities which weren't available in Big Flats, and there wasn't the regimentation. We lived closer to normal lives than you would in a camp situation.

What do you think, as you look back, was the most negative aspect of your CPS experience?

Well, the most negative aspect, in my judgment, was the fact that the government was willing to, in effect, place people in semi-incarceration. We had to be in at a certain time, and you know, a lot of people say, "Well, it's better than being in the army." But for a lot of people who probably would not have been able to take that route, they had to go into the army to survive. When I think back from the standpoint of acceptance in the community, employment opportunities, the person who went into the army received preferences that the person in CPS couldn't even expect. Although I've worked all my life—I've never not worked, so really, it could be said that I wasn't hurt that much. But that was a sacrifice that I knew I was going to have to accept.

Would you say it was your religious background that played the greatest role in leading you to CPS?

I think it was religious. I was very active in youth work in the Methodist church, and at that time there was a lot of discussion and talk about alternative services. I think if you ask me what was the basis on which I was given a 4E classification, it was on the basis that the board felt that I had a religious foundation.

Looking back a generation or so later, do you think you made the right decision to enter CPS?

Would I do it again? I think so. I think so. I have a son who went through Vietnam, and he is suffering.

As a result of his involvement in that war? Did he consider a conscientious objector plea?

I don't think he did. I never tried to press the issue with him. He came out of Vietnam with a disability that he is being compensated for, but he wants no part of it.

Do you recall ever talking with him as he was growing up about your experiences?

Oh yes, yes, but I never said, "Now, this is what I want you to do, and this is the way to go." Because I didn't feel that I could impose my decision on him.

In what ways do you see your life as being changed by your CPS experience?

Except for the period when I was in CPS, I don't think that it has changed my life that much.

It didn't alter your career choice or anything of that nature?

No, I don't think so.

Are you aware of any family bitterness or division resulting from your service?

No. I am one of six children, and my two sisters, I would say, were the least supportive. My brothers were most supportive, but I don't think it had any material effect on our family relationships.

Do you think about CPS much? Does it cross your mind at all?

Occasionally, yes.

And when you do, which memories are the strongest?

Getting out! I just think, "Gee whiz, I wasted all that time." Well, at one time I felt that perhaps the experiments that we did at Welfare Island were helpful to somebody. That would be some satisfaction that could be drawn from that experience. The doctor received the Nobel Prize.

You feel you maybe had a part in it?

I had a part in it, because that was the basis on which his prize was awarded, and there were only a few of us who were involved in it.

So you really were the guinea pigs?

The guinea pigs is right, that's what we were called.

Attendants in Mental Hospitals and Training Schools
William Channel

"Well, the main issue, I think, was, we weren't doing work of national importance, that there was danger of our being isolated in comfort with good food. . . . We had the sense that the government wanted to get us out of sight and out of the way, that there was certainly in time of war a lot more important things that needed to be done."

William Channel, born in Wilmington, Ohio, on 18 December 1919, served three and a half years in CPS. His assignments at Cheltenham Training School and as a recreational director in the Virgin Islands influenced his subsequent career. After obtaining an M.S. in Social Work from Columbia University, Channel worked for the American Friends Service Committee in the Middle East and Hong Kong, directed overseas refugee programs, and assisted migrant farm workers. Since retirement, he has been involved with environmental issues and as a volunteer for the Atlanta Symphony.

Could you describe your formal education?

Well, I went two years to Wilmington College, where my mother was a professor, and then I went to George Williams College in Chicago. Then, in 1953, I went to Columbia to get a master's degree in social work.

What were you doing prior to entering CPS?

I was in college. George Williams College is a five-year bachelor's degree program. Then, we had a notorious Selective Service director who had no use for conscientious objectors or anyone that had anything to do with them. So I went in to ask him what I should do when I graduated. I said, "I know I'm going to be called sometime this summer, and I have a job, and should I take it?" He was very nice, very civil to me. He said, "Certainly there's no use sitting around here all summer waiting to be drafted. Go on to your job, and when it's time, we'll notify you."

This was the head of the local draft board?

Yes, the head of the local draft board. We had a pastoral meeting, a Quaker meeting, and he tried to get the pastor of the meeting read out of the local Rotary Club because he was a counselor to conscientious objectors. See, any CO that came in had his name on it, because he helped them fill out their form 47. So, on the one hand, he was this kind of a person, yet to me he was very civil.

And so, what happened? Did you go on to that job that summer?

I went on, and I didn't get drafted until the end of August, so I managed most of the summer.

And were you through with your B.A. at that point?

Yes, I had graduated the previous June.

What was your family's religious affiliation?

Well, we were Quakers, but we became Quakers when I was about nine years old. I was active in the Friends.

So you felt that being a Friend had a definite impact on your life?

Quite definitely. In fact, all through high school, there was a strong peace movement through the thirties, and I was very much involved in that.

Caught up in the FOR and so on?

Not so much with the FOR as with local things. I remember going to Duke University one summer to a peace conference. All through high school I was a fairly effective public speaker, so I was involved very much. Even in high school, when we didn't know whether there was going to be a war or not, there was no question in my mind that if there was one, I would be a conscientious objector.

It was primarily a religious consideration, then, that led you to enter CPS?

Yes, that's where it started, but I always had a very liberal theological outlook, so that I would have to say that in a way Quakerism led me to a very liberal philosophical and political outlook as well. So that I think they

153

were just as strong. And when I was actually in CPS, I felt that my feelings were as much philosophical and political as religious.

Did your family support your decision? Did they have any role in your making the decision to enter CPS?

No, no, and yet my father supported me. But I always felt, although he was never very verbal about it, he was very active in the local American Legion, and yet he very strongly supported me. In fact, he was always defending the American Legion as not being an all-out hawk group. He said, "You go out there and see how many of those guys want to get within earshot of another gun."

We haven't run into many Friends who also belonged to the American Legion. This is a unique combination.

He was very active in the local American Legion, yet he had none of the hawkish attitudes. My mother, on the other hand, well, I can't say that she was supportive. She thought I ought to find some other way to get out of it. She didn't necessarily want me to go to the army. She tried, all through high school, to get me interested in going to medical school. In college, she wanted me to go into medicine. She used the wrong tack. She kept giving me statistics on how much money doctors make.

I imagine you were probably only making a few hundred dollars during your summer job.

My ambition when I graduated from college was to make $200 a month. I thought, if I had that, that was all I needed; I could live on easy street. But, then, oh, she was always trying to get me to take other ways out. When I was in college, at George Williams College, what we called Tunney's Navy opened up. Gene Tunney [former heavyweight champion] came to try to get physical ed majors to go into the navy as chief petty officers in charge of physical training. And, in fact, that's what an awful lot of my friends did in college. We were all qualified, and Tunney was very anxious to get us. But I never even went to the interviews, and my mother couldn't understand why that wasn't a good way out.

Had your father served in the army?

Yes, in World War I.

You entered CPS in August 1942?

154

You bring the date to me! It was August 24, 1942, and I haven't thought of that date in years!

Were you sent immediately to Big Flats?

Big Flats, yes. Big Flats had opened rather recently, and there were only 30 people there when I arrived. And the main job was pulling weeds four feet tall out of pine seedlings about six inches tall. But when I got there, they asked if I'd work in the kitchen, so I did and enjoyed that very much. But the weed patch was where the action was, and where the high morale was, because the weed patch was the nitty-gritty of the thing. The Forest Service people that were running it seemed to think that they had coolie labor on their hands that they could order about. I don't think a week had passed before the weed patch crew decided they were not going to be supervised by Forest Service people, that we would have to have our own foreman and they could take this or leave it. That was the way it was going to be. And there was great resistance to this. I don't know how they got this negotiated, but we had a post office labor organizer, Lou Taylor, he was a great one to get things organized, and he never stopped labor organizing. So this was arranged very quickly, but there was this constant watching from a distance . . .

That antagonized the men to some extent?

. . . Yes, a great deal.

From everything we've heard, once people were at Big Flats, they wanted to get out and go somewhere else rather quickly. Our sense of Big Flats was that the morale of the camp was never extremely high, certainly not as high as that of some of the other camps we've heard about.

Yeah, I think that's true. We had a lot of discontents there.

What kinds of discontent?

Well, the main issue, I think, was, we weren't doing work of national importance, that there was danger of our being isolated in comfort with good food, we were out of the way. We had the sense that the government wanted to get us out of sight and out of the way, that there was certainly in time of war a lot more important things that needed to be done. A lot of people wanted to get into hospital work.

Did you feel that the work of the NSBRO had been truly beneficial for you? Did you feel that they had worked out the best situation for you, or was there some antagonism?

Well, I think the way some of the fellows expressed it was, "Look how much better off we are than the fellows in World War I." We knew the kind of brutal treatment they had received.

So you felt you had a better deal?

Yes, we certainly had a better deal. But this same feeling gave us, I don't know whether it was a sense of guilt, or . . .

Maybe you had too good a deal? That you weren't suffering enough?

. . . we had too good a deal. We couldn't just accept this as it was and go on, we had to move the thing along to something still better.

You left Big Flats after how long?

I left there around the first of January.

What made you decide to apply for a transfer from Big Flats?

Well, Kenneth Clark, a black who was director of education [at Cheltenham], came up to recruit some people for Cheltenham, a school for black delinquents in Maryland. I didn't jump on this at first, but there was a psychologist in the camp, he was interested, and a couple of other fellows were interested. And I went to the meeting, and I was halfway interested. It was really this psychologist who talked me into it: "Go ahead and apply. Come on, let's do something. You'll be using your talent there. Anybody can pull weeds."

Did he apply as well?

Yes, and he went early. The idea was, Kenneth Clark was trying to change the whole image of Cheltenham. Cheltenham had been totally run by white southerners, had been a very brutal institution over the years. Incidentally, Cheltenham, we learned, was started by Quakers as a private institution and became a state institution. Vance Thomas, the director, had gotten the *Baltimore Afro-American* award that year because he had brought in black

156

staff for the first time. Now they still lived separately and ate separately and had separate dining rooms, but he had plans toward eventually integrating the dining rooms, so he said. But anyway, Kenneth Clark was quite an impressive man. And so I applied and was accepted. I went on to Cheltenham in January of 1943, and it was quite a place. There were these cottages that should have had 35 kids and they all had 50 to 60.

What age were the boys?

Six to nineteen.

How many?

About 350 to 400. They were spoken of as "cottages," but they were old brick buildings that had 12-foot ceilings, and it was a pretty grim place. And so, of course, COs there set about changing the whole treatment of delinquents in Cheltenham. Of course, a lot of these kids there, especially young ones, were only there because they'd played hookey from school. They had no business in a place like that. So it was interesting to see there how nonviolence faded away when you were faced with 60 kids you were alone with and you had all kinds of discipline problems. Corporal punishment became acceptable to a lot of people.

Did your attitudes on this change too?

Well, I think to some extent they did and they didn't. I mean, I certainly resorted to corporal punishment but tried to keep it on an objective level, but found out that it wasn't too objective, and so then I began to reject it again.

How many CPS men were there during this time?

Oh, there must have been 20 of us.

What percentage of the staff was that?

We took over all except one or two—well, let's see, there were about four or five cottage masters that were outsiders. Actually, it got down to be about three cottage masters. Outsiders would come and go because the pay was bad, the hours long, and working conditions were. . . .

So you made up the vast majority of the staff?

Yes.

You talked about the changes you initiated. What kinds of things did you want to change?

Well, we would start in one cottage. I was sort of a floating cottage master. I went down there as a recreation director. I was to go to all the cottages and do recreation programs. I wrote some game manuals, and I'd go around the cottages and help with evening programs. Because you have all these kids on your hands every evening; some had been there all day. We were shorthanded always. So finally, I became pretty much a substitute cottage master. And this was kind of tough, because if you were in the cottage all the time, you got to know all the kids and you got your methods of control in the cottage. But when you were a floating cottage master, you always had to adapt to the methods in that cottage. I would take half of the kids on a morning for long hikes, and we found a creek with a nice swimming hole. In this one cottage, the cottage master was a rather elderly man, so that would mean he'd only have half as many, and then in the afternoon I'd take the other half and we'd go swimming. Then in another cottage, Neil Staley and I would take the whole gang at night out to a place where there were two hills and we'd play steal the flag. We'd run the tail off these kids! And they loved it. And we never lost a kid. The superintendent worried about this.

Children running away?

Yes, we had constant runaways. But you always knew who was going to run away, and you knew when he was going to do it. And you knew you couldn't stop him. You knew that he'd get away, that you wouldn't be able to stop it. But we never lost a kid on any of these excursions. And to this day, when I go out with a group like Audubon Society, to lead a bird walk, I can still tell you exactly how many people I've got. I can spot-count a group. We were constantly counting, until it became subconscious. You always knew how many you had and when one of them lagged behind.

Did you encounter any opposition from the head of the school [Vance Thomas] to any of the changes or innovations that you made?

He was a strange man, very paranoid. And whenever you wanted to do something, you would go up to his office and recognize that you were going to spend two or three hours because he would talk and talk, and he had a great ego. And the way we would do it was that we would introduce the idea at the beginning of the conversation, then let him go on and talk and talk awhile, and then, after you'd been there about an hour, you'd work yourself back to the subject and suggest that this whole thing was his idea in the first place and compliment him on his innovations. We'd assume after that that we'd had his permission, and we'd go ahead and do it. Another thing that we did, at one cottage we had the strongest cell, so that all of the real bad ones were always sent down to our cell because it had a solid steel door.

And the boys would be put in there to spend a night?

For discipline reasons.

For long periods?

Sometimes four or five days, sometimes only a short time. But we had this big clothing room, and so I got the idea that we would make this into a recreation room. We tore out all of the shelves, figured out how we could stuff all of these shelves in the cell, and the cottage was being repainted at the time, so we decided ours was going to be a ship. So we built a ship's rail all around three walls. I have no idea where we got the lumber. We built a ship's bridge at one end of this, and when the painter came in, we told him we wanted him to paint waves up so high and with light blue above that. And this man was the sourest looking man you ever saw, but he looked the thing over; he came in the next morning with two cans of blue paint, dark blue and light blue. He dipped this great big brush and, walking around the room making the most beautiful water line, drew splashes of white caps in. He did a gorgeous job! Then one of the CPS men who was an artist painted the cabin, the bridge, and the wheelhouse and everything on the wall, and then we had the balcony out in the front. And the next day, Mr. Carroll, the assistant superintendent, called me up and said, "I'm sending so-and-so down there to be locked in your cell." I said, "Mr. Carroll, we don't have a cell anymore." He said, "What!" and I said, "No, we made that into our clothing room. We don't have a cell anymore. Sorry." Well, he slammed the receiver down, but that was the last we heard of it. And he sent the kids to another cottage. I think mainly the thing the COs did, in spite of the discipline problems, there was a different attitude toward the kids. We didn't look at them as a bunch of criminals. They and we were under terrible pressures all the time. The last seven weeks I was there, I had 60 kids; the other guy went on leave, and I was alone in the cottage with 60 kids.

You lived in the cottage with the boys?

No, I didn't. A night watchman was in charge from ten o'clock on; most of the cottage masters lived in, but I didn't. There was one room for one live-in cottage master in each cottage, and the rest of us lived in the main building. But I worked from six o'clock in the morning until ten o'clock at night, seven days a week for seven weeks, the last seven weeks I was there.

What would your normal hours be?

Well, I would have half a day off. One person would be on duty in the morning, one person would be on duty in the afternoon, and two together in the evening. So that, in theory, you'd have an eight-hour day. It was always more than that. Another thing which happened was that the white members of the unit—we were a mixed unit—asked permission to eat in what in those days was called the colored dining room. So the superintendent said we could do that, except we had to recognize that all of us couldn't do it all the time, that we should take turns, because of the fact that the dining room wouldn't hold us. So we would change back and forth.

Did you have any blacks in the CPS unit?

Yes.

How many?

Oh, I would say we were at least 50 percent black. There were also some black regular staff members, and one night two of them said, "We've decided that the COs have done enough for black staff members at Cheltenham, and it's time we did something for ourselves. So if you will guarantee that empty chairs will be there tomorrow morning, we're going to eat breakfast in the white dining room." Well, this was a fantastic thing for those fellows to do in those days.

I'm sure!

So the next day, they did. And, of course, the old southern whites, the engineer, the assistant superintendent—there were quite a few there—went down and saw the blacks in the dining room, and they all gathered up in the office, and the superintendent [Vance Thomas] called over and said, "Get those fellows out of there. There's going to be bloodshed!" You see, he had these grandiose plans that eventually there was going to be an archway between these two dining rooms, and then they would merge. Well, he always had these fantastic ways he was going to do things. So the black staff went in and ate in the dining room and, of course, all hell broke loose. Within a day or two, there was a grand jury investigation. Marlboro County grand jury decided to investigate Cheltenham.

Simply because the black staff members had gone in to eat?

Yes, and they decided that this was the fault of all the COs, that they'd started all this, and, of course, they were right. And anyway, they had the superintendent select people to appear before the grand jury, and I don't know why, I was one of those selected. Thomas just picked people, whether he picked his favorites or his least favorites or those he thought could talk a good game. So we went, the inquiry lasted three or four days, and Thomas was on first, and, of course, I knew if he went in there, he would keep them going for three hours. And I was the next one they called in. And I went in, and as soon as I sat down, somebody in the back of the room jumped up and pointed their finger at me and said, "Would you marry a nigger?" and before I could answer, another one jumped up and said, "Do you have a sister? Would you have your sister marry a nigger?" You know, I mean, the hate in that room, you could just feel it. And I soon discovered that I really didn't have to answer any questions, that if I'd hesitate long enough somebody else would ask another question. So I sat there for two hours listening to this kind of stuff and attempting occasionally to answer a question, but my answers were so far out from any of their thinking that they just thought everything was ridiculous.

What was the ultimate resolution of the investigation?

I don't think any action was ever taken, except they vented their spleens on the whole thing. And the dining room was integrated, that's what happened. Thomas was an interesting man, and there's no question that he did a lot of things for Cheltenham. I think that he was a very complex personality. He was as paranoid as could be, and just a nonstop talker and chain-smoker, very nervous and high-strung sort of person.

Was he a Quaker?

Oh no, no. He was out of the prison system. He'd been in Atlanta. I think the way he got the staff integrated was that they were so shorthanded, he convinced people that they couldn't man the place with whites.

How long were you at Cheltenham?

I left there around March of 1944. I was in for a little over a year and a half.

Were there any conflicts between the blacks and whites within CPS at Cheltenham?

No. But I was just going to say that there was this one 80-year-old assistant superintendent, Mr. Carroll, the one who told me about the cell. I was told, after they'd integrated the dining room, there was a very fine dairy man there, a fellow named Dowdy, a black, and they were sitting there at lunch one day—and then I guess I have to tell you that there was an old blacksmith that had a big drippy mustache, and he slurped his soup, he was just the most uncouth individual you could imagine. And right in the middle of the meal, old Mr. Carroll turned around and he slapped Dowdy on the shoulder, and he said, "You know what, I don't know why we didn't do this a long time ago. I'd a hell of a lot rather eat with you than old man Moore!"

You know, one thing that came up in the Orlando camp, there was a racial problem there, they were doing some maintenance work at a black high school, and they generated community antagonism. But there was a division within the CPS group itself, and there was one fellow in particular who felt that raising the racial issue just generated controversy, that his witness was the peace witness, and that he didn't want to introduce other elements that would take away from that. Was there any of that kind of feeling at Cheltenham?

No, not at all. And you know, I think we were all very united on the race issue and saw it as a part of the same thing as the peace issue.

It was certainly a unique experience for the blacks in CPS to have this kind of a relationship with you.

Yes. The interesting thing, whenever one of the kids was mad at one of the CO staff members, [he'd say], "I know one thing, I'd fight for my country." They'd throw this at us all the time, and these guys were big, tough 19-year-olds. I mean, they were rough characters. And this man, the master of the oldest cottage, ran it with an iron fist. But he also, as was said, "had performed the marriage between the American flag and the Catholic Church." And so he had all these flags, crosses draped with flags, and so we knew that he fed these big kids his feelings toward COs, and if they'd get mad, why they'd throw this "fight for your country" bit at you.

You left Cheltenham then in March 1944, and you applied to go down to the project in the Virgin Islands?

Yes, they wanted a recreation director. There was already the unit in Puerto Rico and a subunit in St. Thomas. The Island Council, they were short-handed, they had manpower problems, so they wanted someone to be recreation director. I think they wanted a bacteriologist for the lab and the hospital, and they wanted some teachers too, but Colonel Kosch didn't approve of teachers. Colonel Kosch felt that the one thing you didn't want COs doing was influencing our youth, feeding them this propaganda. So teachers were out. And so I got the post. They also sent down a cook to cook for the unit, in true CPS tradition: they do their own cooking and so on. So two of us went down first, the fellow who was the cook and myself.

What made you decide to leave Cheltenham at that point?

I was disenchanted with Vance Thomas and where you could go, what there was left to accomplish at Cheltenham. This black fellow who was a shoe repairman, he took me to task for leaving. He said, "I thought we were all going to stick it out here until we all left." And at one point where we felt embattled, that's what we were going to do. But this period was sort of over. And I guess the pressures were lessening, and we didn't feel the need so much to hang together any longer there. And I have to admit that there was always a certain spirit of adventure that guided my movements, and I had considered leaving there and applying for the mental hospital up in Cleveland.

That unit eventually was closed down. Cleveland State Mental Hospital, I think it was. Part of the reason—and this was a pattern at a lot of the mental hospitals—was that the CPS unit was perceived as an ongoing source of criticism of the administration. I'm just curious as to how much discussion there was at Cheltenham among the men about the need to go public with some of the problems there, how much of a sense there was that the most important contribution they could make was to bring about basic reforms in the institution. Did you have meetings about that?

No. We almost never had a unit meeting. We'd gather informally in someone's room, but as far as ever having a meeting, except that when there was a crisis to be dealt with, we'd decide what we were going to do. But there was very little of that. Of course, we all had heard about Cleveland. Some people credit that unit for beginning the turnaround in the treatment of mental patients in the state of Ohio. But there's no doubt that the administration wasn't happy with it.

There seemed in many cases to be almost a class separation between the CPS men who came into these programs. I don't know too much about Cheltenham, but certainly at the other hospitals and institutions, COs being better trained, better educated in general, was a point of friction. Was that the experience at Cheltenham?

Quite definitely. I mean, these old white southern types that were at Cheltenham had been there for years exploiting the place for their own benefit, and, of course, they used to take kids to pick their strawberries. And they were very poorly educated. I doubt if many of them were high school graduates. I recall one lunchtime when there were a couple of these men—one had been a railroad engineer, and he was a really rough, tough old southern type—and we had a hilarious time one lunch hour on something stupid, jokes about false teeth or something like that. But anyway, after he went, a CPS man, who had a master's in psychology—all of us were college graduates—remarked, "Isn't it funny the things we're able to find rapport on, something that's totally nonintellectual? Here we really had a good time today together." It was really earthy type of things.

The other thing that was interesting was that, of course, they were very antagonistic toward us all through this time, and the day that I was having my last meal before leaving to go to the Virgin Islands, this old engineer, he got up, and he came around, and he shook my hand, and he said that he hoped I'd enjoy my next job and the line of work, and he was very cordial. And then he left, and a CPS friend said, "You know, he really meant that." It was interesting how we did find some means of communication over the years.

Was the Virgin Island unit administered through Puerto Rico?

Puerto Rico, yes. Rufus King was the director, although we supposedly had our own director. There were only two of us there for a long time. One was the cook, and then I was doing recreation work, and coaching the athletic teams at the two high schools, one at each end of the island. Then I started going out to all of the country schools. I'd get on the bus in the morning, it was a wonderful experience, with all of these people with their big bundles on their head and their chickens and their sheep and their goats. And if somebody wasn't in place, we'd drive all around town looking for them. I'd eat lunch at the school, and then I'd go out and stand on the road and wait for the bus and go down to the next school, so that I'd get all these out-of-the-way country schools. And I'd have physical education classes through the whole school, one class after another. And out at Diamond School, there was the most wonderful, well-read principal at that school that you could just spend hours with. He could talk to you about Shakespeare, Proust, anyone. He was just a remarkable man, stuck out here as the headmaster.

What kind of accommodations did you have?

We were in what they called the marine barracks. Now actually, this was a part of the school property. It was a two-story building; we lived upstairs, there were classrooms downstairs. And the kitchen and the place we ate was the little cook house and kitchen for the big house that we were living in originally. And then the cisterns were there, and part of the school yard was our yard, and there was a huge tamarind tree over the place, and there were a lot of old cannonballs laying around. We stacked these up and developed our own version of lawn bowling using these old steel cannonballs.

Did you continue in St. Croix doing this work until your discharge?

Yes, I was there for two years.

Did you feel that your discharge in March 1946 was unduly delayed?

As a matter of fact, I didn't leave when my discharge came. What had happened would have been very upsetting to Colonel Kosch, but after the superintendent of schools had brought us down there, he resigned and went to teach at Castaner in Puerto Rico. And the assistant superintendent, a black woman, became the superintendent of schools. So the day she became superintendent, she called me in and said, "Now what you're doing is fine. This is great, it's good for the kids, but we're short of teachers. And you, here you're a college graduate, so the only thing for you to do is teach." I said, "What would Colonel Kosch think of that?" And she said, "Has Colonel Kosch been down here?" So she asked me, "What would you like to teach?" I said, "Well, I can teach general science, and I like to teach history and geography." Probably the two subjects that would upset Colonel Kosch the most!

When was this that you started teaching?

I think this was the second year. I think it was probably the school year beginning in 1945. And then I guess I was discharged in March, and they asked me if I'd stay on and teach out the rest of the school year.

Was there any moonlighting at any of the camps? Was there any such opportunity for men at Cheltenham, for example?

No, because we were too far out, isolated. We moonlighted in St. Croix, we taught adult education courses. We got a dollar a session, which was their going pay for anyone who taught.

You had a real problem with the local community at Cheltenham, but certainly it sounds as though in St. Croix you had very good relations with the community. How about Big Flats?

We didn't have any contact with the community. Big Flats was isolated. The town of Big Flats itself was a wide place in the road. And so we had no community contacts there. At Big Flats there was a place over at Painted Post that some of us used to go [to] on a truck, another nursery, to do some work. I know I painted the roof of a big barn there, and there was some forestry workers there that were sort of distant to us. But one day it was pouring rain, and we all sat in a barn together shelling chestnuts for seeds, and we had a great time together, and after that we were always friendly. After any personal contact, even though they didn't agree with us, why a lot of the antagonism seemed to melt away.

Was the shared commitment that you and the other men had to nonviolence and to pacifism a sufficient bond to unite the COs within the camps, or did you find that there were conflicts?

You had very fundamentalist church groups: the Jehovah's Witnesses and other small fundamentalist groups. You had people who were really philosophical and political objectors. For instance, there was one fellow at Big Flats who said one time, "Oh, I won't fight in this war, but that doesn't mean I wouldn't fight in any war." And someone said, "You mean a revolution, for example?" He said, "Yes." And so there were great differences. I don't know that they brought about conflict, except that it was hard to ever come to a consensus on issues.

Had you ever considered going 1AO?

It never entered my mind as the slightest possibility.

And so the fact that you weren't going to be receiving any money in CPS, that never entered into it?

No, no.

What was the most difficult aspect of CPS for you?

I suppose it was just plain long hours and hard work at Cheltenham. And the kind of pressure you were under there. And particularly, on a couple of occasions, I had to go and take charge of this cottage of older boys, and since the cottage master ran this place with an iron hand, he ran it in such a way that would ordinarily make it difficult for anyone that came in to try to take over, but you always suspected, for his own ego reasons, that he wanted anyone who came in while he went away to have problems. And when you were faced with Cottage 3, you sort of took a deep breath, like you were going into the den of the lions. And yet I can't say that I ever had any difficulty.

What was the most satisfying aspect of CPS?

That's something I never thought about. Because there are two kinds of satisfaction. Just to live in Christiansted [St. Croix] in 1946, before it became what it is now, a tourist trap, just being on that spot was personally satisfying, but that's a separate kind of satisfaction. I think the changes we felt we made at Cheltenham were the most satisfying thing. For some of these kids, we provided an opportunity for them to laugh for a change and have a good time and really get rid of some energy and forget themselves.

What was the least satisfying aspect of CPS?

You know, that's a funny thing, I never felt bad morale in CPS.

Looking back now, a generation later, do you have any doubts about your decision to enter CPS?

No, no.

Do you see your life being changed in any particular way for having served in CPS?

I don't think so. Friends of my mother and father used to say to them that they shouldn't let me do this, that it was a big mistake, that this would be a stigma that would be with me for the rest of my life. But I can't see that it has been. I don't see that it's ever affected my employment.

No professional limitations?

No. I have never concealed it. The only thing, I have occasionally applied for a state or government job where military service gives you points in civil service. But since I've never gotten one of those jobs anyway, I don't know that that has made any difference. I think now World War II is so far away that it doesn't mean that to anyone. Also, I've found that when I'd say that I'd been a CO, I'd be asked immediately, "Are you a Quaker?" And I had to answer yes, and it seemed to me that this sort of made a difference. I was unhappy about that, that this should make a difference. The other thing is that it's never been a problem in my hometown. Of course, I haven't gone back for many years, but when I used to go back, I'd be invited to speak at the Rotary Club or at the college or at various gatherings.

In what ways did the CPS experience affect your career decisions afterward?

I don't really feel that they did. I feel that this was a link in the whole chain, that I was already pointed in that direction before I went into CPS. I went into George Williams College with the idea of going into YMCA work but became disenchanted with the YMCA in the process and was interested in settlement house work. So when I got back, I followed right into that career, and then after I came back to Columbia for a master's, the dilemma was, what to do now? I had gotten my degree in community organization, and I didn't want to get into the usual community council, having meeting after meeting with these heads of organizations and getting in this rat race, and my wife said to me, "Well, rather than do that, I'd rather go back to St. Croix and fish for a living." So I said, "Well, rather than fish for a living, I'd rather call up the [American Friends] Service Committee and work for nothing." She said, "All right, let's do it!" So I wrote a letter to the Service Committee and got a letter back saying, "We knew you were graduating from Columbia and wondered when we were going to hear from you." And so I went off to Israel for four years with them. Then went to Hong Kong following that for three years. And then came back to the Philadelphia office and was there for three years as director of overseas refugee programs and then came down to Florida to work with migrants in 1965.

One of the things that came up toward the end of CPS was a concern on the part of many to continue the kinds of communities that had emerged, to develop intentional communities. Had that attracted you at all?

Never! I am very anti-intentional community. In fact, I hold the view that people that are looking for intentional communities are those who can't function in society on their own.

Do you have any recollection of the general treatment of CPS in the popular press?

At Big Flats there was a flood on the Chemung River, and we had built a dike down there, and some of them were down watching the dike and the bridge during the flood. And there was an emergency on the other side of the river, and a doctor was trying to get there. And so the fellows went out and checked the bridge and walked across the bridge with the doctor's car, so we got awfully good press out of that. Even before that, a writer from the Elmira paper came out to interview, and she wrote a very positive article because she was impressed with the people she met—medical students, architects, doctors, college graduates—so the only press we got was positive. Now I'm sure we got bad press at Cheltenham after the grand jury investigation.

The person in public life that most of the peace groups reached out to in terms of hoping to have her serve as something of a spokesperson for CPS was Eleanor Roosevelt, and that turned out to be very unsatisfying.

Yes, I recall that column where she said these people really aren't serving their country, if they were really serving their country they'd be in the army, or something like that.

Right, that they really weren't entitled to any benefits, because they were doing nothing. Did that surprise you, that she would have that attitude?

No, no. I recall that it surprised some people.

You would think, with her sensitivity to people who were victims in any sense, looked down upon, or subject to personal abuse—but in this case. . . .

Well, Franklin Roosevelt was so totally emotionally tied into this war, and his hatred of Hitler was so consuming, that I guess she couldn't live with him and. . . .

One thing that's come up, mainly in the letters of some CPS men, was the sense that World War II was "the great experience" of your generation, and there was this ambivalence—not doubting the correctness of having gone into CPS, but a sense of not taking part in this central experience. Did you share any of that?

No, I didn't, but you know, two or three weeks ago, I'd been working in Sebring for a couple of months, and in the motel room where I was staying, there was this television series about World War II, and I had that feeling then. That made me think about this and what those fellows had gone through together.

Paul and Jayne Wilhelm

"The minister that married us wrote a beautiful letter to my mother about the boys at camp. It was the most reassuring thing that my mother got, to have a nonparticipant in the whole thing say that the boys were really fine fellows. I mean, there was this whole business that they were yellow cowards who were sneaking away from the whole thing."

Paul Wilhelm, born in Blytheville, Arkansas, in 1916, trained as an architect before entering CPS. He married his wife Jayne (born in Tacoma, Washington, in 1917), while assigned to the camp in Powellsville, Maryland. Paul subsequently participated in a medical experiment and worked as an attendant at a mental hospital in Philadelphia. Jayne taught for 25 years at Germantown Friends School before her death in July 1981. Paul was a principal player in the urban renaissance of Wilmington, Delaware, in the 1960s. He also taught at the University of Pennsylvania and has been a consultant on ecologically sound development. He recently completed a study entitled Civilian Public Servants: A Survey of 210 World War II Conscientious Objectors *(1990).*

Did you have trouble getting your CO classification?

(*Paul*) Yes. They called me in about every time they met for about a year.

Did you have a strong religious upbringing that would've assisted you?

Oh, I did, but my draft board didn't want any conscientious objectors. And there were two brothers that had gotten a CO classification, and they didn't want any more. Every Tuesday they would threaten to have me put in jail if I didn't come in. And then every Friday they would promise me a commission and something cushion-safe in the army, and then on Tuesday it would start over again.

Did you appeal?

Yes. At the crucial time, after I had presented the presidential appeal, the case was turned over to the Department of Justice. The minister of the church that we attended got together a delegation that came to the court and testified for me, because I'd been active in young people's union and Sunday school and all parts of the church.

You weren't a Quaker at that time?

No, we were Baptists. The judge said that he had decided that I was not a serious conscientious objector on religious reasons until the minister brought the board of deacons in.

(Jayne) Paul had also been the president of the Y group at Washington University.

(Paul) I had had a lot of activity, but I had not been a pacifist.

Had you been involved with the FOR?

No, I'd never even heard of the FOR until I got into camp, but I was active in the campus Y and Sigma Chi and architectural affairs at the campus, but not one of the campus radicals. One of the big laughs to me was that the campus pacifists all signed up for the draft.

What was your family's reaction when you decided to choose CPS?

Well, they didn't understand, but they were supportive. They thought every good boy should go fight Hitler.

And obviously, Jayne supported you too.

Yes, but not as a pacifist until A. J. Muste talked her into it.

Maybe you could tell me a little bit about the background of the Muste conversion experience.

(Jayne) In the summer of 1941, Paul and I got engaged. And then I visited my family and explained to them all what a great guy Paul was and how he was going through this terrible decision making. And, of course, there was never anything in my background that would have given me the idea of being a CO. There weren't any pacifist organizations that I knew of in Montana.

You supported him, but you probably didn't understand at this point.

I didn't, I just would say, "I'm not going to say anything about this until I know more about it." But I kept reading all these books. Paul was inducted on the first anniversary of CPS. He went down from Plainfield to the Maryland camp at Patapsco. He had arranged for me to stay with a family who lived in a house up the hill, and they were a very unsupportive kind of family. They didn't like the idea of these COs down there in the CPS camp. But there was an older man and a wife who had been a nurse, and she had three children of her own but was also boarding a child for the Jewish Charities. She and I hit it off pretty well. She suggested that if I wasn't going to do anything else that summer, I could come down and stay in their house with them and take charge of the baby while she took the other children off to visit her parents down in the South somewhere. And so it sounded perfect, because Paul and I then would be together for the first time on a regular basis.

It worked out beautifully, it was a really wonderful summer, but one of the first visitors to the camp was A. J. Muste. And he was so marvelous, the kinds of questions he would pose were the kind that don't have any answers, that you can't say yes or no to. He gave me an afternoon. The guys were out in the fields, building outhouses and other useful things, they were maintaining the park for the city of Baltimore, and so A. J. and I just sat there. He was so matter-of-fact about the whole thing. It was an unemotional thing, I didn't have to defend myself, I didn't have to defend Paul, we just talked. And at the end of the time, it was just clear to me that there was no other good way. That no matter what they said about the value of the war and the grandmother being attacked and all these lovely things that they envision, there just was no other better way to do it, to think about the world.

So at the end of that summer, not only were you still supportive but you understood and you shared Paul's pacifism.

Yes. So I used to go to all the camp meetings, I just was a camp follower.

(*Paul*) Then they closed the camp. We had built all the privies and the big parking lot that they wanted, and so the project was pretty well finished.

Did you maintain contact with your family?

(*Jayne*) Yes, they were writing letters and making phone calls. My sister married a paratrooper, and he was one of those noble lads who was the first one up when they thought the Japanese were going to invade Alaska. And then they went over and were the first ones at Anzio, and he was badly wounded on the very day that I came home with Paul for the first time. And at the end of those weeks, Mother said to me, "Well, Jayne, I certainly don't agree with you, but I think it'll be all right if you'll stay in Philadelphia." She liked Paul, but it was the pacifist thing, and they kept saying, "You must think of your future. What is your life going to be? How, if you have children, will you ever let them face the whole thing? He's cut off his whole future. You'll have no success. He may be a very fine fellow, but why do you sacrifice your future?" They pulled every stop out.

But that didn't deter you?

No. We had the funniest wedding of all time, I'm sure. I guess everyone's wedding is memorable, but this was especially so. I asked for the day off to celebrate our birthdays, since everybody knew that Paul and I had the same birthday, and they thought that was a reasonable request. So I went down there, finishing my wedding dress as I went, and got there after six o'clock for an eight o'clock wedding. I was, at that point, not sure that anything was going to come off. And I was in the shower, and the air raid sirens blew, and they had a blackout.

(*Paul*) A guy borrowed a school bus, and he had to make five trips to get everybody to the church.

(*Jayne*) So we were finally married at ten o'clock. Then we had a reception. The guys had baked us birthday cakes, and we had a wedding cake. We cut the cake with a brush ax, and we marched out under an arch of brush axes. By the time we got through the receiving line, half of the guys had already gone, they wanted to get back to camp. On the first day of our delayed honeymoon, I was interviewed for a job at Germantown Friends, and then Paul went out to Byberry while I went up to Germantown.

(*Paul*) The superintendent at Byberry was enthusiastic to get help. He was in bad shape. The hospital had been built for 4,500 patients, and they had 6,900 patients there. And I was the 29th CPS attendant.

And how many regular?

There were less than two dozen.

(*Jayne*) It was awful.

You're talking about less than 60 attendants for 7,000 men.

(*Paul*) Men and women. But we only worked in the men's wing.

(*Jayne*) There was a women's service in mental hospitals, and a lot of the wives worked that. In fact, some of the marriages that occurred were between women who had come to work at Byberry, who then met these boys in the unit.

(*Paul*) We had a really good bunch there finally at Byberry. It got up to about 120 people, and there were some awfully good men in there. We did have a training course at Byberry.

When you first got there or later?

Later. My first job at Byberry was with no introduction and no training whatever. I was told to report at a building. When I got there, I was the only attendant. The nurse brought me into this dayroom with about 325 epileptics with these instructions: "These men, when they're about to have a seizure, become very combative, and here's a pillow and a tongue depressor wrapped in adhesive tape. If you can possibly get this between their teeth, and if you can possibly get a pillow under them when they have a seizure, to keep them from hurting themselves, do it." And she gave me these and pushed me through the door and locked the door behind me. And here were these people marching around the room, just milling around the room. The plumbing had all broken down. Some of them were carrying feces. Very few of them had any clothes on at all. The stench, I'm telling you. . . .

I'll bet you were in a state of shock.

I was really in shock. And there were about three fights going on. Well, I was busy, I'll tell you that, but I was shocked!

How did you and the other men in your unit resolve the issue of using force or physical coercion with violent patients?

We had interminable arguments all through CPS.

About this issue?

About everything. But whether to use restraint was one argument we had. But just from a practical point of view, I had the ward where the nurses sent people to die or people whom they were unable to control. I came in, for example, one day, and an 11-year-old kid without any conscience was gouging out the eyes of an old man. And there had been a lot of hassle about what to do with this kid—he'd been in three or four wards and buildings—whether to keep an 11-year-old in restraint, for example. And another patient had syphilis in the maximum degree and was very combative, and they put him in my ward. I came in one time and found him in complete restraints, and when I took him his food, I let him out, and he grabbed me by the testicles, and I automatically cauliflowered his ear! And then we all felt so badly about it that all the shifts on the ward concentrated on him, and in four months we had him out. But boy, he got his pills when he was supposed to get his pills, and he got his shots when he was supposed to get his shots!

But that was a kind of conscience reaction for using violence. We tried not to, but it was very hard. We had very bad patients. I worked in "B" Building for a while, which was for violent patients, and we used a lot of wet-pack treatments where you take a sheet and soak it in cold water and wrap the guy who was violent in that so he couldn't move. There was hydrotherapy there, but there was just too many, you couldn't do it. In "B" Building you had three attendants, but there were three wards, and you couldn't get guys to manage that.

Probably the same thing with shock treatment.

We had overlapping shifts so that we could help with shock therapy, and I got to where I wouldn't do that.

Why?

Well, that patient I was telling you about was getting shock therapy before we'd started giving him the medication, and I worked on that with him, and I think that's why he attacked me. I think he was not being helped by shock therapy. It's a terrible thing.

Does the violence of it bother you?

Yes. If a patient resisted, boy, he resisted in force. It was a scramble to get some of the big male guys through shock therapy.

And I think, too, that if you believe in a nonviolent approach, that that kind of thing . . .

. . . And if you don't believe in it, you certainly can't talk them into it. I couldn't really believe Byberry. "A" Building was for incontinents, and you could smell it 100 yards away. All through the hospital, the plumbing was broken down. I got released from Byberry, but I wasn't cured, believe me. I don't think it did my mental health any good.

Were there major differences among the men at the camps?

There were a lot of guys who came there who didn't believe in CPS.

(*Jayne*) The minister that married us wrote a beautiful letter to my mother about the boys at camp. It was the most reassuring thing that my mother got, to have a nonparticipant in the whole thing say that the boys were really fine fellows. I mean, there was this whole business that they were yellow cowards who were sneaking away from the whole thing. And, of course, the men were so furious. What they wanted to do was to get into the relief and rehabilitation.

(*Paul*) Yes. That was what we had hoped for, that we would be trained to go to Europe or Japan or somewhere. And when that relief and rehabilitation program was killed, that was the worst.

(*Jayne*) Because everybody who had any ambitions to help, to mend what was being torn apart, had really wanted to get involved in that.

Did you think of volunteering at all for medical experiments?

(*Paul*) Oh yes, I was a guinea pig in the vitamin A experiment at Byberry. We had to be bled every day, and I still have scars here, as though I were a dope fiend, from that. And then the guy who had all the results of the thing in his head died of a heart attack just as it was winding up. Nothing came of all that bleeding. We got awfully needle-shy.

Were you told sufficiently, do you feel, about the nature of the experiment before you volunteered?

I guess so. We were eager to volunteer for something. Gee, you didn't feel you were making much headway on the wards and with patients. We wanted something worthwhile.

Did you ever participate in any slowdowns or protests at any of the camps?

I can't remember. I know that at Powellsville, which was a former Civilian Conservation Camp, there were two big buildings full of bulldozers and all kinds of power equipment. Our power was manpower. We were given hand-saws and brush axes. And there was a sporadic discussion of going on strike to get to use the equipment, but you always ran up against the fact that what you were doing was taking down those beautiful cypress trees, clearing swamps.

(*Jayne*) Which nobody wanted. And you knew that it was—*ecology* is a word that's thrown around a lot now—but you knew that this draining of swamps was not helpful, that the Audubon Society and others had said that the swamp was better as a swamp.

(*Paul*) At Byberry there were a lot of things that we were discontented about. And guys were always, in the last couple years, walking out and going to jail. Even at Patapsco, for instance, there were very radical political objectors and very passive Jehovah's Witnesses and fundamentalists. And so at Patapsco, there was big talk about a strike for a while.

(*Jayne*) Well, that ferment created the awareness in the government that they had to provide a government camp.

Was there a lot of criticism of the NSBRO on the part of these men?

(*Paul*) Yes, and of the [American Friends] Service Committee and of Quakers.

(*Jayne*) They wrote new words to old songs, and that was the feature of every evening meeting, to sing the radical songs.

What were their biggest complaints about the NSBRO?

(*Paul*) Well, at Patapsco the men were fed for 13¢ a day, and the food was terrible. When Douglas Steere [professor at Haverford College and pacifist philosopher] came to camp, he spent all night in the kind of gum beats [prolonged discussions] that we used to have. We got him up at five o'clock, and we took him to breakfast, and the breakfast was fried cornmeal mush with syrup, and that was one of the best breakfasts we had. And Douglas, not being awake enough to be his usual charming, polite self, [was] revolted and said, "What's this?" Then he became himself and said, "Oh, splendid, splendid." So fried cornmeal mush was always "splendid."

Did you ever consider going 1AO?

Oh, sure. As a matter of fact, when I went into the Quaker camps, I didn't know anything about them. I thought if it was not for me, I would try to go 1AO.

Finances might've been a consideration too, because then you would've gotten paid and gotten dependency allowances.

When Jayne became a pacifist, that did it. There was no problem.

What kind of an effect did CPS have on your relationship? Do you think CPS strengthened it or put strains on it, or perhaps a combination?

Well, it certainly put a terrible strain on Jayne the first couple of years that we were serious about getting married. We had been engaged for two years, and I had said to her that if she didn't marry me on April 16, 1943, it was all off. And so she was in a terrible bind between her parents and me.

(Jayne) Well, I don't know. As I think about it, what Paul wanted from me was a commitment that I wasn't really ready to make. I was perfectly willing to marry him knowing that I believed in him, but not necessarily believed in what he was doing.

(Paul) I kept saying to her, "Love me, love my dogma."

Did you notice any changes in each other during this period because of the strain?

There were a lot of times Jayne would sit silent and not participate when she was under these pressures. But other than that, she was game.

(Jayne) I think the whole CPS experience for Paul was an unsettling kind of thing. His life had been very purposeful and directed before he went into camp. And the whole camp experience was tough, because all of the efforts that he made to do what he really was interested in doing were peripheral to this coping. He designed an outhouse for the Patapsco project that they said was the best one that had ever been designed. It turned out that the

179

man who was in charge of the parks down there was still here later in Philadelphia, and he remembered those marvelous outhouses.

What was the most difficult aspect of CPS for you?

(*Paul*) That ward at Byberry, the epileptics the first few days, had my adrenaline up. But week after week we had at least 60 patients in bed, and every day they'd send us more. They'd sit in the aisles. And those in bed, we just couldn't cure the bed sores, and they were incontinent, and the cockroaches were four inches long.

What was the most satisfying aspect of CPS?

That's interesting. In general, learning the Friends' methods of doing things, worship and business.

(*Jayne*) And meeting the guys.

(*Paul*) And meeting people.

(*Jayne*) The men in CPS were the great thing about it. Our son is a conscientious objector. But he spent all of his early life being just a normal kid to me. He had toy guns, and, I mean, we never gave him one, but if he wanted to spend his money for it, we didn't tell him he couldn't have it. When he went out to college in Cleveland, he began going to meeting out there. He had gone to meeting with us and first day school and the whole thing, and he'd been, of course, to Germantown Friends, indoctrinated in that way. But he went to college in 1964 and in 1966 was very much involved with the student revolts and everything. But he never actually participated in the SDS or those kinds of things.

When he got drafted, of course, they didn't classify them right away, but finally there came the time that he had to be classified, and he received a 1A classification and then fought it. He didn't decide to be a CO until that actually happened. And then he really put on a convincing effort, and as a result of that, he said, "Now I'm not going to work in a mental hospital, but I'll find the kind of job that'll be the right one for me."

(*Paul*) He did, that son of a gun! I'm so proud of him.

(*Jayne*) He took a job in Boston at a group called the Interfaith Housing Corporation, because by that time he had decided he wasn't going to be an electronics engineer or a history major, that he was going to be an architect.

And so the Interfaith Housing Corporation had a whole lot of property that they were renewing, and he had to live in an apartment in one of these buildings and explain what was going to happen to the tenants and help with the reconstruction and doing the planning. He lived there for about a year, and then when that building was renovated, he moved out. But he continued to work with them, and as a result of that, he stayed on with the man who was the architect after he'd finished.

Is your daughter a pacifist as well?

Yes, I think she was more of a pacifist all along than Mark. She was very active in Young Friends. She's very artistic. She went to Syracuse to college in 1969 and participated in the antiwar student movements—all the kids went to Washington. So did we, of course—a great family feeling—we were all protesting together!

Looking back now, a generation later, do you have any doubts about your decision to enter CPS?

(*Paul*) I have no doubts about pacifism, but I've become much more religiously oriented with pacifism.

But might you have refused to register or gone to jail or gone 1AO, or do you think if the situation was the same, you'd choose CPS again?

I haven't faced that. I don't know that I'm ready to now. I don't like hypothetical questions like that.

(*Jayne*) Well, we think Mark missed out on the friendships that we were able to make because there was the community and the feeling among the men and their wives and girlfriends that we were all in this together. And, of course, if there hadn't been CPS at the time, I mean, when you think about what happened in the First World War, there was no sense of community then either. I don't think that I could've gone as far as I have under the circumstance of the First World War, it would've been much more difficult. CPS certainly helped me.

(*Paul*) I think now I would go to jail if that were necessary.

In what ways do you see your life as being changed by the CPS experience?

Well, it's introduced me to Philadelphia Quakerism.

So you became a Friend as a result of that introduction during CPS?

Yes.

(*Jayne*) It changed everything.

(*Paul*) Yes, totally.

William and Wilma Ludlow

"Force was restraining, but with concern and respect for the person you were restraining, whereas violence was what was recommended by the old bughouse attendant who told us, 'The first thing you do when they come in is you beat them up, and you won't have any more trouble with them.' "

William Ludlow, born in Madison, New Jersey, in 1911, developed as a pacifist through reading, Quaker work camp, and involvement with the Fellowship of Reconciliation. This process deepened with his marriage to Wilma Chitterling (born in Caldwell, New Jersey, in 1912), a woman who shared his pacifist idealism. Ludlow entered CPS in February 1944 and served as an attendant at a mental hospital in Williamsburg, Virginia. Wilma worked as an attendant there as well, and both Ludlows found it a harrowing experience. After the war William worked in urban planning and development, and Wilma, despite the negative experience at Williamsburg, worked for 20 years as a psychiatric social worker in Pennsylvania. She died in 1981.

How did you become a pacifist?

(*William*) Well, I went to Princeton and graduated in 1933. I was in the Woodrow Wilson School of Public and International Affairs, and I think I majored more in American history than anything else. I was pretty much of the opinion that wars were senseless things. For example, some of our courses were on the causes of World War I, and the way it was handled afterwards obviously succeeded in sowing the seeds for World War II. So I would say that I was intellectually against anything that had to do with war, but I didn't have a very strong emotional commitment, at least when I came out of college.

Did you have a fairly strong religious background at home?

Yes, Presbyterian. My grandfather was a minister, and I went to Sunday school.

But it wasn't necessarily a pacifist background?

No, not at all.

What did you do after graduation?

I worked for my brother for a year in his architectural office. He was just starting out his practice then, so I did practically everything. After I'd worked a year, I didn't have very much to do in the summer, and the minister of our Presbyterian church asked me if I would help in the church vacation school, and I was assigned to the junior department, headed by a Miss Wilma Chitterling. I had an idea that she was going to be some old gray-haired hag. So I walked into the room, and there she was in a yellow dress with a red scarf, and I was very taken at first sight.

(*Wilma*) He was supposed to be my assistant, and when he walked down the hall looking very much like a Princeton graduate, I thought, "Holy Moses, what's coming?" I expected a pimply high school boy, something of that shape. Well, he bummed his brother's car and took me home that day for lunch, and every day that week, and on Friday night he proposed, and I turned him down flat. But he asked me if I'd go to the movies on Saturday night, and he apologized for proposing to me, because he wasn't in a position to marry anybody, and that made me so mad, I guess that's why I married him. His family rose up in holy horror because I was not a debutante; his brother, after all, was courting a debutante with money, and my family was anything but that, so we had to put it off a year.

Did you come from a family where there was quite an emphasis on religion?

Yes. My mother was very conventionally religious, fundamentalist, and I was kind of interested in whether there was anything to this immortality stuff. I was pretty way out. And so, as I started through college, I began to think, "How am I ever going to find out about all this?" So I was torn between being a schoolteacher or going into philosophy. I graduated from Drew University, and then I got a scholarship to go on, so I picked systematic theology and comparative religions, with some sort of lunatic notion that I would go to India and offer my services and my training to Gandhi. So I guess I got the pacifist bug sooner. I read a book on Appalachia, *Schoolhouse in the Foothills* or some such, and vaguely got involved with the Save the Children Federation. And I went to work for them mostly on publicity, and then I began reading letters from one of their workers in the mountains, and I volunteered to go down to Tennessee. I worked for several months in a coal-mining town that was suffering from a failed strike. The Depression hit there before it hit the rest of the country, and it was a pretty bloody place, people got killed there. And I forgot to mention that I was the lead in a play at Drew called *The Enemy* about a pacifist family in Austria during World War I. So I think my ideas had begun to solidify before his had. Then when I came back from Tennessee, we were married.

What were you doing while Wilma was in Tennessee?

(*William*) I was working for my brother, and I began to get interested in city planning. So I looked around and finally got a job in Chicago as an apprentice with the National Association of Housing Officials. From the time I first met Wilma until we were married a year later, I was in Chicago in this training program. When my year of training finished, I got a job in Washington, where the New Deal was just really beginning to sprout in resettlement, starting to build "new towns" like Greenbelt, Maryland, and Greenhill outside of Cincinnati. Well, after I got the job, we were married about four days later and had a short honeymoon. Then we got a little apartment in Washington, and I worked there for a year until that department was phased out.

We got involved in Washington with what we called "the Group," which used to meet every Saturday night. And we used to discuss all the problems of the world and what to do about them. We were interested in pacifism, consumer cooperatives, and work and socialism. We joined the FOR and were quite active in it. We got to know a lot more about Quakerism. And I moved around from one job to another when something opened up I was interested in. Then I got a job with the Tennessee Valley Authority, and we were down in Knoxville for two years. And we started an FOR group there.

(*Wilma*) I got fired in Knoxville.

How did that happen?

Well, I had this master's degree in theology and comparative religions, and the Minister's Council [in Knoxville] needed someone to teach Bible in the public schools, and I don't know how they discovered me, but anyway, they offered me the job. I said they didn't want to hire me because I was not conservative in my theology. And they said, that was all right, as long as I stuck to teaching only the Bible. So I said okay. I started my Bible teaching with the Jews fleeing Egypt, and I described it as the first walkout in history. You know, you can do all sorts of things with the Bible. I was getting along all right, not coming to any disaster, I didn't think, and then they asked me to give a talk to the Minister's Council on consumer cooperatives. One of the ministers got up and said, "All people who are interested in cooperatives are communists, and if she believes in cooperatives, she's a communist, and she's no fit person to teach Bible in the public schools." I got fired. After I got fired, I started writing letters for the *Knoxville News Sentinel* on international affairs, and they published them all, and finally, I had a column called "Mrs. Ludlow Says."

(*William*) About this time, around 1938, it was very apparent that war was coming fairly soon, and we got interested in Quakers. In Knoxville they had a Quaker church with a minister. And, of course, we were very active in the FOR at that point. And so by that time we were all set, and I knew I was going to be a conscientious objector.

So certainly by the time the United States became involved in war, you had a very strong record of involvement in pacifist organizations.

Yes. At that time I was deferred on account of my job with the federal government. I was working mostly on postwar planning, and at one point my boss wanted me to do a survey about how to handle the establishment of war industries. My boss was a very understanding guy, and I explained to him what my position was and that I didn't want to do it, and it never came to a real showdown. He said, "All right, I'll send somebody else."

When did you enter CPS?

In February 1944. I had already had an interview in Baltimore with my draft board and had no problems getting my conscientious objector status.

How did your family feel about your going into CPS?

My father was a very strong supporter of the war, but he accepted my position. He was retired at that time, and he used to write to servicemen and was very active in war-connected things.

You were assigned to Big Flats. What were you doing there?

Chopping down trees in snows about two feet deep. Then summer came. I wasn't interested in weeding, so I got on the kitchen crew. Wilma got a good job with the Child and Family Services in Elmira, and she had an apartment there.

What made you decide to apply for a transfer?

Well, Big Flats, you know, is supposed to be an induction camp, and the camp director was putting pressure on me to go somewhere.

(*Wilma*) You first applied for the jaundice experiment, [but] I raised Cain.

(*William*) So then I applied for Williamsburg and was accepted there. I was at Big Flats about a year altogether. At Williamsburg we could only have a room together if she worked at the hospital.

What was your job?

(*Wilma*) Attendant. When I resigned, it left 15 attendants, night and day, for 1,200 patients in the women's section.

(*William*) The entire men's section staff consisted of conscientious objectors at Williamsburg. See, you're right next to Newport News and all the big army installations there, and everybody could get good jobs and good pay.

Tell me about work at the hospital.

(*Wilma*) It hit me very hard, because I knew absolutely nothing about mental illness. I knew there was such a thing, that's all I knew. And I think it would have been very difficult to tell the difference between me and the patients. Our room was on the top floor, and it had been condemned as unfit for patients, bars still on the windows, wooden construction. There was a ward on the first floor, and you worked a 12-hour shift. Oh, a whole lot of dramatic things happened at that hospital.

Tell me about some of them.

Well, the conscientious objectors who arrived before us were locked on the wards with the patients and without a key for 12-hour shifts.

(*William*) They would let them out to have a couple of meals.

(*Wilma*) But the hours changed, so that instead of having a 12-hour shift, you had a break, what was it, an hour in the afternoon?

(*William*) The superintendent bettered the hours a little bit. First, when you went there, you worked seven to seven, or the night shift seven to seven, and every other Sunday you got a half-day off.

(*Wilma*) But you spent that half-day off thinking what you were going to do the next day.

Incredible. It must have been almost a case of being shell-shocked when you first began to work. What kinds of things were going on?

Well, I had tremendous guilt feelings over—well, my childhood fantasies were of St. Francis kissing the leper sores and all that kind of stuff. I hadn't made it at all. My image of myself working with the mentally ill—I would calm their raging spirits—didn't do anything but make mine raging. And so I had a tremendous feeling of guilt about that. Later I applied to the government employment agency, and they sent me out as a case worker to Norristown State Hospital, and I worked there for close to 20 years expiating my guilt.

Do you feel that the level of patient care improved significantly at Williamsburg because of CPS participation?

There's no doubt about that, the attitude of the conscientious objector was *so* different.

How long did you work at Williamsburg?

Three months. I had a job waiting for me with the Department of Public Welfare in Newport News, if I could find a place outside of the hospital to live.

Were you successful?

That was one nightmare because of all of the big army installations with all of the wives there too, and there was prejudice against conscientious objectors in Williamsburg, and there were no rooms. And when I finally did find a room, I stayed on at the hospital for a couple of weeks because the woman who was supposed to come back on the ward, her husband was going overseas and she wanted two weeks off to be with him. All right, I thought, I stuck it out this long, I can take two more weeks of it. I think I was in a haze. By that time, I was working on a tuberculosis ward all by myself.

(*William*) I remember you used to go over and see the doctor, and he gave you pep pills to be able to stay on the wards and tranquilizers to go to sleep afterwards.

And what were you paid, do you recall?

(*Wilma*) I don't know, but I was paid more than he was.

(*William*) She was getting the going wage, which was then very, very low.

(*Wilma*) Fifty-eight dollars [per month], or something like that. Anyway, when I finally did find a room and moved out, it was in a house that this woman rented, and I had to room with her. I was kicked out of there when the landlord found out she'd rented a room to the wife of a conscientious objector. I lost my room, and I was out of the hospital, and I remember one total nightmarish day when it was very hot, going from house to house ringing doorbells saying, "Do you have anyplace where I could stay and live? You know, anyplace, maybe just a cot in the cellar." Towards the end of the afternoon, I hit a house that belonged to a Professor Phelan of William and Mary College. He opened the door and started to say no, and his wife came to see who was there. She said, "You look dreadful, you poor thing, what's the matter? Come and sit down." So they got me a little glass of wine, and I sat down. It was a room with books in it and comfortable chairs, so I burst into tears. So they said, "We're going away on vacation tomorrow, and we have a dog. Will you take care of the dog? You can have our house."

And then their next-door neighbor was Dina Willing of William and Mary College, and she was there to be sure I didn't do anything I shouldn't. And she came after church one day and said, "I used to be a conscientious objector in the First World War, and I got thinking about you, and I thought 'Well, I'm going away,' and you can have my house." And so I moved to her house, but she was a little short thing, and I'm not, and she had her house furnished to scale. There was hardly anything to sleep in, or sit in, or anything else, it was all built to her scale. I finally found an old guest house, and we moved in there, and it got to be known as "AWOL Camp," because we were the hangout for whatever. And I had a job near Newport News.

Tell me a little bit about your experiences at Williamsburg.

(*William*) I was on the admissions ward first, and the first day was terribly scary. There was a big rangy guy who was in there and fairly violent, messing around the ward. I had had no experience; they had a training course that met once a week, but we were thrown right into the wards. The day shift wasn't too bad, because there were three attendants on and, of course, the doctor was available some. After about a week, you became acclimated to the patients. We used to go over to the violent ward to bring patients for shock treatment. Sometimes five guys would carry patients the 400 or 500 yards from the violent ward to the admissions building where the shock treatment would be administered. We'd have one on each leg, one on each arm, and one up at the head. Shock treatment was the main treatment they were given.

(*Wilma*) There was no psychotherapy, and there were no tranquilizers or anything like that.

Was there any difficulty for you and for your unit resolving the issue of using force on these patients? Did that conflict with your pacifist commitment?

(*William*) No, the difference was between force and violence. Force was restraining, but with concern and respect for the person you were restraining, whereas violence was what was recommended by the old bughouse attendant who told us, "The first thing you do when they come in is you beat them up, and you won't have any more trouble with them." Well, that just illustrated the difference between force and violence; if somebody had to be restrained, call on another attendant. Also, there's the matter of attitude. You restrain somebody while caring for them, respecting them as a human personality and even loving that person, which also involves discipline. When you love your children, you discipline your children, as well as being nice to them. So that you apply force with an attitude to protect the person and to protect the social environment in which you and he are involved so as not to harm that person physically.

One of the most heartbreaking experiences was, there was a whole family in there, and one of them had been a judge. He had been in there about 20 years on the deteriorated ward, which was outside, and that's where they rooted around in the muddy yard and made noises like they were pigs. When they ate, they put their heads right down and ate out of the plates.

Were there any suicide attempts while you were there, or perhaps any deaths of patients through negligence? I know that occurred before the arrival of CPS men.

I remember going into the toilet room and there was a patient to whom I had given a razor; I'd gone out of the toilet room for just a minute. I came back in, because you never allow them to have a razor unless you're there all the time, and he had the razor blade out and was sawing at his wrists.

(*Wilma*) But in sort of a lackadaisical fashion.

(*William*) Well, he was bandaged for about a month on his wrists.

What were some of the psychological effects, either for you or for people you knew, of working in a mental hospital?

(*Wilma*) A good many of the CO wives simply couldn't take it. I would say that even though I did take it, I couldn't.

(*William*) Those who couldn't take it went home to stay with their families.

(*Wilma*) There was an incident when two of the patients eloped or escaped, stole a car, and went to Florida.

(*William*) The superintendent had just put in so-called escape-proof screens.

(*Wilma*) A thousand dollars' worth.

(*William*) Yes, they kicked them out, and the superintendent said, "We haven't got proper coverage on the ward." So he shifted all the hours so that everybody had to work a 72-hour week with no days off. And there were a lot of meetings. The group decided they weren't going to work those hours, and they continued following the old schedule.

(*Wilma*) They wanted to hire regular attendants.

(*William*) But they weren't able to, they were just beginning to be able to hire other people coming out of the war installations. So the Department of Public Welfare of Virginia brought a case against the conscientious objectors. However, in defense of the superintendent—since I'm a bureaucrat and government administrator myself, and political scientist—in my view, he had no real alternative, as a strict administrator, which a hospital superintendent has to be, because he deals with some rough problems and he's got to be a strict guy. When his employees refused to obey his orders as to shifts, he had no recourse but to take the strongest disciplinary measures he could, in the interest of the hospital. In a hospital situation, where you are dealing particularly with mental patients and you didn't have the drugs they have now, you had to be able to order attendants to do things and do things fast. Now if they had been ordinary private hired help, he could have fired some, or docked their pay, or anything he wanted, but they were CPS men. They were assigned to him. The only alternative that he had then was to go to Selective Service, which was ultimately in charge of these men doing what was considered a full day's work. He had no alternative but to do that.

(*Wilma*) But the funny thing of it was the Richmond newspapers and the way they covered it, about conscientious objectors refusing to take care of mental patients.

(*William*) Now there's a lot of guys in CPS who think that this is a free-floating world. As we get more technology and more civilization, you've got to have more social disciplines, and you've got to have them particularly at those points in the social and cultural system where there is danger to life and limb, and that includes mental patients in a mental hospital.

(*Wilma*) Bill was no longer on the wards by this time. He had been writing a paper for the superintendent on prognostication for mental hospital populations, tied up with city planning and plans for expanding the hospital. He was kind of out of it.

(*William*) I had a very plush job; I sat right outside the superintendent's office and saw all the Selective Service people come in their uniforms.

(*Wilma*) All of Hershey's brass hats.

(*William*) And they had conferences over this, and then they went on down to Norfolk to see the district attorney. In the meantime, of course, Paul Comly French and the administration from Washington were keeping close tabs on the situation and working with Selective Service.

(*Wilma*) And you were already in the process of being transferred to Puerto Rico.

(*William*) At that point, I had rather a tough decision. I had a friend who was a New York City planning commissioner, and he was working as a consultant to the Puerto Rico planning board, which had just started. This was when the Popular Democratic party came into power under the leadership of Luis Muñoz Marín. Rex Tugwell was appointed governor, so this was where the New Deal went. Tugwell had been head of the New York City Planning Commission and had been too radical and had gotten eased out. You now had a Puerto Rican government with a leadership that wanted to raise up the country using New Deal ideas and more government ownership, and the planning board was part of that.

Of course, I had been following the New Deal from one job to another really. I was slated to be on detached service to work for the Puerto Rico planning board. I was just waiting for them to work this through. And so I knew I was going, and here were these charges. We had a meeting, and I had to choose whether I was going to stick with the group or say, "Oh, I've got a plush job waiting, I'll keep out of it." We all put our names down, and I put mine down with them. This was part of the conspiracy, because there were petitions that involved practically everyone who was a CO in that unit. Well, after about three days, word came down that the charges were dropped. The war was over, and the peace churches administration in Washington had finally convinced Selective Service that this was a silly charge to press at this time.

You went on down to Puerto Rico then?

We went down in November of 1945, and I got discharged about a year later, and I stayed on another year with a salary.

It was quite a welcome change, I'm sure, after Williamsburg.

The conscientious objectors were really revered in Puerto Rico for what they did. There was practically no health care back in the mountains. They would bring the patients in who couldn't see, and they had a doctor who would do cataract operations, and they would go out seeing. So to be a conscientious objector in Puerto Rico was immediately a tremendous thing. You were not only accepted but respected for the work that was being done down there.

What did you do, Wilma?

(*Wilma*) I went back to school teaching at St. John's School; it was a private school in Puerto Rico.

Did you ever consider going 1AO?

(*William*) No, handing out the bullets was the same as firing them.

What was the most difficult aspect of CPS for you?

You know, it's hard for me to remember anything that was very difficult that lasted very long.

Even Williamsburg?

I guess Williamsburg when I first got there and worked on the deteriorated ward. It was pretty rough, and if you were on at night, you were there all by yourself and you had to be very much on your toes because things could erupt. It was very hard to even telephone to get help if anything should break out at night.

What was the most difficult aspect for you, Wilma?

(*Wilma*) Working at the state hospital at Williamsburg with so little preparation and very little support, because most of the wives were having an even worse time or had cleared out. I stayed even though I couldn't take it. I don't know why I always have to prove that I can take something when I can't. I get a headache for that reason.

Did you see changes in Wilma, particularly during the Williamsburg period?

(*William*) Oh, she went through a terrible time really. I would say that Wilma is always a person who rises up in a crisis and resolves it. That's right, when things get tough, why, you're really right there.

What was the most satisfying aspect of CPS for both of you?

Well, I think detached service in Puerto Rico, because I got back into my professional career right away, and in the same line that I had been doing before, which was where the new things were happening. And when Rex Tugwell went to the University of Chicago to found a planning school, I went up there to teach and get my Ph.D.

What was the most satisfying aspect for you, Wilma?

(*Wilma*) I think a sense of community, particularly in Elmira, but it went straight through, to a degree. I think there would have been more of a sense of community in Williamsburg if more of the wives had stayed.

(*William*) I'd say that CPS was a great experience, and I wouldn't have missed it for anything.

(*Wilma*) Well, also it led to my finally becoming a psychiatric social worker, which I found very satisfying.

So it changed your life in that respect. Looking back now, do you have any doubts about your decision to enter CPS?

(*William*) No, not about the decision. I think this came from Evan Thomas [peace leader and brother of Norman Thomas] some years ago, that if you become a conscientious objector because you think it may change things, you are then being practical. You can't be a conscientious objector and think you are going to change views necessarily; you are a conscientious objector because you can't do anything else. And look, pacifism's got no answer to the war situation or the war system, or the military-industrial government and now university complexes, because the top people in the universities are the people who are always going off to Washington to consult, and there is federal money coming into the universities.

(*Wilma*) In other words, he used to believe that someday they'd give a war and nobody would come. If we didn't go, we'd be starting a trend. Oh, I think in a sense we sort of did, we stopped a war, the Vietnamese war, and even my son, who I think was going through a delayed adolescent rebellion.

He was a paratrooper in Vietnam?

Yes. I remember he went to Drew University, dropped out, and said he was going to sit around here and wait until they drafted him. He said, "If I do go into the military, I know perfectly well I can never walk in this house again," and I said, "What nonsense, of course you can." Well, he went through the whole damn thing and came out with views about the same as ours, I'd say.

What are your feelings about the administration of CPS by the Historic Peace Churches?

(*William*) Well, I think that the Quakers were in an untenable position in that they had to go by the rules that were set down by Selective Service, and they had to administer whatever discipline was prescribed by Selective Service. As I look back on it, my expectations of Quakers at that point, or what Quakers could do, or how they acted—you read all the stories of the great Quaker heroes—and when they got into a position of being almost part of the government, why, they made a lot of compromises. But after CPS, we were still Quakers, and we went to meeting in San Francisco at Berkeley, and Wilma worked for the American Friends Service Committee when we were in San Francisco. However, when we came to Philadelphia, we found the Quakers of Philadelphia are quite different from the Quakers we had known in several other cities, in their sort of establishment and "in group," and we never felt too much at home.

6

REFLECTIONS ON THE CPS EXPERIENCE
Hoosag Gregory

"I began feeling that the people who had refused to register at all were the ones who had done the right thing."

Hoosag Gregory, born in Massachusetts in 1918 to Armenian immigrants, came to his pacifist commitment through reading and reflection. He served two years in CPS before deciding to enter the army. After the war, he earned a Ph.D. in English literature at Harvard. He taught at Case Institute of Technology, Bates, Northwestern, and San Francisco State. In his retirement, Gregory learned Armenian, enabling him to translate into English an autobiographical account written by his father. He died on 20 July 1995.

Did you have a strong religious upbringing?

No, not at all. My parents had a somewhat simple notion of religion: you do something for God, and God does something for you. God hadn't really done very much, either for them or for the Armenian people as a whole, although that didn't stop millions, or hundreds of thousands, of Armenians from remaining firm Christian believers.

But my parents were definitely, I think, shaken in their religious belief. And we grew up in a town where there wasn't an Armenian church anyway. I don't think I heard either of my parents say a single prayer, all the time that I was growing up. Nevertheless, when an Armenian priest came down to Bridgewater to baptize whatever unbaptized Armenian children there were around, they invited him to the house, and I and my brothers and my sister, all four of us, plus a few other children in the neighborhood, were baptized, using a galvanized tin tub that was in our bathroom. I guess my mother washed clothes in it or something.

It sounds as though your decision to enter CPS had nothing to with religion.

No, it had nothing to do with my religious affiliation.

What considerations made you choose CPS?

Well, when I was at Bates, that was probably where it began. Teachers had us read war literature, war fiction, so I read novels that portrayed the futility of war.

Were you reading All Quiet on the Western Front?

Yes, *All Quiet on the Western Front,* Dos Passos's *Three Soldiers,* and *Farewell to Arms,* and also several books of nonfiction that I was either required or encouraged to read by my college teachers. And then the college was a religious foundation, Bates, and I probably got more religious feeling from going to chapel at the college. Chapel was required, so we would go five times a week, but the college religious groups were led by students who tended to be antiwar too.

Did you have, for example, students who were involved with the Fellowship of Reconciliation, the War Resisters League, or the Quaker camps, anything of that sort?

At that point, no. Actually, I can't really be at all specific about the affiliations of the people who came to the college and who gave pacifist speeches, but I remember being quite persuaded that war was an evil and that anyone who really was intelligent and civilized and ethical wouldn't go to war. The whole business about the "atrocity" stories during World War I influenced me, how hatred against the Germans was built up and how it was only later that more people realized that this hatred was based on stories that weren't true, were propaganda. I was really singularly uninformed about current events for somebody who was first in his class. I used to get terribly good grades in all my courses, but I was a pretty narrow kind of student, and in fact I remember when I sat before a committee of the professors at my college, who were trying to choose a candidate from Bates to try for the Rhodes scholarship, that one of my professors asked me, did I know who "the sick man of Europe" was, and I didn't. I had no idea what he meant by "the sick man of Europe," and yet I was the child of Armenians who had this woeful history with the Turks.

I just cite that in order to indicate that I wasn't well informed. I had read quite a lot, but it was mostly novels, poetry, drama. I had taken courses in history, a few, and courses in other subjects, but I wasn't someone who was a serious reader of a good newspaper each day, so whatever I knew about what was going on in the world trickled down to me. For example, I had the vaguest notion of the Spanish Civil War. It was going on all the time I was at Bates, and the only way I had any particular awareness that it was going on was that I had a teacher or two who mentioned it occasionally. So for somebody who was supposed to be a bright student, I was pretty damned stupid and ignorant.

Did you have any trouble once you decided to ask for a CO status? Did you have difficulty from your draft board?

Yes.

It had to be on the basis of religious persuasion, didn't it?

Yes. I asked for a form that you had to fill out if you wanted to apply for an exemption as a CO. I was asked to tell what had made me decide to become one. So I think what I said to the draft board, which was probably the reason that they rejected my application first time around, was that I didn't belong to any church, although I attended Sunday school a fair amount growing up and was exposed to religion, at Bates particularly. That I wasn't even sure that I believed in God. I think I said something like, the God I believed in—we had read 20 or 30 pages of Matthew Arnold in English literature, Matthew Arnold had said that God was that power not ourselves which makes for righteousness, and that that was the God that led me to object to war.

But your draft board didn't appreciate that.

No, no. Not at first, anyway, and I said that I simply couldn't conceive myself killing anyone, only because somebody else told me to do it. And they turned me down. And I remember telling someone, who I knew was a pacifist, at the University of Illinois, that I had been turned down. And he said, "Well, you can appeal." And I said, "Oh, can I?" So I appealed. And they wrote back and gave me a date for a session with the draft board, I think sometime in January 1941. So when Christmas holidays came, I decided just to quit graduate school and go back to Somerville, Massachusetts, where my parents were living at the time. My father was working as a leather sorter in a tannery in Greater Boston, and so it was Somerville that I went back to, and it was the Somerville draft board to which I was appealing.

I remember going on the evening when I was to have the interview, and there were about 11, 12 other people in the room with me. The draft board called each of them in and talked to them. Finally, I was the only one left in the room. Then I went in, and they just asked me questions such as, "What would you do if . . . ," and I really don't think I gave any great answers. You know, "What if a German were attacking your mother and sister?" I said I really didn't know what I would do, but I certainly wouldn't have it in my mind that I wanted to kill them. If I had the courage, I would try to do what I could to prevent whatever evil they intended to commit, and if in the course of trying to prevent it, one of them got killed, I couldn't help that. But somehow that seemed terribly different to me from signing yourself into this huge army with decisions made by some central office, and being sent off to meet someone you never saw before in your life. They just kept asking questions and letting me talk, and when it was over, they said, "Thank you," and I went home. After some days I learned that my appeal had been granted. I was told there wasn't a camp open at that time, but that as soon as a camp was opened, I would be sent to it. So then I worked in a restaurant, busing dishes, for a few months.

You went first to Royalston, Massachusetts, in June 1941?

Yes, that sounds about right.

Was your family supportive?

No. They were thinking at first of the shame that I would bring on myself, and the way in which it would affect my whole career and waste all my years of academic work. That was the vision they had, and so they were really bitterly against me for doing it, at least my father was. My mother felt rather glad that I had done it, but no, they weren't supportive. But as the war went on and I paid occasional visits home and took some of my camp friends with me, they met them and the world didn't seem to be falling around my ears. They, even my father, began feeling rather glad that I had done it, not on the basis of any kind of principle, but simply that I wasn't risking my life anywhere.

What about your brothers, were they drafted?

Yes. One of the twins went into the army and became a dental officer, and the other one went into the navy and became a navigator on a plane.

They weren't critical, though, of you?

No, no. As a matter of fact, they had no strong convictions. They read the newspapers even less than I did.

And what they did was what almost everyone else was doing.

Yes, although in a way I'd be a liar if I didn't confess that I didn't like the vision of risking my life in battle. But I don't think that that was the reason that I became a CO, that I simply couldn't stand the thought of battle, but I was certainly glad to be out of it while I was out of it. Then, ironically, it turned out that even when I said, "Take me," in a sense I still remained out of it, because they never asked me to do anything that was combatant.

But you did enter the army, as 1A, combatant?

Yes, but I was never asked to do anything combatant. I had to learn how to fire a rifle, although I can't say I learned much, because I never did it after I took the marksmanship test.

Were you posted in the United States?

I didn't leave New England all the time that I was in the army.

What kind of work were you doing?

After basic training, I was sent to Fort Adams in Rhode Island, and I was a ward man in the hospital there.

Ironic, isn't it? Doing the same thing that you were doing in CPS before you went in.

Yes. It was very hard work, we got practically no time off, but after I had done that for several months, the rumor began making the rounds that our unit was going to be sent to Europe. So I thought, "Ah, this is it, now even though it's just as part of the medical unit, I'll be sent to Europe." And then, oddly enough, at the last minute, I was picked out of that unit and told I wasn't going with the others to Europe, that I was to report to the Climatic Research Laboratory in Lawrence, Massachusetts. And it happened, I think, because when I was at Camp Devens, getting basic training, I made very good friends with a young Irish-American guy, who was a physicist. I remember at one point in the course of a conversation he said to me, "I know where I'm going after we leave here, I'm a physicist, and I'm being sent to a laboratory," and, "If I could arrange to have you sent there, would you be glad?" and I said, "Sure!" I mean, I had said I was going into the army, but I wasn't terribly eager to go and fight. So that's where I was sent.

So were you a lab assistant for him?

No, the chief work of the laboratory was testing different kinds of soldiers' equipment in controlled temperature rooms, mittens, uniforms, and sleeping bags in cold rooms.

Were you a guinea pig?

Yes, test subject.

Which is just what so many men were doing in CPS.

Yes. So I was a test subject there, and after I had done that for a year or so, the colonel who was the head of the laboratory, called me in and said, "I see by your records that you have an M.A. in English. We've been told that we have to write the history of our laboratory, and I wonder whether you would like to do that?" And I said, "Sure!" So there began the most boring job I ever had in my life.

Writing the history of the lab?

Yes. All that they really wanted was summaries of all of the tests that they had made and the results. So I had my office, and I would go in and sit down at a desk and fall asleep after lunch. I wrote 700 or 800 typewritten pages about all the tests the laboratory had done during the few years that it had been open.

And did that take you through to the end of the war?

That carried me through to the end of the war. Then I applied for Harvard Graduate School. I had done very well on a GRE exam, so I went to Harvard.

Let's go back. Can you tell me just a little bit about those first few days at Royalston?

I remember thinking it was wonderful, it was really like going to a camp run by the young people who were in the religious groups at Bates.

That was a Friends camp?

That's right, yes. A lot of my fellow campers were people who had been to college. I remember just the general feeling that we had a very good time there. We worked hard.

You were doing forestry work there?

Yes, forestry work, but actually the hardest part of it, and what we did most of the time that I was there at Royalston, was digging water holes, for water to fight forest fires. During the three months or so that I was at Royalston, there was a big forest fire that burned down about 1,500 acres. So we had an exciting two or three days with backpack pumps fighting the forest fire. I don't mean to say that we quenched the flames with our backpack pumps, but they were trying to hold a line against the forest fire. They put us on the side of the road, and then if a spark from the other side jumped over the road and started a spot fire somewhere behind us, the idea was to run with your backpack pump to where the spot fire had blazed up and do what you could to put it out. So that did happen a number of times, and it was all very exciting. Digging the water holes was harder work than I had ever done in my life, but I had the feeling that it was good for me, it was body-building work, pickaxe and shovel.

So you felt good about what you were doing, although you probably would not have characterized it as work of national importance.

Digging the water holes and clearing out the trees that had blown down, all of that I felt had some significance, but it wasn't of earth-shaking importance. I enjoyed being out of doors, and we had good meals, plenty to eat, I put on weight, I got a terrific tan, and I felt very popular among the campers there. We did a lot of singing, and girls from Smith and Mount Holyoke would come occasionally and put on little dances for us, you know, our USO or whatever. So it wasn't bad, I really quite enjoyed it.

Then one day this man came from the Catholic camp in New Hampshire, his name was Dwight Larrowe, and he told about how they were trying to start a Catholic camp at Stoddard, New Hampshire. It had started, but they needed four or five more people to make up the minimum number required to keep the camp open. He wanted some of us to volunteer to go. I went, and so did several others.

What was the appeal of doing that?

There was something about him I admired. I think I've always been a hero worshiper. There was something about him that was very, very attractively sincere and earnest. He was a good man and a dedicated man.

So you packed up and took off. How long were you at Royalston before you went to Stoddard?

About three and a half months. I think it was early in October that I and a few of my fellow Royalston campers went to Stoddard.

What particular work were you doing there?

Mostly clearing out hurricane blowdown.

From the 1938 hurricane?

Yes, and digging water holes again. During the whole time I was there, there wasn't any forest fire to fight, so I didn't have the excitement and the slight risk that there had been at Royalston. Stoddard was a much poorer camp than Royalston; nevertheless, there was plenty to eat and having enough to eat is a great part of my life. It was a much more serious and earnest place than Royalston. At Royalston I really did have the feeling it could have been a summer camp of college students sympathetic to Christianity.

Was the shared commitment to nonviolence a sufficient bond to develop a real sense of community within the camp?

Well, there was a sense of community, but it was a community within a larger group. There were people outside the community that did share some sort of earnest feeling about nonviolence and spiritual development and all of those other things. In fact, at one point I used to think of the campers as being divided between the men of spirit and the sensualists, and this in spite of the fact that I am a big eater and having a good meal is terribly important to me and I always ate well. But at Stoddard—and I don't think this was true at Royalston—every meal began with the saying of grace. There were several people among the campers who completely ignored the grace that was being said and were heaping their plates. Two guys particularly became almost symbols to me of everything I disliked about this part of the camp group. I thought of them as the "chief sensualists," although all I meant, I suppose, was that they were people who didn't really have a thought or a feeling that seemed to go beyond their senses.

When did you meet Dorothy Day?

It was sometime in the late autumn of 1942. Several conscientious objectors were arriving at the camp, and so I was asked to show one of them how to use an ax. It was perfectly silly, but while I was showing him how to use an ax, I cut my own foot. So I had to be taken back to the camp and have the thing bandaged. Then I caught cold and developed this really quite bad pneumonia and lay in camp for 12 or 13 days, and it just wasn't getting any better. This was before penicillin and sulfa drugs were available to civilians. The doctor finally said that I ought be taken to the hospital in Concord, New Hampshire. I lay there for another two or three weeks and lost about 35 pounds during the whole damn thing. Dorothy Day was paying one of her visits to the camp, and I had really never talked with her during any of her previous visits.

She would come up every two or three months?

Yes, I suppose about that often.

What was your impression of Dorothy Day?

Well, I had heard a lot about her before she came, and I remember at first feeling a bit disappointed, because she seemed very flat and drab as a person. She made no effort at all to be an attractive woman. I didn't think she spoke terribly effectively either; she spoke in a rather flat, unexciting way. But then, I guess after I had seen her several times at the camp—maybe it was simply because I was more and more impressed by the depth and strength of her commitment—I began finding her more impressive. I had wanted something more colorful, more like the Grand Inquisitor chapter of *The Brothers Karamazov*. I had literary expectations.

Did you discuss Dostoyevsky with Dorothy Day?

Yes, I had heard that she read and liked Dostoyevsky. So when she came to visit me, I brought up Dostoyevsky during the little conversation we had. I forget even what she said or what I said about it, but we had a chat about Dostoyevsky, and she was very kind. Someone I found much more colorful than she was an old man who came with her on one or two occasions, who was apparently the man who inspired her to found the Catholic Worker movement, Peter Maurin. He was much more colorful, he could have come from one of those Marcel Pagnol French movies. But Dorothy Day, I couldn't see in any movie or play.

I get a sense that your attitudes toward CPS were beginning to undergo a change.

Well, I found some of the men more impressive examples of what I think of as a pacifist than others about whom you might say, "What the hell are they doing here"? And even though the work we were doing in the woods wasn't useless, we were in a sense being kept away from the rest of the community, and therefore it would be better if COs were where other people were and not sort of shoveled off, hidden away. The idea of work in hospitals and so on sounded good to me, which is why, when I had the opportunity, I volunteered to do that. I suppose one of the things that was happening to me during that time was that I felt there must be some way in which I could more fully be what I wished to be in becoming a CO. Have you read anything by Gerald Heard?

No.

I guess reading Gerald Heard made me feel something that seemed to tie in with the thrill that I got out of reading the Grand Inquisitor chapter in *Brothers Karamazov*. That there is such a thing as disciplined spiritual self-development. One thing that Heard emphasized in his books was the importance of meditation, the importance of silence, and what he called "alert passivity." So I started getting up earlier than all the other campers and meditating an hour before anyone else was stirring, except for the cook, and then before going to bed at night I meditated another hour, just sitting in silence, waiting for whatever came, like a one-man Quaker meeting. Anyway, I guess reading Gerald Heard made me feel, it's not enough just to say, "I don't believe in war," you ought to have some sort of nonviolent power, potency, so that it wouldn't just be a question of turning the other cheek and getting destroyed because you didn't believe in violence, that somehow you ought to be able to exert . . .

A compelling power . . .

. . . like the Christ in "The Grand Inquisitor." So in my own loose and slaphappy way, I was poking along towards something of that kind. I wanted somehow to be more potently saintly. Again, you see, it was all a very egocentric kind of fantasy. You look at someone with love in your eyes and his defenses crumble. I don't mean to say that the people who achieve this are egocentric, but I think that I was; my version of it tended to be.

Some people would say that Gandhi perhaps was very egocentric.

I think he probably was too. But anyway, that was one of the things that was brewing in me; I wanted to become some sort of actively saintly being, and I didn't think I could really do that simply by being in the camp. Come to think of it, I didn't even have any influence worth a damn on my fellow campers when I tried to exert it. Because I remember one day I was acting foreman of the group that was working on a water hole and the "sensualists" were part of the group that I was supposed to be foremanning. They weren't really working the way the rest of us were, and I simply didn't have the resources to get them to do anything that I thought they should do, so in the end I was reduced simply to denouncing them and telling them what a couple of hypocritical fakes they were.

Was that a factor, perhaps, in your volunteering for the mental hospital work at Highland Hospital?

Yes, yes. Actually, I thought that was a good cause. Here are people who are mentally ill, and the people who work with them ideally should be kind and loving and somehow able to impress them in a way that would make them want to get better.

You were at Highland for about six months. What was that work like? What was the feeling among the men there?

There was something about the setup there that didn't encourage the same kind of communal awareness among the COs as in the camps.

Why do you think that was?

I think it was primarily that the COs no longer had their own community. The community was Highland Hospital, with all of its doctors and nurses and presided over by this octogenarian despot, who was not a bad man, named Dr. Carroll. He was also head of the hospital when Zelda Fitzgerald died there, whenever that was. But anyway, I became part of Highland Hospital, I wasn't really part of the CPS unit, we didn't have meetings.

You had classes though, didn't you?

Well, the classes were given by Dr. Carroll on psychiatry. He gave a little course on psychoses, their symptoms and definitions.

What kind of work were you doing?

The way a typical day would be was, I would go to Miss Bailey, who was the nurse in charge of us all, and she would assign me to a particular patient. They had a small number of patients. I'd spend several hours with one patient, take him for a walk and bring him back and lock him in his room, but it didn't amount to much more than being a custodian. You really didn't have conversations with any of the patients. You know, I have some stories of patients who were more colorful and interesting than others.

For example?

Well, I had a patient named Dewey Bridges, who had a disorder called tabes dorsalis, which meant that he lost all feeling of tension in his bladder muscles, so he didn't know when he needed to pee. So—this was at Duke University—so I would take two urinals to him, not just one. His bladder would become so full and distended that he finally would get the idea that it was necessary to get rid of some of this, and he'd fill one urinal, then I would pass the other one to him trying to avoid a drop falling to the floor. Then, when he had done all the peeing that he had to do, he would stand there and look at me with a very deeply sad, grave expression. On one occasion, he said, "Oh, Dewey Bridges, they've gone and done you a terrible wrong, for there's no more water in your body. You climbed to the top of a tall tree, and there was no water, you came down to the ground and rubbed two dry sticks together, and there was no water. Oh, Dewey Bridges, they've gone and done you a terrible wrong, for there is no more water in your body." I've never forgotten that. Another time he was locked in a special room because he was smearing feces over the walls. I had taken something to him in the room in which he was locked, and he tried to push his way out of the room, and I pushed him back in, and he again stood there with this deeply melancholy look on his face and said, "You struck me, you struck me, you struck my little wife Annie, who is in my stomach baking a chocolate pie."

That raises another issue of interest to us: some of the methods of control and some of the treatment, particularly, of course, electric shock treatment, hydrotherapy, insulin shock, and simply the necessity sometimes to use almost violent methods to control violent patients. Did this ever create any kind of a conflict for some of the men?

Well, I don't know about others, but I wouldn't say it created a conflict. In a way, I was disappointed that I hadn't been able to whip up enough spiritual power to do it without using physical force. But there were a number of occasions in which I had physically to force a patient, I mean, the time I pushed Dewey Bridges, gently, but nevertheless pushed him back into his room. Or another time, there was a patient named Tony, who was a very pathetic patient, who had been at Highland over 30 years and who almost never said anything during all the hours that I spent with him. I was assigned to him quite a number of times, and I remember one occasion when I had brought him back from his walk. Usually he would go back into his room in quite a docile way, and I would close the door and lock it. But on this occasion, he stood there and didn't seem to want to go in, so I pushed him gently into the room, and he stood there, looked at me, and said, "What would you do if you were in here and I was standing out there?" Then he lapsed into vacancy again. That made me feel terribly strange.

Another time—this is funny, I think—I had a patient named George who was a hebephrenic-schizophrenic, and when I took him out for a walk, every so often he would stop. I mean, the idea was that one walked behind the patient. Every so often he would turn around and look at me and go, "No-no," then he would turn around and go on walking. On one occasion, he turned around and instead of just looking at me and doing his "no-no," he came up to me and started pummeling me with his fists. So I grabbed his wrists and wrestled him to the ground until he indicated that he would be a good boy. Then I let him up again, and we resumed our walk.

One of the things that made Highland Hospital fun for me was that there were two baseball teams, each of them made up of patients and workers. We had uniforms and shoes with spikes and everything, and I was a left fielder on one of the baseball teams, and as a matter of fact, I was terribly proud of myself because I had the highest batting average of anybody on either of the two teams. I was playing for the team that was opposing Dr. Carroll's team, and he was the pitcher for the other side. And I don't know what the reason was, but I was the only one who seemed to be either willing or able to hit his pitching quite hard, so I had a batting average of something like .420 against Robert Carroll. Anyway, when George started going at me with his fists, I thought, "I've got to do something to stop this," so I went and I borrowed the catcher's mask from the baseball equipment room and when I went out for a walk with George, I put the catcher's mask on, and he'd turn around and look at me, grunt "no-no," and then continue walking.

Actually, I had fun at all these places. At Highland Hospital, as a matter of fact, I even had developed a great crush on a woman who was about 15 years older than myself, who was a psychotherapist. She had been a patient herself some years back. She was an intelligent woman on the staff at the New York Public Library. Dr. Carroll helped her, and then she began doing some psychotherapy there herself. I never really questioned her enough to even know how much of a gap there was between the time that she was a patient and the time that she did whatever psychotherapy she was doing. I met her at a New Year's dance at the hospital, and we somehow seemed to be able to talk to each other very easily. She was really a lovely person, in fact, she had a lot to do with my going into the army.

Could you explain?

Because she simply couldn't see my pacifism at all.

And did you find that you had difficulty explaining it to her?

Yes. That raised questions in my own mind, and another thing was spending a lot of time with mental patients, and reading books by Jung and Freud about neuroses and psychoses, and then beginning to feel I have a lot of that in me and I wonder how real my conviction that I shouldn't fight is. If somebody that I really cared about were threatened—I mean, the question the draft board asks sounds sort of comic when it is repeated often, "What would you do if a German were attacking your mother?" but actually it is a valid question. What *would* you do? What do you think about conduct in such a situation? I think I came to feel that if I could do nothing except simply turn the other cheek, it would be better if I fought.

In a sense, it was Gandhi's own analysis of the situation. His feeling was that if you can't develop power in nonviolent direct action, it is better if you are a soldier. I think I came to feel something quite close to that myself. In college I had never really had much awareness about psychiatry and mental disorder. The feeling that I probably wasn't all that healthy psychologically and emotionally began making me suspect my reasons for having decided to be a CO. Also, just as I went from Royalston to Stoddard because I admired something about Dwight Larrowe, I wanted this woman that I had fallen in love with, I wanted her to think well of me, to be proud of me.

You transferred from Highland to Duke, and she stayed, obviously, at Highland.

Yes.

You were at Duke for only three months before leaving CPS. What moved you in that direction?

210

At Highland Hospital there was zero intellectuality. You had these little routines, you performed them, you did as good a job as you could. At Duke there were weekly clinics that the attendants were allowed to attend and different cases were discussed and analyzed. There was a library to which we had access. I don't even know where the books were at Highland Hospital; they must have had books there, but we weren't encouraged to use them. At Duke we were actually encouraged to look at the books that were available.

Were you working there in the mental ward, or were you working as an operating room attendant? I understand that the men were doing both there.

More the mental ward.

And you were moving toward this final decision to leave CPS?

Well, actually, I began developing another fantasy, and that was that if I get out of the army after having gone into it, what I would like to become is a psychiatrist.

And, of course, you could do that with the GI bill in the army; you couldn't do it through CPS.

Except that, after having been in the army and coming out of it, I decided I had to go back to something I could handle more efficiently and quickly— get a Ph.D. in English. So when it came down to snuff, I didn't want to start from scratch, to become a psychiatrist and go to medical school, all of that. I decided, well, I had better stay in English. Then as time went on, I decided to look for psychological help myself and went into analysis. So the movement there was from feeling, I want to become a psychiatrist, healing and curing people, to finding a psychiatrist who would heal and cure me.

I still don't understand why after three months at Duke you decided to go into the army. Was it just something that gradually grew until one day you said, "I've just got to do this," or was there another particular incident that triggered the decision?

Maybe it was reading another book. I started reading Nietzsche when I was there too, particularly *The Genealogy of Morals*, in which Nietzsche makes what at that time seemed to me a devastating attack on Christianity and the ascetic ideal. That was really what I had been . . .

. . . Basing your whole argument on, or much of it anyway?

. . .and I think it was Nietzsche more even than Jung or Freud who had made me feel my pacifism was really a symptom of sickness, not really an expression of health. So I think that as much as anything. During the whole time I was at Duke, I hadn't seen my psychotherapist friend at all. I can't quite remember what happened to her at that point. I think it was maybe during the time that I was at Duke that she went back to the New York Public Library to work in her librarian's job.

So she really was no longer a factor? You were not in any close communication with her by the time you made the decision to go in?

No, no. As a matter of fact, I think that I had made a kind of advance toward her before I left Highland, and she in a very, very gentle but firm way had discouraged me. She was really a wonderful person and made me feel, "It's been wonderful, and is, and we are great friends, but I'm much too old for you, and it just wouldn't make for a happy relationship." So maybe that had something to do with my readiness to leave Highland and go to Duke. Although years later, when I was at Fort Adams, Rhode Island, I still wrote to her and she wrote to me. I did meet her in New York, and we went to a couple of plays together, and it was there that she told me that she was marrying a Scotchman, who was much older than herself. She was at that time about 43 and he was 65. That was the end so far as our continuing to communicate with each other was concerned.

Did you know anyone else that went into the army from CPS?

Actually, that reminds me of something else, I don't know how important, that I left out. I began reading more about the nonregistrants.

The absolutists.

Yes. I began feeling—this again just shows really what a volatile and unstable kind of person I was—I began feeling that the people who had refused to register at all were the ones who had done the right thing.

There are trade-offs and compromises, and what they had taken was the purist approach?

They were the ones who had really stood 100 percent for their belief, whereas we who had said, "Okay, I'll go to a camp and do your forestry work, etc.," that we somehow had sold out. I am reminded at this point of a rather horrible and perhaps slightly comic development. Another camper and I got to be quite buddy-buddy, and I was always talking to him about my thinking that the only logical thing was to leave camp and to be picked up and put into prison. And blimey! if he didn't go and do it! Because I had presented it to him so persuasively.

So you did have power on some levels.

Yes. He used to call me "Sage." My name is Hoosag, and he mispronounced it "Hoosage" at one point, and then he shortened it to Sage because he was really impressed by my . . .

. . . your brilliance and your wisdom.

. . . Yes! So anyway, poor John went to prison. I don't know whether we'd kept in touch in some way. We must have, because when at one point he was sent on parole from the prison he was in to Rochester, New York, where his wife was working, I went out and paid them a visit, and I felt terribly guilty.

We were talking, also, about blacks in CPS, and I came across this comment in the newsletter from Highland. It said, "We've become 'adjusted,' for instance, to the color line and at the same time have made some real friends among the hospital's colored employees." Do you remember that being an issue at Highland, working with blacks?

No, I don't remember it so much at Highland as I did become aware during the time that I was in Asheville, where Highland is, of course, and Durham. I did become aware of the color line in both those communities, mostly while riding on buses, and I remember particularly, I think it was in Asheville, that this famous black choir had come to give a concert. It was the Wings over Jordan Choir, and they had a national reputation. And I went to the concert, and five-sixths or six-sevenths of the hall was just for whites, and this one little bit in the upper right-hand corner was a place where blacks could sit. I remember that struck me as just terrible.

Did you experience any harassment or any sense of discrimination while you were in CPS from people in any of the local communities?

Actually, not much. I would say that most of the people who picked me up when I was hitching a ride were really more *interested* than anything— "Ah, isn't that interesting . . . blah, blah, blah," but on one occasion, the guy stopped the car and said, "Why don't you get out, I don't want to be giving a ride to somebody who isn't willing to fight for his country." I got out.

Do you see CPS as having had any discernible impact on your later life?

It wasn't so much having elected to be a CO that had the impact on me. The psychiatric work obviously did. It made me turn to psychiatry personally. But I suppose, even though I didn't feel as articulately critical of other COs and the people in charge of the camps as others did, I did gradually build up the feeling that we were really a fairly impotent part of the community, and there was a sense in which we weren't functioning in the real world. So in the sense of making me turn both through psychiatry and in other ways towards a more practical orientation, I gave up thinking of myself as the Christ-to-be or any of the rest of it. I began feeling, "Look bud, heal thyself." For quite a long time, I actually became quite anti-Christian, because of the Nietzsche influence. Then little by little, I began turning toward religion, but on quite a different basis from before. Maybe I believe in God, but a very different kind of God, more than I'm willing to admit that I do, and maybe I believe in prayer in a way that I wasn't thinking of before. Before, prayer was, for me, a road to power. More and more, starting in my middle thirties, which was a dozen years after I was a CO, I began thinking of prayer as a source of enough strength to cope with the difficult realities of my life, and not as a way in which I was going to become some sort of Olympic champion of spirituality.

To control others. It was more of a release for yourself.

In that sense, [being a CO] certainly, I think, had an impact on my life. I continued to feel that Dorothy Day and Peter Maurin had done great things, but I think I didn't feel as much as I had before that this was the way for me to continue trying to live. I don't turn really to books about that kind of spiritual development very much any more. I'll read a book, for example, like Philip Toynbee's *Part of a Journey*. He was literary critic for the *Observer* for quite a few years, Arnold Toynbee's son. It is just an account of his day-to-day struggle to be in touch with things that made him feel a little bit more whole. I became more humble. The poems that still mean more to me are the poems that are quieter, like

> Vigny was chilled,
> By the silence of God.

> He misconceived
> The soul of Christ.
> For Son and Father
> To converse
> Silence sufficed.

There I'm talking as much about my attempt to establish some sort of communion with my own father, with whom I felt so deeply out of touch, as with God.

J. Benjamin Stalvey

"I think from a political standpoint you can't justify pacifism, so it has to be morally and ethically based."

J. Benjamin Stalvey, born on 9 December 1908 in Pittsboro, North Carolina, was working on his doctorate in political science at the University of Illinois when he was drafted into CPS. After serving two and a half years in CPS, Stalvey completed his degree and began teaching in the Political Science Department at the University of Miami. He took a two-year leave of absence in the 1950s to serve in Geneva as European director of the American Friends Service Committee's international seminars. He has continued to be interested in programs promoting international understanding and is now professor emeritus of political science at the University of Miami.

Did you have a strong religious upbringing?

I had a traditional Methodist upbringing, but not in the sense of pacifism. I really had had no pacifist training at all in my church, and the other members of my family didn't agree with me.

What considerations led you to choose CPS?

Frankly, I think it was the study of history. I had a senior graduate course in recent European history and concentrated very heavily on the First World War. And as I read books, such as Fay's *Origins of the World War*, dealing with the First World War, serious questions were raised in my mind as I read more and more about it. And then when I went to Lambeth College, I was office mate with the professor of religion there, who was a man substantially older than I. We talked a great deal, and he was a very strong pacifist. He was a native South Carolinian, but he was very broad in his view on race and these various things, and so that, I think, further confirmed my position.

I declared myself a pacifist at Lambeth College. And quite frankly, I think that was one of the reasons that I felt that I was almost obligated to follow through on it, even when some serious questions came up in my mind because of the difficulties my wife would face. For example, when I was faced with the final determination of what to do, in a way I think I felt I would be

216

letting some of my former students down if I didn't go through with it, because I had taken such a firm pacifist stand. Of course, I was still committed, but there were these problems.

Did your wife share your pacifism?

Yes, she did.

You discussed this decision with her in great detail?

Yes. As a matter of fact, before we were married, we had discussed this and racial matters and so on, and we were in agreement.

You mention difficulties that she would face with your going into CPS.

Well, financial particularly. She had been a public school teacher before we were married. We were married in 1936, and this was in 1943, so she had not taught during those years. And she really didn't have many other qualifications for earning a living, and, of course, CPS made no provisions for families—or for the persons themselves, for that matter.

In spite of that, she was supportive, but the rest of your family was not?

Well, we really had no contact. You see, my family all lived in North Carolina, and my wife and I had lived in Tennessee and then moved to Champaign-Urbana, and so we had very little contact. We were not a close family really. I continued to keep in touch with my parents, and they were sympathetic but. . . .

Did they give you any financial support?

No, they were not in a position to.

Had you considered going 1AO because of the financial problems?

Slightly. I didn't seriously consider it, because I felt that I could not compromise that much. I really felt that if I went into the military, I would go all the way. I just didn't feel that I could accept that alternative. Fortunately, my wife was able to get a position as house mother of a cooperative [at the University of Illinois] under the auspices of the Wesley Foundation. She stayed there and got her room and board, and she was able to do a little bit of work from time to time at the foundation as a receptionist, which earned a little bit of cash. Then she occasionally did substitute teaching, which enabled her to get a little bit more, so she managed that way. She wasn't able to contribute to my support, although a friend of mine, a former student, did make contributions on my behalf to the American Friends Service Committee.

You entered CPS in 1943, and you were first assigned to Big Flats for the basic indoctrination?

Yes. Actually, this was before Big Flats became the indoctrination center. It was converted into that while I was there, which was a primary reason why I went to Trenton. I was asked to stay on at Big Flats to help with indoctrination, but there were so many there who I thought had more reason to stay than I did that I just didn't feel that I was justified.

You weren't out weeding?

No, I was out on a project. I mean, this personnel work was on the personnel committee of the camp. I was not personnel director of the camp or anything. The Service Committee did plan to have me go to Trenton as personnel director there, but the men there didn't know me, and they would have none of it. They didn't want the Service Committee sending someone out there as personnel director, and I probably felt the same way. It was partly because of that that I decided I wanted to go on to Trenton anyway; I felt it would be a good idea for me to go. I am glad to say that I was accepted. They knew that I was the one who had been proposed as personnel director there, but they elected me as their educational director, so I guess I got along all right with them.

How long were you at Big Flats?

I was at Big Flats over a year.

What was the nature of your work?

One of the reasons, frankly, that I wanted to leave Big Flats was the project. It was the most boring project, particularly in the spring and summer. The winter was not too bad, because we were out in the woods doing selective cutting, but getting out on your knees all day pulling weeds out of grass was about the most boring type of project. You couldn't even be reasonably close together. I wanted to get away from it. Trenton was much more interesting. It was an irrigation project, building dams and leveling, a lot of big machinery. I didn't operate any big machinery. I was always on construction crews at Trenton. Part of the time, of course, I was education secretary.

Did you stay at Trenton until your discharge in November 1945?

Yes. I was in the process of being transferred to this training school for retarded persons, I believe it was in New Jersey, but then the end of the war came, and I knew that the older people would be discharged earlier, so there was no use in transferring me. So I stayed at Trenton until I was discharged.

Did the fact that you had a dependent have any effect on your discharge?

I think it may have, although I think they went more on the basis of age. I was older, of course, I was about 33 when I was drafted, so I guess I was 35 or 36. So I think they were, for the most part, both in military service and in CPS, discharging the older persons first. But I guess a dependent did make some difference.

Did you experience any harassment while you were in CPS?

No, I didn't, but being older and traveling, for example, in civilian clothes, people would not be as likely to wonder, "Well, what's this guy doing out of the army?"

Were your CPS units accepted by the local communities?

Not too well. Big Flats was worse than Trenton. Trenton was, of course, a very, very small community, and a lot of Indian mixed breeds were there. But, for example, the project foreman at Big Flats was not at all understanding or sympathetic. The man at Trenton was a very decent sort of person. He had actually been a Congregational minister, and then he had left that, and he had been a CCC foreman. Then he was called in to this, and he was the man under whom I worked directly on the construction. He was a rough-talking person, profanity constantly, but he was a very decent sort of man. He knew what he was doing, although I doubt if he had more than a fifth-grade education. We would be putting structures in some of these canals, ditches, and he would look at the blueprint and say, "Goddamn it, that won't work that way." He got a pencil and a rough board, and he would scratch out something, and he would say, "Do it this way," and it would work. So the situation generally was pretty good in that respect.

Did you have a generally positive feeling about CPS while you were in it?

Mostly yes, but I got discouraged about it. I was on the verge of leaving at one stage; I seriously considered it, I wrote my wife about it.

What would you have done?

Gone to jail.

You wouldn't have gone into the army?

No, I wasn't considering going into the military, no. I just got to the point where I felt, even this is too much of a compromise, and, of course, we were draftees, I mean, we were accepting the draft. We were under Selective Service. I felt that maybe the Mennonites, Brethren, and Friends were going too far. I never did seriously consider applying for the government CPS camps that were established late in the period, but I did get to the point that I felt the Service Committees ought to get out, that the religious organizations ought to get out.

Was there any particular issue that brought that to a head for you, any particular sign of compromise on the part of the NSBRO or the Service Committee?

Not particularly, so far as the Service Committee. The NSBRO, yes. I mean, I am sure you got this over and over again from people, of the antipathy toward the NSBRO which existed among the men in camps, because I think rightly or wrongly—and as I look at it from this perspective, I think more wrongly perhaps than rightly—we tended to feel that the NSBRO was simply an arm of Selective Service, that it was doing the dirty work for Selective Service, and that carried over to some extent toward the Service Committees. Of course, I had no contact with any of them except the Friends Service Committee, and I don't recall any particularly bad specific incident that caused this feeling. I just grew more and more to feel that this was too much of a compromise.

How many men were in the camp at Trenton when you were there?

I can't remember. I think maybe 125 or so.

Were the men at Trenton mainly from one religious group?

No, there were Methodists and quite a number of Quakers in the camp. I don't recall that there were any Mennonites or any Brethren, although there may have been. There were quite a few Jehovah's Witnesses [JWs], and then I remember there were First Century Christians. They were a group, mostly blacks, who were, I think, a very orthodox, conservative group, hard-working, very conscientious, as were the JWs, I might say, they were hard-working people. And then there were some who professed no religion at all, quite a few of them, as a matter of fact. Incidentally, at Big Flats I was there with Aaron Orange. He had been at one time the vice-presidential nominee of the Socialist Labor party. And he told me that when he registered in New York City as a conscientious objector, they asked him his religion, and he said, "Marxism is my religion," and they accepted it.

Were there any Catholics at Trenton?

Yes, there were quite a few Catholics. As a matter of fact, they pretty well ran the small Catholic church there in Trenton and had meetings at the camp also.

With all of these disparate groups, was the shared feeling of nonviolence enough of a common bond among you all or did you pretty much go your own way?

Well, I would say there was a common bond among about half. There were quite a few who did not participate in the camp meetings or meetings for worship. I didn't participate much in the meetings for worship, but the regular camp meetings I participated in, and about half did regularly. But there were quite a few who had nothing to do with anything. Well, these JWs did not participate in these things, nor did these First Century Christians. Then there were evaders in CPS, as there were anywhere else, some of them who I don't really think had any deep commitment, but several who were sick all the time and didn't work.

Were there any serious differences among the groups?

Oh yes. The most striking one I can remember, I think this was at Trenton, was over the showing of *Birth of a Nation*. This went on at camp meetings for week after week after week, and some of the blacks, not all of them, were vehemently opposed to showing *Birth of a Nation*, and some of the whites, I guess, were rather vehemently for showing it. But this went on and on, and finally one fellow, who was not a Quaker, said, "Well, shall we vote on it, or shall we use the Quaker method of deciding it?" And they said, "Well, what is the Quaker method?" "Consensus, the sense of the meeting." And they said, "Does that mean if there is any opposition that it doesn't go through?" And he said, "That's what it means." "Well then, let's use the sense of the meeting." And so he was using that really as a parliamentary device to get his aim, and he was a white person, but that was one of the most striking ones.

Were relations good between blacks and whites in the two camps?

I think so. There was a certain amount of, I would say, self-imposed segregation in some cases. I think certain of the blacks preferred to be separate; I don't mean in the sense of eating, for example, or in meetings or anything of that kind, but I mean just around the camp they tended to be together.

Did your wife visit you while you were in any of the camps?

Oh yes, she visited me on a number of occasions.

Was your wife forced to change her living habits during the time you were in CPS?

Yes, to some extent, but not a great deal. I mean, since we had been living on this very limited stipend . . .

You were prepared.

Yes. I suppose in some sense she was maybe even better off living there in this cooperative house with the girls. She had pretty good meals, I guess, and she had a room.

Were you able to develop any relationships with people in the surrounding communities?

222

Not a great deal, although in Trenton the relations were reasonably good. We had some contact with the people, since it was predominantly the mixed-breed Indian population. They were themselves, of course, discriminated against, so there was sort of a mutual feeling, although there wasn't a great deal of contact. I think the Catholic group did have a fair amount of contact with the native population in the church, so it must have worked out. But there was no conflict, except one occasion that I remember. One fellow had been maybe having a little affair with the wife of one of the halfbreeds there. And her husband may have been in military service, at any rate, he was away. I know he threatened to kill this man and actually came into the camp, but I guess it was handled some way. But for the most part, I would say the relations were very satisfactory.

What was the most difficult aspect of CPS for you?

That's a really difficult question to answer. I suppose the feeling of being unable to do anything that I thought was at all constructive, just to be more or less put away like that in sort of a busy-work type of thing, although actually I did, as I said, have more feeling of accomplishment at Trenton. But the feeling that whatever competence, whatever ability, whatever training I had was not really being utilized in as effective a way as I thought it could have been.

Do you think this was an additional factor when you considered leaving the camp?

Yes, I think so. This is sort of tangential to this, but I remember that, while I was at Trenton, I wrote to Francis Wilson, who was my faculty adviser at the University of Illinois and under whom I had been doing my dissertation, and said, "I just feel that I can't go on with this when I get out. It seems to me so meaningless, the dissertation doesn't have any meaning. It seems to me that I ought to do something that really relates to what this is all about, particularly, of course, something involving pacifism and the role of conscientious objectors." And he wrote back a very understanding letter and said, "Well, I can appreciate your feelings, but since you have gone so far with this, I think you would be foolish not to go ahead and finish it. Then you can do the things that you really want to do, that you feel are important to do." I think it was good advice, and I did follow it.

Did you work at all on your dissertation while you were there?

No, no, there was very little privacy and very little opportunity to get away. One or two did. There was a fellow at Trenton while I was there, he was an economist and doing some research while he was there. He must have been a much better disciplined person than I was.

Did anyone moonlight in any of the camps that you know of?

Yes. I did. I worked in potatoes out in Trenton. During potato season, I went out every night that I could, and in fact, I took a week of my furlough one time and spent it on the farm there. Unfortunately, it rained a good part of the time that week, and I wasn't able to work very much, but I went out regularly, as did quite a number of others.

Do you think that the CPS experience basically strengthened your marriage or put strains on it?

I think it put strains on it. Yes, I think it put strains on it more than it strengthened it.

What kind of strains?

Well, just the separation and the separate life, and we were each, to a certain extent, going our own way.

Did your wife seem to have changed when you saw her after CPS?

Yes, to some extent, and I think maybe I had. Yes, I think it was difficult, to say the least.

Was there a satisfying aspect of CPS?

Well, I think the feeling of actually doing something that would be helpful. I never got that feeling at Big Flats, although I know a grass nursery is needed, it's useful, but I couldn't feel it. At Trenton we were developing an irrigation project, we were leveling land, we were putting in structures to irrigate this wheat land which had been completely despoiled in the dust bowl earlier. So yes, I felt a great deal of satisfaction in certain things. For example, I taught a course in American government, although there weren't very many who took it.

Looking back, do you have any doubts about your decision to enter CPS?

Yes, in a way I do. I have said to students on occasion, "If I had really been fully aware of the extent of the brutality, the viciousness associated with

Nazism, I don't even know that I could have justified the position, taken the position that I did, even though I still would have felt that this is not the answer, this is not the solution." Reinhold Niebuhr said that it's just the lesser of two evils, going to war; you don't actually destroy evil by killing the people not really responsible for doing these things. But I don't know. I remember Clarence Birdhall was a professor at the University of Illinois, and he was chairman at the time that I was drafted. He had been professor of international relations, and I went in to tell him that I was leaving. I had to leave before the end of the semester, but he had made arrangements to take care of things, and as I was about to leave his office, he said, "Ben, let's go into a classroom, I want to talk to you a little bit." So we went into a classroom and closed the door, and he said, "How can you justify taking this position?" I said, "Only on the basis that I think it is morally and ethically wrong to engage in war." And he, of course, brought up the types of things, the brutality—and I don't know if even he was aware of the extent of it— the viciousness of this system, and we had to eliminate it. Perfectly valid arguments from his standpoint, but I could only fall back on my strong moral conviction in regard to this.

I recall one time in CPS I was talking to another man who was trained in political science, he had been on the faculty of either Swarthmore or Haverford, and I was saying that I thought you could justify pacifism on a political basis. He said, "I completely disagree with you. I don't think there is any political basis upon which you can justify pacifism." And I agree with him, I think he is right; I think from a political standpoint you can't justify pacifism, so it has to be morally and ethically based.

In what ways do you see your life as having been changed by your CPS experience?

Well, I think I have been more deeply concerned about my fellow man. Before I got out of CPS, I didn't know what the situation was going to be professionally. Of course, as you probably know, at that particular time it was a seller's market, so I didn't find it a rough time at all. Incidentally, I might say that when I first almost halfheartedly wrote to the University of Miami about a position, I wrote in detail about my war experience; I explained exactly what my position had been, because I didn't want them to consider me under any false illusions on that.

Are you aware of any limitations, professional or otherwise, that your being in CPS has created?

No, I am not, and I really have been surprised at that. When I went to Duke, the chairman of the department—who had negotiated my going there—a few days after I got there called me into his office, and, of course, I had known him as an undergraduate, and he said, "Ben, I want you to know that you are free to do and say whatever you feel like saying. I want you to know that you are not under any restrictions whatever." I said, "I do not feel that the classroom is the appropriate place to propagandize for pacifism or anything else. I do appreciate your attitude." And here it was not publicized at all, but, of course, the administration all knew about it, and some of the faculty did. I didn't either tell it or conceal it unless it came out in the course of a discussion.

Again this is tangential, but it does relate to this. One of the men who came here at the same time I did and stayed only one year, a man who had been in the army, he told me that he learned shortly after arriving that I had been a conscientious objector. And he said, "Oh, then you're the one that this woman was talking about." He had met some woman's family, I guess, here in Miami, shortly after he had come here. The woman had originally lived in Jackson, Tennessee, where, of course, I had been on the faculty of Lambeth College. She was now living somewhere in Miami, and I don't know how it came up, but I guess he said something about being in the Political Science Department, and she said, "Oh, that's the department where they have that slacker, isn't it?" And he didn't know who she was talking about, and so then when he learned about that, well, he and I were very close.

But another man, who was a postal carrier—we met them, I guess, through some church associations or something—he had been in the military, and she, I believe, had been an army nurse. And one night they were in our apartment shortly after we came to Miami, and again, I don't remember how it came up, but in the course of the conversation it came out that I had been a conscientious objector. He jumped up from his chair, came across, and extended his hand, "I want to shake hands with you," and we were pretty close after that.

Do you think about CPS very often, and if you do, what memories are the strongest?

No, I don't really think about it. Although it's interesting, every now and then I will have a dream which takes me back to it, and as a matter of fact, now that you raise the question, I do recall that on at least one occasion I did dream that I was drafted back into CPS.

Do you classify that as a good dream or a bad dream?

It was a bad dream, yes, it was a bad dream.

William Stafford

*"Everything that has been stable in your life before you can no longer count
on. Your neighbors don't feel the same way. You can't tell how someone is
going to react when they learn who you are. So that when you meet a
stranger, there's this interval of finding out how much reality that person
can bear."*

*William Stafford was one of the nation's most respected poets. Winner of the
National Book Award for poetry in 1963 for* Traveling through the Dark *(1962),
recipient of a Guggenheim fellowship in 1966, consultant in poetry in 1970 to
the Library of Congress, poet laureate of Oregon, and dedicated teacher at Lewis
and Clark College, William Stafford's reputation as a major American poet owes
much to his experiences as a conscientious objector serving in Civilian Public
Service during World War II. He was born in Kansas into a nonconformist
home and became a committed pacifist during the 1930s. His reflections on his
CPS experience at the camp in Magnolia, Arkansas, were the basis for his
University of Kansas master's thesis, published in 1947 as* Down in My Heart.
*His unflinchingly honest development of such themes as his alienation from
society and the sense of community he experienced with other pacifists helps to
explain his tremendous appeal to many young people during the Vietnam War
era. Stafford died on 28 August 1993.*

Could you describe your life prior to entering CPS?

I was born in Hutchinson, Kansas, on January 17, 1914. My formal education was extremely extended, all the way through a master's degree in Kansas.
Then I went on for a Ph.D. at the University of Iowa, but that was after the
war, in the early 1950s. At the time of being drafted, just after Pearl Harbor,
I was a graduate student at the University of Kansas. I believe at the time I
was drafted, though, I did have a graduate assistantship to teach "engineering
English" for the English Department.

*At the time of your entrance into CPS, did you share your family's religious
and political views?*

My mother and father were not really formally affiliated with any religion.
They had a general benevolence toward religion. So I can't say I had a strong

religious upbringing, except that I did go to Sunday school a lot; it was the social thing to do in little towns in Kansas. That's where the ice cream socials were, that's where young people met. So I didn't have it strong from the family, but I got it sort of strong from the surrounding society.

Where did you go to Sunday school?

Any convenient church, any church that had a meeting place and nice girls, that's where we went. That was sociability. And it also had the other part too. In fact, when I was drafted, the commander of the American Legion in the town where my family was living at the time I was drafted was also a Sunday school teacher. And I had gone to his Sunday school class. So they needed a reference, and I gave them the commander of the American Legion. He was really great about it. I think I saw his letter to the draft board.

He really supported you?

He wrote a letter and said, "What Bill says today is the way he's been for years. We've talked in Sunday school class about these things."

That's the best American Legion story I've heard.

I really suspected him of being subversively a CO in the American Legion. They didn't know it, and he was selling insurance, so he didn't tell them; just the same, I doubt he would have dropped those fire bombs.

Were you active in any pacifist organizations in the 1930s?

At the time of entrance into CPS, I was the most extremely political member of our family, I believe. Actually, it was everybody else who changed at that minute the war came. There was a very strong peace movement, religious movement, during the thirties. That's where I was. The consideration that led me to choose CPS was that everybody else was going somewhere else and I was headed straight down the line as a pacifist. By the time I was drafted, I was a member of the Fellowship of Reconciliation, and this was at the University of Kansas, and there was a driving group of the FOR there. The principles of the Fellowship of Reconciliation we all knew and had their literature, and this was sort of drifting along with the general tide of social consciousness.

That was a part I always felt—maybe it was my age, my age bracket, drifting from the Depression into the thirties—the feeling that society hadn't done what it ought to. Read all kinds of things. Henry George, *The Grapes of Wrath*, everything I read very strongly influenced me. So that would be everything from *Les Misérables* to *War and Peace*, all of Tolstoy, all of Thoreau. When I was sent off to camp, my landlady, who was a Quaker, Rose Morgan, gave me a copy of the *Journal of John Woolman*. She never did say, in so many words, how she felt about my being a CO. But when I read the *Journal of John Woolman*, I knew how she felt. It was all a part of that drift. And we did go to church and Sunday schools. And those lessons we listened to, and they are still echoing in our ears.

Did your family agree with your decision to enter CPS?

The family was supportive. My parents were explicitly, and wholeheartedly, I believe, friendly. My brother went into the air force. My sister's husband went into the navy, so my position was not typical, but emotionally they were supportive.

What were your CPS assignments?

I served in Magnolia, Arkansas, Santa Barbara, California, and Belden, California, and then I went back and served in the headquarters of the Church of [the] Brethren for the last of the four years I was in CPS. I started as assistant educational secretary, and I ended as educational secretary, at the time that I got out.

Was the 1AO position an option for you?

Did I consider going 1A0? You couldn't do that with assurance at the time of World War II, I mean, you couldn't choose that. You could say, all right, I'll be a drafted person in the army, and then you could ask to go 1A0, but you no longer have a choice—I mean, you're under military orders, and they decide. So that rule was changed during the war when Lew Ayres— one of the most recognized of COs, he was an actor—wanted 1A0, and they wouldn't guarantee him, and so they said, "All right, go to CPS," which he did. A few weeks after he went in, they said, "Okay, we'll guarantee you 1A0." But most of us couldn't get that leverage. I mean, he was just too conspicuous. I think it shook them up a bit.

If it had been guaranteed, would you have gone 1AO?

I think I still wouldn't have gone 1AO, because I believed that the military effort was directed toward subjugating somebody else. To participate that much—everyone draws the line somewhere, even Hitler, somewhere, and I would have drawn it somewhere this side of becoming affiliated with the military.

Did you ever consider going to prison?

Yes, and in fact, I assumed that was a very likely possibility. I mean, we didn't really know what was going to happen. And in fact, when we got to camp, we still didn't know what was going to happen. There were people who showed up at camp and said, "Where are the bars?" you know, or, well, I can go further than that. There were people who ran camps who thought they were running prison camps. In fact, the person who was running the Santa Barbara camp patrolled the periphery with his gun the first night we were there. That's a story for you. He set a shotgun trap at camp—you know, these things are unbelievable now. He was there, but he didn't know what kind of people he was going to be dealing with. And he was a World War I hero. At first we disbelieved it, but he was some kind of sharpshooter. And he began to be friendly with the COs. He was hopelessly sociable; we were all out there together. And soon there wasn't anybody else to talk to, he was talking to COs, and pretty soon he was kind of partisan, sort of a General Hershey, a local General Hershey. Part of the stance of being a CO was to win these people over, so he was not challenged, he was just benevolently looked at when he gave some of the orders. You know, "Fall in," or something like that, he got a million reactions, but none of them military or none of them challenging. It would just be better if he didn't say things like that, so he quit saying things.

Once you got into CPS, did you at any time think that perhaps you were not making a strong enough witness in CPS and that you were not doing work of national importance? Did you seriously consider going to prison?

I never seriously considered it, for a reason that is very easy for me to find my way back to. I assumed that the role of the person who had the attitude I had is not to give people any kind of temptation to increase their coercion of me. However far they would come, I would encourage them to go that far. If they had said, "You can go home now," I would have gone home, because I didn't think it was my job to seek out extra pressure in order to register my protest against pressure. I thought my job was to decrease the pressure, and I still feel that way.

Your comment about the feeling of being almost in a prison camp initially, not knowing what you were going into, reminded me of something you discuss in your book [Down in My Heart]. *You describe a meeting between the CPS men and the forest rangers in a new spike camp, and you say, "Here were men planning their imprisonment with a considerate gentlemanly foreman." I thought that was a very intriguing thing to say.*

Let me put another circle around this thought. We all felt in our local situation that we were behaving under the covering guidance or menace of impending closing down of force on us, of other people, who had other ideas, and these Forest Service men had men over them, people, the society, and they had to behave a certain way in order to get along out there. We were aware of what was back of them. And they were ready to become aware of what kind of people we were. They had very odd ideas of what COs were, I mean, grotesque.

And you were given no idea about what work you'd be doing?

Well, as I remember, no. They asked me what kind of administration I'd like to be under, and I said, "Friends," because that was the only peace church I knew. And then the word came that I'd been sent to the Brethren. I didn't know what the Brethren were; that's how little I knew about it. So I was on a bus, and I remember going into Texarkana, and I spotted a young man there who looked hale and hearty and about my age, and I suspected, and I went over and talked to him and said, "Are you by chance going to Magnolia?" and he said yes. And then when he knew I was going there, then we could talk freely, and we compared notes. We knew nothing. We were just supposed to go there, and we were met and taken out to camp.

Was Magnolia an old CCC camp?

Yes, it was an old bunch of barracks. Morris Keeton showed up in the bunk next to mine, drafted right out of Harvard, Ph.D in philosophy. And one of the country boys came up to him the first night, Morris told me this later, and said, "Where are you from?" He said, "Harvard." He said, "What have you been doing there?" He said, "I've been studying for my Ph.D.," and this country boy said, "You ain't ever worked, have you?"

Did they tell you how long you were going to be in?

No. People talked 15–20 years, you know, how ever long it lasts. And that was one of the things that faced us, or maybe that was just part of the psychology that we were given. Saying, you know, you can't anticipate when it's going to end.

You said, "Living in CPS had become our custom," that you never really sat down and talked seriously about what you were going to do next year or when you got out. It just seemed that you were going to be in forever.

Yes, we didn't dare count on it. It was the indeterminate sentence. The soldiers had it too. Maybe that was part of the national psychology too, we'd better dig in for as long as it takes.

Who was the most impressive person you met at these camps?

In some ways, Morris Keeton was, in terms of having a coherent, intellectual life and being a positive and effective social tactics kind of person. I thought I learned a lot from Morris Keeton, and all I learned I loved. So he was one. But there were a number of very impressive people that I met, the kind of people I wouldn't have had the chance to become acquainted with if it hadn't been for this forced pushing together. I guess I didn't meet any overwhelming writers. I was sort of aware that some very influential people in this field were at CPS, like William Everson. Some other writers too were in camp, and I would hear about them, but I didn't meet them.

Did you have much of an opportunity to write while in CPS?

Yes, and many of us wrote a lot. The camp was full of newsletters, diary keepers, long letters home, even journal keepers. There were several who got into literary life later; for instance, Robert Lowell immediately occurs to me. He was a CO, but he was not at camp, he went to prison, and he would have been impressive. After CPS, I did get to talk to him, but I didn't know any writer of that degree of effectiveness in Civilian Public Service. A lot of forensic talents were exercised at camp. There were many meetings, things were thrashed out at great length in camp meetings. Actually, some of the leaders were impressive to me, W. Harold Row, and certainly Andrew Cordier at Manchester. I was trying to think if I met any saints.

Did you meet any sinners?

Yes, I met a lot of sinners, and in fact, I suppose one of the things that is so obvious is that CO camps were filled with conscientious objectors, they weren't filled with saints. There were all kinds of people there, people you wouldn't really want to meet. But prevalently, it was a pretty impressive group, mostly maybe because their circumstances forced them to examine their inner philosophies, so there was a lot of that, a lot of "tough inner self" kind of people.

Was there concern over how to follow through with the pacifist commitment in one's daily life?

Yes, this was cooked over and over again in camp—your motives and effectiveness, possibilities, social strategies, later modes of conducting your life. Conversations on the job, long meetings in the evening, reading, you know, the power of nonviolence and so on. There was an awful lot of this. In fact, that "mode of conduct" theme was probably one of the main distinctions in camp—concern about it. Vegetarianism is an example. Some of the most distinctive people I met were vegetarians, partly just from following out their implied conviction about life.

And how about the impact of Gandhi?

Yes, Gandhi was one of the saints; I mean *satyagraha*, ashrams, and so on, these terms that in the sixties became popular in college, were everywhere in CO camps.

What were some of the negative effects of CPS?

I think that CPS service was very hard on a lot of people. It turned some of them into professional gripers, people who can't do without a losing fight with society; I mean, they go around looking for it. I sense that in a lot of young people as a result of the Vietnam War experience. They cannot settle down to being positive and expecting-good-from-their-society kind of citizens. They just feel they've been betrayed, and that they will be again. I don't like that, I don't want to be like that.

On the other hand, CPS service, in relation to other kinds of experiences that you could have had during the war—you know, I've talked with the men who were in the armed services who at the sound of a truck backfiring would cower under the table and shake. And so I know that others had much worse experiences. So it just depends on what you relate this experience to. I don't think it's a positive experience ever to have your life interrupted by fiat from the state; you're sent somewhere, you're held in camps, your associates are chosen for you by other people. I can't see it as a positive experience. But a whole generation was having an experience that was worse than mine. So I don't say "worse" as compared with other people's experience; I just don't think it was good. I think it's better to have a life that is chosen by yourself, in which you have expectations of results from your present endeavor instead of a great big hiatus in your life when you don't know. It's just like a big earthquake in your life.

What about the gripers? You mentioned that there were some, and that they expected to be victimized, they expected everything to go wrong.

Yes, and I think this was a progressive thing as the years went by in CO camps. People became more and more frustrated. And there was less forgive[ness] toward administration, both church and state. There were more people who were rebelling against the existence of the compromise of CPS, people going over the hill, into prison, disappearing, or just becoming troublemakers. So they set up government camps for these people to go to, because they didn't feel that they wanted to cooperate with the church, or the church didn't cooperate with them, or the church shouldn't be involved.

Did you know some of the men who went to the government camps? And what did you think of them?

Yes, I knew quite a number of people who went to government camps as a kind of step toward prison. Really, that was for the hard-liners.

Do you think there was a justification for the government camps? Did that seem to indicate a failure of the original Historic Peace Churches?

I felt it a kind of failure, I guess. I hadn't thought about it in this way, but it was a place that some people wanted to go, and so I didn't feel anything very acute about it. But when I think about it, I think it indicated that the community that was established in the CO camps and run by the peace churches was breaking down in a certain way, and this belief in the effectiveness of what we were doing was eroding.

Why?

Well, the war went on and on, and once you begin to analyze your position, one possible way to go is to think that you're not opposing enough. You know, the war is still going on, why don't I stop it? And how shall I stop it? Well, I'll get more insulting toward General Hershey, or I'll declare that I'm going over the hill and they'll have to detach some police to find me. Things like that.

You referred to CPS as almost like being in the middle of an earthquake. I thought that was an interesting choice of words.

Yes, everything that has been stable in your life before, you can no longer count on. Your neighbors don't feel the same way. You can't tell how someone is going to react when they learn who you are. So that when you meet a stranger, there's this interval of finding out how much reality that person can bear.

Did you experience any of that alienation even before entering the camps?

During the war, my father died; my mother went to live with my sister; most of my friends, maybe all of my earlier friends in school, had gone into the army or air force or marines, and many of them were quite antagonistic with my position, strangely. I felt it when I would see them before I had to go to camp. So that part of the earthquake was quite drastic; my friends were, at least for the duration of the war and a while after too, more antagonistic to my position than the general populace was. I think it must be some kind of psychological thing. They knew me, and I had done this, and it was kind of an affront.

A personal thing.

Yes, a personal thing. It wasn't the sort of thing you could just shunt aside, the way you could with a stranger, and start all over again. I was right there. But I think that's an endemic part of my life now. How much of the truth is it practicable to allow a person you meet in a hurry? This stretches out endlessly before me when I think about it, all these gradations. In camp I became very much aware of that; I had always assumed people up and down the street, you know, this is *our* country, this is *our* town. Suddenly, it's *their* country, it's *their* town. And I'm more foreign. In fact, even before I left college, it was like that. Some of my college friends were really mad at me. They'd say, "I think you ought to be killed." That was kind of a jolt.

Do you think that the length of the war challenged CPS?

Yes, of course. I hadn't thought of this before, but in a way, what was happening was that later parts of the draft were bringing in people who were a part of the wartime society. I mean, we were part of the peacetime society. We were suddenly sent off to camps, and there was kind of a momentum about this. But the people who were later drafted were products of the war years in some ways, and they began to come in, and there was discouragement.

Did you recall talking to any of the men when they were considering transfer-ring into the government camps?

Yes, we all talked about it. People would, you know, telegraph ahead, months ahead, in their conversation, what they were thinking of doing. Because there wasn't any secrecy. I mean, I was not aware—I sometimes thought about this in the intervening years. Did I know anyone in CPS who was subversive? You know, some fascist, Nazi, Communist, or something? Well, no, I didn't, I don't think they could have survived, because everything was out front in conversations with others. It didn't occur to us that a fellow prisoner, in effect, was someone we had to trim our language to: "I think I'm going to get out of this place," and, "If you stay here, you're really cooperating with the war effort," and so on. Conversations like that would go on, so you would know what people were thinking of doing. In fact, sometimes they would send letters to Selective Service saying, "As of such and such a date, I won't be here, but if you want to find me, I'll be at such and such a place." They just wanted to hand Selective Service a hot potato.

Did they feel in a sense betrayed by the NSBRO and the Historic Peace Churches?

Some of the people did. I knew these people felt that way, but I didn't, I couldn't understand them, with my sympathies. I always felt 100 percent harmony with the efforts that so far as I could tell were being made by the NSBRO and by the peace churches. The idea of Harold Row somehow betraying the peace effort or something like that never occurred to me. I thought he was effective, and I still think that he was probably as troublesome a person as anyone could want to be opposed to war—adroit, winsome, very hard to get mad at. I liked the way they were doing it.

You were married after having already served in CPS for two years. Was your wife supportive of your CO position?

I really think that my wife wavered a bit. She was supportive of me, but also the society had just a lot of clout, and my brother was in the air force, and he was heroic, and I think she wavered quite a bit. There wasn't any problem about our marriage, but difficulty because I was in CPS, from other people and also inside herself.

Do you think that some of the CPS people bothered her because their commitment was perhaps so intense?

Yes, I'm sure that she was bothered by the intensity of some of the people. It was partly that she felt somehow excluded from some of the CO activities. She wasn't in a camp, she wasn't all that much involved with some of the commitments of the COs. And my brother Bob, who was in the air force, had a lot of appeal for Dorothy when we visited him. I could tell that she couldn't help feeling that maybe Bob was doing the right thing. So she felt much more wavering than I felt.

She said that she came from a rather protected childhood, and that she'd never met people quite like the COs.

Yes, and some of them were—well, *scary* is too strong a word, but sort of overwhelming people, I mean, very strongly opinionated and literate and vocal, flourishing, even arrogant people. So I could understand her feeling of some nervousness in their presence and not knowing whether she was being included or not.

Did you feel that CPS put any extra pressure on your relationship?

I believe that CPS did. Because you don't have an income, you don't have any prospects, your clothes aren't any good, your place in society is not at all exalted. I say all these things assuming that it's all right to have good clothes and to have a good place in society and be respected by others, and you're missing all those things.

And you can't plan. That must be one of the most difficult things, not being able to plan.

This is it, you can't plan. You know, how long is this thing going to last? One [year]? Twenty years? Forever? And also, I think it has a diverging effect being under that kind of stress. I think military service would be the same way. I don't think being drafted is a good thing, no matter which way you go. And it puts a strain on your relations with anyone who isn't drafted. It's just there, and I wouldn't want to link it or overstate it, but I do think it's there.

Did any of your friends experience severe difficulties with their marriages?

Well, again, this works various ways. I think some of them had more reliable, long-term, and sustained relations with women as a *result* of being COs. I mean, the kind of women who did cleave to them were extraordinary people. I think I knew people in CPS who never would have made it in the open market, getting married, who found this interest with particular women. I think there's been some of that too.

Would you say that kind of thing could happen in the military?

Yes, yes, right. So you know, chance factors like this operate so much, it's hard to tell where the prevailing effect would be. But I think there was buffeting for all people who were involved in those buffeting times.

Do you see many parallels between the position of a CO in CPS and a man in the military?

Yes, many more parallels than anyone who wasn't under the draft would see. In many essential ways, their situation is strikingly similar. The earth quakes for all of them. For instance, if I could meet a military person in wartime as a CO in circumstances in which we wouldn't be displaced by the kind of intensity of the society around us about the justice or injustice of the war, we immediately have many things in common. You know, how long are you in for? When do you get furlough? What kind of food do you get? How do people treat you? We're both prisoners, and when war comes, it's already all over for those who are involved in it. Freedom's ended. That's what conscription means.

What was the most difficult aspect of CPS?

It was just the uncertainty whether we were doing any good, whether we were just being shunted aside and not doing any witnessing. Also, it was harrowing; World War II was harrowing. People were going abroad and getting killed; the whole thing was a very difficult time. But life in general, I thought, was difficult, especially difficult for people in the armed forces, so I wouldn't make any distinction about us. It was just difficult, your life was all torn apart.

What was the most satisfying aspect of CPS?

The most satisfying aspect of CPS service: great company. I mean, it took a war, a draft, getting people together, a luminous, great, astounding group of people. I never would have in my life been able to meet such good people as I did in CPS. I think of the whole host of speakers who came through to see us from all parts of society: writers, ministers, peace workers, political people.

Do you still feel that bond with them?

We used to say, there's a golden network all across the country, and you can travel from station to station on our own kind of underground railroad.

I do have that feeling, and sometimes it's disconcerting, because there are people whose ways of life are quite foreign to mine who sometimes show up, and they've got that kind of claim on me: "Hey, we're both COs."

What was the least satisfying aspect of CPS?

The least satisfying aspect of CPS service was, it was bleak. We lived in barracks; it was hard work, building roads, fighting forest fires, and all the arbitrary part of it, everything that comes when your life is upset. It's like going to prison, it's like a prison camp. All those benchmarks in your life are foreign—your government, your school system, your minister, your family, your neighbors, the mayor, the police force. You can't count on the police. I mean, it's better if they don't know who you are if you're walking down the street. That's the difference. Well, of course, in a way you learned what all minorities learn I guess: it's better not to be seen. Become invisible.

So you felt that then and still feel that now?

I still feel that. I mean, once the earth shakes, it's never that firm again. That's sort of the feeling I have.

Looking back a generation later, do you have any doubts about your decision to enter CPS?

I always have doubts, though in which direction I'm leaning, I don't know. I mean, maybe I should have gone to prison, maybe I shouldn't have accepted alternative service—that's one possibility. Another possibility: I don't really seriously entertain the thought that I should have gone into the army. I was a citizen in the strongest nation in the world. Other nations had a lot to fear and, I think, still have a lot to fear from the United States. I'm told by my president, by everyone around, that our nation is the strongest in the world; then I'm told that I'm supposed to help strengthen it. Fantastic! No, I still think, as a citizen of the world, I did the right thing in CPS. I'd do it again.

In what ways do you see your life as being changed for having entered CPS?

I think my life has been changed a lot. For one thing, it put some fervor in my voice just then when I answered that question. The sensation of being within a society that you prevalently and overwhelmingly really accept and like, but being different on a few crucial things, puts a lot of stress on many things in your life. After CPS, my life changed a lot. For a while, it was sort of touch-and-go about jobs. These things were explicit. People would give opinions about how it was to have been either in the service or being a pacifist. I've been surprised sometimes at getting jobs. But there was always that tremor—is it going to happen? And then, my life has been changed because every public issue since that time—including the intervening wars, Korea, Vietnam—these things have kept alive those old vibrations. Strangely, during the Vietnam War I found myself welcomed, maybe even almost made a hero, by the vast majority of people in college. This rattled me. I didn't necessarily think that was right at all; I was not a hero. But to them it was as if I had the foresight of being 25 years ahead of my time. It was their point of view. So I've been shaken both ways.

Are you aware of any professional limitations that you have experienced as a result of having been a CO during World War II?

Yes. There are a number of incidents. I was offered a job at the University of Colorado by the chairman of English a short time after CPS. And then I read the catalog, and I saw that every student at the University of Colorado, every male student, had to serve in ROTC, and so I told the chairman that I couldn't teach in a school where students would be forced to do what I wouldn't do myself. He gave me quite a lecture on how foolish I was. Then, that was true at another job, at the University of Utah, same story. So there were many colleges at that time that I could not consider. So those were overt and actual incidents. This was always hovering about other jobs.

I think almost everyone in camp expected it'd be a lot worse than it was. They were all set for a lifetime of hovering on the periphery of society. Furthermore, I think the CPS experience and the awareness of those limitations strengthened an impulse in me to be an around-the-edge rather than in-the-middle kind of citizen, kind of [a] guest of the state—*in* but not *of*, always having in mind an exit somewhere, always thinking that there are going to come issues pretty soon when we'll have to go through this again. So it has made me a kind of habitual intellectual hippie in academic life. My nature is not to be critical, but my stance has been to be ready to be critical as a result of this. So all sorts of such things happened as a result of having been a CO. It extends to today.

I was wondering, beyond employment, if you had ever, for example, applied for government grants or Fulbrights or travel abroad?

Yes, I have a number of reflections about this. For one thing, about 25 years after CPS I was invited to go abroad on this USIA [U.S. Information Agency] trip. I did a double take and thought, "Well, whatever my record is, it must look pretty good to the government," and I was sort of surprised. I was glad, and I thought they were right—it was okay for me to go abroad, because I never have at all felt subversive or anything like that. But I was a little bit surprised. So that was kind of a milestone.

In a way, it closed a door or answered a question that may have been there.

Yes, it did. There is another angle on this, and that is, there were advantages that have come to me because I was a CO, and these are no more justified than the disadvantages, but they're human. For instance, there are people who may have felt—in some kind of a subtle psychological way—guilt about their participation in the war. And they have been extra nice to me. And maybe extra generous. And a few of them have been overtly so. Even school administrators have gone out of their way—this would be an extreme, but it shows what way I'm leaning—to give me a better job than my qualifications might qualify me for. Because they didn't want to be the kind who held any grudges against a CO. And they might even have had a secret underlying current in their lives that made them feel like COs themselves. It would be strange, wouldn't it, if the COs who thought they would be discriminated against actually had a strong tide going in their favor that other people aren't even conscious of.

Sweet justice.

Sometimes I felt that people have said things that made me see that really deep down they still hold a grudge. I noticed that.

You mean, even today?

Well, yes. I mean, they could say it even today; the examples I think of are from the past. When I was in graduate school, I remember a group there, hearty fellows who had been in the war. And one of them opined to my wife that they talked it over and they thought it was all right that I'd been a CO. Well, I could think of another way to phrase that, things like that.

It's interesting that you'd taken this stand during World War II and then Vietnam comes along and you're a hero.

Yes. I felt sort of fakey about this, visiting colleges in the sixties. I had a special entrée, but on grounds that were shaky to me. I didn't think they understood *our* war.

That's why I think the CPS experience is unique.

That's right. I think of what Robert Frost said, "They will not find me changed from him they thought they knew, only more sure of what I thought was true." Something like that. But I was consciously avoiding the lifelong stance of quarreling with my society. I wanted to forget it, get back to nonstrenuous—I wanted the earth to stop shaking.

You indicated that some people may have gone overboard to do nice things for you, perhaps because of guilt. I wonder how many men you have talked to who were in the service now say that they wish they had done what you did during World War II?

Many of them say that. I discount it. But to me, a surprising number say that. I think it's partly the disgust many people have felt about recent wars and a kind of belated recognition—I guess that's not too strong a word to use from my side—a recognition of what committing yourself to the orders of the military can mean. A realization of that. And maybe even a really long, arching look back at World War II and realizing that they were right at the point of doing things they couldn't really in conscience do, if they hadn't been so stampeded. We're back to that atom bomb thing again.

What were your feelings about that?

I think Harry Truman's decision to drop the atom bomb was a justification of the CO position. My side had just done the unspeakable act. And when I think of what the supreme commander decided to do, I realize that if I had to do it over again, would I swear to uphold the actions of such a supreme commander? The answer is, no, no way.

Were you in CPS when that occurred?

Yes, yes I was.

What was the reaction of those around you?

I guess we were surprised at the ultimate devastation, but not all that surprised at the decision to use it. In a way, I'm disappointed in myself for not feeling more clearly a morally decisive thing had happened. I didn't feel it—it's just another bombing. But looking back on it, I feel really terrible about it. To think that we could all drift into a position of doing something so unspeakable.

A CPSer in your book Down in My Heart *observed, "War was the wrong way of attaining ends many agreed to be good."*

Yes, this was a very common way to see it in CPS. Grant others the justice or justification of their position, but disagree with them about the means they are using to attain it. The assumption that all people are trying to do right. We just have to figure out what the right thing is.

Early in your book, you talk about the unique situation of being forced to rebel against other human beings in order to avoid participating in the larger violence that was engulfing the immediate society.

In a way, it's a strange thing. COs, who were pacifists, are the only activists. I mean, they're the only ones who are saying no. And everyone else that is going in is saying yes. So it's a strange kind of reversal in society. And there were a lot of "nay"-sayers in CPS.

Of course, your very action is then arousing antagonism in those around you.

Yes, it is. So you're aware of what the effect of the original decision is. It's around you all the time. And you might drift into the army, into the marines, and into extreme combat conditions. And into medals of honor and so on, through inertia. It's a strange thing. I think a lot of the COs drifted into CO camps for the same reason, inertia. I mean, they were part of the church. The church said no, so they say no. And in fact, there were people that were sent to camp who didn't even know they were saying no. They were Brethren, so the draft board said, "Oh, you're Brethren," and they sent them to camp. They thought they were going in the military. We think we're talking about the same thing. No, we're talking about different groups who came from different directions and were put into this slot. So the camps were full of quietists and activists. It was a strange mix.

How often do you think back about CPS, and what memories are the strongest?

I don't think back about it very much. I mean, it's not a special time at this stage in my life. But I don't avoid it, and the memories that are the strongest are those in-group feelings of solidarity, the result of the out-group hostility you endure.

7

CONCLUSION

On 31 March 1947, the Civilian Public Service program discharged its last assignee. Since the first camp had opened in Patapsco, Maryland, in May 1941, close to 12,000 men had participated in CPS. Well before the ending of the program, it had received close scrutiny from all sides.

The Historic Peace Churches had mixed but generally positive assessments of this institution they had helped to create. The Mennonite history of CPS saw it as "a success" that would show "the way to the further course of nonresistant groups under similar circumstances."[1] The Brethren Service Committee, in a March 1946 statement, offered a more guarded but still positive reading, calling CPS "a working compromise between church and state." Although it had proved "inadequate for the achievement of all ends sought by pacifists," the Brethren Service Committee acknowledged CPS as "a true community of men who hold in common at least one ideal—objection to war."[2] The Friends found the least to applaud in CPS. Raymond Wilson, a principal Quaker lobbyist for the CO provisions in the 1940 draft act, later concluded that "there is no satisfactory solution for the problem of conscience under conscription—only a series of more or less unsatisfactory accommodations."[3]

While weighing their experiences with CPS, the Mennonites, Brethren, and Friends had to deal with a more disturbing fact: why had their peace witness proved unpersuasive to such a large portion of their adherents? Why had so many chosen the military over CPS?

The Mennonite Peace Problems Committee noted, in August 1943, that "all too large a number of men in our younger ages have failed to meet the test of conscience and have entered the army voluntarily, choosing rather to surrender the faith of their fathers, even under the most favorable circumstances, and become a part of the war machine." Looking at the period 1940–47, and including all of the Mennonite branches, 46.2 percent chose CPS, 14.2 percent entered the military in a noncombatant capacity, and 39.5 percent accepted a combatant assignment in the military.[4] The proportions of men entering CPS from the Brethren and Friends fell well below the

Mennonite standard. World War II had exposed the vulnerabilities of a peace witness and led each of the churches to reexamine its peace teaching.

CPS furnished an additional legacy for the Historic Peace Churches. Some of their members, and a wider array of outsiders, saw complicity in the churches' relationship to the conscription process. The *Christian Century* complained that the Historic Peace Churches were "as directly involved in running a part of the Selective Service System as are draft boards."[5]

The Selective Service System itself had few doubts about the Civilian Public Service program. Its existence, "in a period of concentration camps, slave labor, and other features of totalitarianism elsewhere," exhibited the openness of American democracy. For Hershey and the Selective Service System, CPS had been a viable compromise, respecting consciences but doing it in such a way as to avoid a backlash that would weaken national unity in wartime. In their judgment, although "extreme groups were not completely satisfied, the System's policy apparently met with general approval."[6] Selective Service Director Lewis B. Hershey believed, however, that the program would survive best with the lowest public profile. Testifying before the Senate in February 1943, Hershey noted that "the conscientious objector, by my theory, is best handled if no one hears of him."[7] Hershey's assumption about the need to protect CPS men from a hostile public was challenged in a study conducted by the Princeton University psychologist Leo Crespi. Crespi's data established that the presumed public attitude of extreme antagonism toward COs in wartime proved not to be the case. Rather, "the largest proportion of the public expresses no rejection of CO's whatsoever, and more than a majority would accept them during this war as friends, or closer."[8]

For the men of CPS, no simple statement could adequately convey their experience. For some who chose CPS, their decision remained constantly at issue and subject to revision. For others, there was no real "decision": choosing a course of action other than CPS would have been so alien to the values of their community that they never considered it. The nature of the war itself challenged or buttressed their choices. The emerging revelation of the Holocaust, followed by the stark newsreels of the liberated camps, undercut the moral certitude of some CPS men. Others saw in the atomic bombings of Hiroshima and Nagasaki confirmation of the correctness of their choice.

Some experienced the grinding realities of CPS more keenly than others. Their decision had alienated family and friends, and the isolation of CPS camps deepened that mood. The lack of pay caused additional pressure, particularly for those with dependents. Only 35 CPS men would be released for dependency reasons from Pearl Harbor until the end of the war. For many men, entering the military looked increasingly attractive, and more than 900 would follow that route.[9]

Far larger numbers had a decidedly different experience of CPS. Family and friends either supported or accepted their decision. Most eventually found work that, if not of national importance, contributed meaningfully to the well-being of others. They found their camps and units flawed communities but nonetheless filled with opportunities for intellectual stimulation and spiritual growth. They made lifelong friendships there.

For some, CPS furnished an opportunity to examine issues of violence and pacifism, of obligation and resistance, in a deeper vein. CPS men can recall the seemingly nonstop discussions even after the passage of almost half a century. Not all were enamored of this philosophizing. One man insisted that all "the 'do-good' instincts I had were drained in CPS. Meetings, causes and group action bore me. I had my fill of meetings and verbose egotists in camp."[10]

The vast majority of CPS men, asked whether they would make the same choice again, quickly say yes. Ironically, the choice of CPS or its equivalent was never available after World War II. Selective Service characterized CPS as an "important exercise" that must "be guarded historically; it may have great future significance in connection with fulfilling an obligation for duty within the limits of faith."[11] Despite that assertion, alternative service for conscientious objectors after World War II consisted solely of individual assignments. The Historic Peace Churches readily accommodated themselves to this, and Selective Service found it a less demanding arrangement. Indeed, if CPS had still been in operation at the time of the Vietnam War, it would have faced extraordinary demands. During World War II, for every 100 inductions into the military, there were 0.15 COs. As the war in Vietnam heated up, and as opposition to it intensified, the ranks of conscientious objectors grew rapidly. In 1968, the number of selective service registrants classified as conscientious objectors rose to 8.5 percent of those inducted into the military. The following year it reached 13.5 percent, in 1970 25.6 percent, and in 1971 42.6 percent. In 1972, with the phasing down of American forces in Vietnam and the winding down of the draft, for the first time in history more men were classified as conscientious objectors, 33,041, than those inducted, 25,273.[12]

The decision to enter CPS, as important as it was for each man, had a broader resonance. The churches from which they came and to which they returned would be significantly affected as well. Fundamentalist churches, historically wary of psychiatry and therapy, had members returning from work in mental institutions who had seen the uses of psychological intervention. Catholics who had been in CPS, particularly Gordon Zahn, would lead a debate in the Catholic church that brought issues of peace and disarmament to the forefront in the 1960s and 1970s. All of the Historic Peace Churches would inherit a generation of leadership from the ranks of CPS.

In both dramatic and less dramatic ways, CPS would leave its mark on the struggle for peace and justice over the ensuing 50 years. CPS men served as a cadre of draft counsellors during the Vietnam War. One of the men from the Minnesota starvation experiment still gives slide lectures to community groups on world hunger and the experience of starvation. Others are active in migrant programs and in forums to develop international understanding. The idealism that led men into CPS during World War II still animates a remarkably large number of them. William Stafford's pledge, that "we have just begun to not fight," proved remarkably prophetic. Five decades later, on issues of peace and social justice, they are still honoring it.

Notes and References

Chapter 1

1. Edna St. Vincent Millay, "Conscientious Objector," in *Collected Poems: Edna St. Vincent Millay*, ed. Norma Millay (New York: Harper & Row, 1956), 305.

2. Selective Service, *Conscientious Objection*, Special Monograph No. 11, Vol. 1 (Washington, D.C.: Government Printing Office, 1950), 105.

3. Ibid., 260–61.

4. Ibid., 117.

5. John O'Sullivan and Alan M. Meckler, eds., *The Draft and Its Enemies: A Documentary History* (Urbana: University of Illinois Press, 1974), 124–25.

6. Secretary of War, *Statement Concerning the Treatment of Conscientious Objectors in the Army* (Washington, D.C.: Government Printing Office, 1919), 16.

7. Secretary of War, *Statement*, 8–9.

8. Walter Guest Kellogg, *The Conscientious Objector* (New York: Boni and Liveright, 1919), v.

9. Secretary of War, *Statement*, 8.

10. Harlan F. Stone, "The Conscientious Objector," *Columbia University Quarterly* 21 (October 1919): 272.

11. Albert N. Keim and Grant M. Stoltzfus, *The Politics of Conscience: The Historic Peace Churches and America at War, 1917–1955* (Scottdale, Penn: Herald Press, 1988), 68.

12. National Service Board for Religious Objectors (NSBRO), *The Origins of Civilian Public Service* (Washington, D.C.: National Service Board for Religious Objectors, n.d.), 10.

13. George Q. Flynn, "Lewis Hershey and the Conscientious Objector: The World War II Experience," *Military Affairs* 47 (February 1983): 1.

14. O'Sullivan and Meckler, *The Draft and Its Enemies*, 181.

15. E. Raymond Wilson, "Evolution of the CO Provisions in the 1940 Conscription Bill," *Quaker History* 64 (Spring 1975): 4.

16. NSBRO, *Origins of CPS*, 21.

17. Keim and Stoltzfus, *The Politics of Conscience*, 113.

18. NSBRO, *Origins of CPS*, 25.

19. Ibid., 27.

20. Selective Service, *Conscientious Objection*, 164–65.

21. Melvin Gingerich, *Service for Peace: A History of Mennonite Civilian Public Service* (Akron, Penn: Mennonite Central Committee, 1949), 85.

22. Robert Ludlow, interview with John O'Sullivan, 22 November 1977, New York City.

23. Cynthia Eller, *Conscientious Objectors and the Second World War: Moral and Religious Arguments in Support of Pacifism* (New York: Praeger Publishers, 1991), 65.

24. Ibid., 64.

25. Mulford Q. Sibley and Philip E. Jacob, *Conscription of Conscience: The American State and the Conscientious Objector, 1940–1947* (Ithaca, N.Y.: Cornell University Press, 1952), 124.

26. U.S. Senate, Committee on Military Affairs, *Conscientious Objectors' Benefits*, 78th Cong., 1st sess., 17 February 1943, 17.

27. See Heather T. Frazer and John O'Sullivan, "Forgotten Women of World War II: Wives of Conscientious Objectors in Civilian Public Service," *Peace and Change* 5 (September 1978): 46–51.

28. Paul Hume, interview with John O'Sullivan, 30 December 1980, Washington, D.C.

29. Lawrence S. Wittner, *Rebels against War: The American Peace Movement, 1933–1983* (Philadelphia: Temple University Press, 1984), 73.

30. Eller, *Conscientious Objectors*, 31; see also Sibley and Jacob, *Conscription of Conscience*.

31. Peter Bennett, interview with John O'Sullivan, 6 June 1978, Philadelphia, Pennsylvania.

32. *The Reporter*, 1 October 1943.

33. "Our Mental Hospitals: A National Disgrace," *Life*, 6 May 1946.

34. Gingerich, *Service for Peace*, 223–25.

35. Ancel Keys, "Human Starvation and Its Consequences," *Journal of the American Dietetic Association* 22 (July 1946): 584–85.

36. Ancel Keys et. al., *Later Stages of Rehabilitation Following Experimental Starvation in Man* (Minneapolis: University of Minnesota, 1946), 49.

37. "Men Starve in Minnesota," *Life*, 30 July 1945.

38. Albert N. Keim, *The CPS Story: An Illustrated History of Civilian Public Service* (Intercourse, Penn: Good Books, 1990), 43.

39. Norman Kriebel, interview with Heather T. Frazer, 12 November 1980, Villanova, Pennsylvania.

Chapter 7

1. Harold Bender, quoted in Gingerich, *Service for Peace*, vi.

2. Leslie Eisan, *Pathways of Peace: A History of the Civilian Public Service Program Administered by the Brethren Service Committee* (Elgin, Ill: Brethren Publishing House, 1948), 471.

3. Wilson, "Evolution of the CO Provisions," 15.

4. Guy Hershberger, *The Mennonite Church in the Second World War* (Scottdale, Penn.: Mennonite Publishing House, 1951), 38, 39.

5. Editorial, *Christian Century* 60 (22 September 1943): 1064.

6. Selective Service, *Conscientious Objection*, 331, 5.

7. Senate, *Conscientious Objectors' Benefits*, 23.

8. Leo Crespi, "Public Opinion toward Conscientious Objectors: 3. Intensity of Social Rejection in Stereotype and Attitude," *Journal of Psychology* 19 (1945): 260.

9. Ibid., 311.

10. Paul Wilhelm, *Civilian Public Servants: A Survey of 210 WWII Conscientious Objectors* (Washington, D.C.: National Interreligious Service Board for Conscientious Objectors, 1990), 36.

11. Selective Service, *Conscientious Objection*, 250.

12. Selective Service, *Semiannual Report of the Director of Selective Service for the Period July 1 to December 31, 1973* (Washington, D.C.: Government Printing Office, 1974), 32.

Bibliography

American Friends Service Committee. *The Experience of the American Friends Service Committee in Civilian Public Service under the Selective Training and Service Act of 1940*. Philadelphia: American Friends Service Committee, 1945.

Brock, Peter. *Twentieth-Century Pacifism*. New York: Van Nostrand Reinhold, 1970.

Bush, Perry Jonathan. "Drawing the Line: American Mennonites, the State, and Social Change, 1935–1973." Ph.D. dissertation, Carnegie Mellon University, 1990.

Chatfield, Charles. *For Peace and Justice: Pacifism in America, 1914–1941*. Knoxville: University of Tennessee Press, 1971.

Cooney, Robert, and Helen Michalowski, eds. *The Power of the People: Active Nonviolence in the United States*. Culver City, Calif.: Peace Press, 1977.

Cornell, Julien. *Conscience and the State: Legal and Administrative Problems of Conscientious Objectors, 1943–1944*. New York: Garland, 1973.

Crespi, Leo P. "Attitudes toward Conscientious Objectors and Some of Their Psychological Correlates." *Journal of Psychology* 18 (1944): 81–117. See four subsequent articles in *Journal of Psychology* 19–20 (1944–45).

Durnbaugh, Donald F. *Pragmatic Prophet: The Life of Michael Robert Zigler*. Elgin, Ill.: Brethren Press, 1989.

Eisan, Leslie. *Pathways of Peace: A History of the Civilian Public Service Program Administered by the Brethren Service Committee*. Elgin, Ill.: Brethren Publishing House, 1948.

Eller, Cynthia. *Conscientious Objectors and the Second World War: Moral and Religious Arguments in Support of Pacifism*. New York: Praeger, 1991.

Flynn, George Q. *Lewis B. Hershey, Mr. Selective Service*. Chapel Hill: University of North Carolina Press, 1985.

Frazer, Heather T., and John O'Sullivan. "Forgotten Women of World War II: Wives of Conscientious Objectors in Civilian Public Service." *Peace and Change* 5, nos. 2–3 (September 1978): 46–51.

French, Paul Comly. *We Won't Murder: Being the Story of Men Who Followed Their*

Conscientious Scruples and Helped Give Life to Democracy. New York: Hastings House, 1940.

Gingerich, Melvin. *Service for Peace: A History of Mennonite Civilian Public Service.* Akron, Penn.: Mennonite Central Committee, 1949.

Grimsrud, Theodore Glenn. "An Ethical Analysis of Conscientious Objection to World War II." Ph.D. dissertation, Graduate Theological Union, 1988.

Guetzkow, Harold Steere, and Paul Hoover Bowman. *Men and Hunger: A Psychological Manual for Relief Workers.* Elgin, Ill.: Brethren Publishing House, 1946.

Hershberger, Guy Franklin. *The Mennonite Church in the Second World War.* Scottdale, Penn.: Mennonite Publishing House, 1951.

Hurwitz, Deena, and Craig Simpson, eds. *Against the Tide: Pacifist Resistance in the Second World War: An Oral History.* New York: War Resisters League, 1984.

Keim, Albert N. *The CPS Story: An Illustrated History of Civilian Public Service.* Intercourse, Penn.: Good Books, 1940.

Keim, Albert N., and Grant M. Stoltzfus. *The Politics of Conscience: The Historic Peace Churches and America at War, 1917–1955.* Scottdale, Penn.: Herald Press, 1988.

Kellogg, Walter Guest. *The Conscientious Objector.* New York: Boni and Liveright, 1919.

Lemke-Santangelo, Gretchen. "The Radical Conscientious Objectors of World War II: Wartime Experience and Postwar Activism." *Radical History Review* 45 (1989): 5–29.

Levi, Margaret, and Stephen DeTray. "A Weapon against War: Conscientious Objection in the United States, Australia, and France." *Politics and Society* 21, no. 4 (December 1993): 425–64.

Moskos, Charles C., and John Whiteclay Chambers II. *The New Conscientious Objection: From Sacred to Secular Resistance.* New York: Oxford University Press, 1993.

National Interreligious Service Board for Religious Objectors. *Directory of Civilian Public Service: May 1941 to March 1947,* revised and updated. Washington, D.C.: National Interreligious Service Board for Conscientious Objectors, 1994.

National Service Board for Religious Objectors. *Directory of Civilian Public service: May, 1941 to March 1947.* Washington, D.C.: National Service Board for Religious Objectors, 1947.

———. *The Origins of Civilian Public Service: A Review of the Negotiations during the Fall of 1940 between Government Officials and Representatives of the Churches Most Immediately Affected by the Drafting of Conscientious Objectors.* Washington, D.C.: National Service Board for Religious Objectors, n.d.

O'Sullivan, John, and Alan R. Meckler, eds. *The Draft and Its Enemies: A Documentary History.* Urbana: University of Illinois Press, 1974.

Pacifica Views: A Weekly Newspaper of Conscientious Objectors. New York: Garland, 1972.

Robinson, Jo Ann Ooiman. *Abraham Went Out: A Biography of A. J. Muste.* Philadelphia: Temple University Press, 1981.

Robinson, Mitchell Lee. "Civilian Public Service during World War II: The Dilemmas of Conscience and Conscription in a Free Society." Ph.D. dissertation, Cornell University, 1990.

Sareyan, Alex. *The Turning Point: How Men of Conscience Brought about Major Change in the Care of America's Mentally Ill.* Washington, D.C.: American Psychiatric Press, 1994.

Schlissel, Lillian, ed. *Conscience in America: A Documentary History of Conscientious Objection in America, 1757–1967.* New York: E. P. Dutton, 1968.

Sibley, Mulford Q., and Philip E. Jacob. *Conscription of Conscience: The American State and the Conscientious Objector, 1940–1947.* Ithaca, N.Y.: Cornell University Press, 1952.

Sibley, Mulford Q., and Ada Wardlaw. *Conscientious Objectors in Prison, 1940–1945.* Philadelphia: Pacifist Research Bureau, 1945.

Stafford, William E. *Down in My Heart.* Swarthmore, Penn.: Bench Press, 1985.

Stone, Harlan F. "The Conscientious Objector." *Columbia University Quarterly* 21, no. 4 (October 1919): 253–72.

U.S. Secretary of War. *Statement Concerning the Treatment of Conscientious Objectors in the Army.* Washington, D.C.: Government Printing Office, 1919.

U.S. Selective Service. *Conscientious Objection.* Special monograph no. 11, vol. 1. Washington, D.C.: Government Printing Office, 1950.

Wachs, Theodore Rickard. "Conscription, Conscientious Objection, and the Context of American Pacifism, 1940–1945." Ph.D. dissertation, University of Illinois at Urbana-Champaign, 1976.

Wilhelm, Paul. *Civilian Public Servants: A Survey of 210 WWII Conscientious Objectors.* Washington, D.C.: National Interreligious Service Board for Conscientious Objectors, 1993.

Will, Herman. *A Will for Peace: Peace Action in the United Methodist Church: A History.* Washington, D.C.: General Board of Church and Society of the United Methodist Church, 1984.

Wilson, E. Raymond. "Evolution of the CO Provisions in the 1940 Conscription Bill." *Quaker History* 64 (March 1975): 3–15.

Wittner, Lawrence S. *Rebels against War: The American Peace Movement, 1933–1983.* Philadelphia: Temple University Press, 1984.

Zahn, Gordon C. *Another Part of the War: The Camp Simon Story.* Amherst: University of Massachusetts Press, 1979.

Index

The Authors

Heather T. Frazer holds a Ph.D. in history from Duke University and is a professor in the History Department at Florida Atlantic University in Boca Raton. Her research, publications, and teaching focus on women, India, the British Empire, and modern England.

John O'Sullivan holds a Ph.D. in history from Columbia University. He is a professor in the History Department at Florida Atlantic University. His publications include two books on conscription. He teaches courses on World War II and U.S. foreign policy.